The
RADIO FRONT

THE BBC AND THE
PROPAGANDA WAR 1939-45

RON BATEMAN

The
History
Press

In memory of my parents Ron and Joyce, who
experienced the terror of aerial bombardment

First published 2022

The History Press
97 St George's Place, Cheltenham,
Gloucestershire, GL50 3QB
www.thehistorypress.co.uk

British Library Cataloguing in Publication Data.
A catalogue record for this book is available from the British Library.

ISBN 978 0 7509 9664 8

Typesetting and origination by The History Press
Printed and bound in Great Britain by TJ Books Limited, Padstow, Cornwall.

MIX
Paper from
responsible sources
FSC® C013056

Trees for LYfe

CONTENTS

ACKNOWLEDGEMENTS

At the time of writing, Britain was in the grip of the Covid-19 pandemic that resulted in strict limitations being put in place regarding access to essential archived material. I am most grateful to those institutions that were able to facilitate limited access to vital documents under very difficult circumstances. I would particularly like to thank the staff of the Churchill Archive Centre in Cambridge, The National Archives in Kew, The Netherlands Photo Museum and the Priestley Archive in Bradford for their friendly co-operation.

Special thanks also to the Orwell estate, the J.B. Priestley estate and the BBC Written Archive Centre for granting me permission to reproduce original material. Thanks also to Dr Rosa Matheson for reading through the original manuscript and offering useful suggestions, and to Karen Mortimer for assistance in 'cleaning up' certain images.

I would also like to give a special thank you to the contributors who wrote the Foreword and the Introduction to this book. Now into her nineties, Dione Venables still has vivid memories of living in wartime London in a household dominated by 'wireless', and still hopes to discover more about her father's wartime activities in connection with radio. Richard Blair's father, George Orwell, was also involved with wartime radio as an architect of propaganda for the BBC's Eastern Service. He too provides us with many valuable observations in the pages of his wartime diaries.

It was Orwell who once described the process of writing a book as being 'a horrible exhausting struggle'. I was under no illusions that the task of disentangling the complexities and controversies of the BBC's wartime radio propaganda programme would not turn out to be just that, although I firmly believe it to have been well worth that struggle!

Ron Bateman, July 2021

FOREWORD

BY RICHARD BLAIR

When I was asked by the author if I would write the Foreword to *The Radio Front: The BBC and the Propaganda War 1939–45*, I immediately thought of my father, George Orwell, and his time at the BBC, where he described the corporation as being a cross between a 'lunatic asylum and a girls' school'. One hopes that as there is now a larger-than-life-sized statue of him outside the BBC, that forgiveness has been granted. At the time of his employment between August 1941 and November 1943 as talks producer for the Eastern Services, he would have been regarded as just one of many employees. Although he had several published books and was regarded as an interesting and, indeed, influential writer, it was after he left the BBC that his final two books, *Animal Farm* and *Nineteen Eighty-Four,* would propel him into the mainstream pantheon of one of the great English writers of the twentieth century.

When the BBC was founded in 1922 under its first director general, Sir John Reith, and his lofty ideals, its motto was 'Nation Shall Speak unto Nation' and it was the embodiment of neutral and honest broadcasting. However, it didn't take the government long to recognise the power that this new form of communication could have in conveying important information to the population of not only Great Britain, but also the British Empire and other countries. Here was a powerful tool capable of being abused for the benefit of those countries who sought to spread disinformation and to bend the people to the will of the controlling authorities. Is it not interesting that some populations are more compliant to higher authority than others? It soon became clear to world governments that it was necessary to control the broadcasters of radio, and thereby control the population. 'In the land of the blind, the one-eyed man is king', goes the saying. As war approached with an inevitability that many failed to recognise, it was left to a few visionary people like Winston Churchill to see the danger. Mr Bateman relates an insightful story that during a meeting between British diplomats and Hitler in 1938, where both sides were 'wooing' India, which wanted independence, Hitler showed his real hand by suggesting, if there was resistance, 'shoot Gandhi, if that fails shoot the Congress and keep shooting until they acquiesce'. This was persuasion by terror. This was how, by various degrees, Germany subjugated the German population with the power of radio.

Once the Second World War had started, the government was able to instruct the nation through the BBC as to how people were to behave as martial law was introduced: blackouts, travel restrictions, rationing, opening and closing of public establishments, air-raid instructions and a long list of 'dos and don'ts'. There is no doubt the government tried to temper the rigidity of wartime conditions with entertainment on the radio, such as *It's That Man Again*, otherwise known as *ITMA*. The lighter part of the BBC was broadcast on the Forces Programme, while anything more serious was on the Home Service. Interestingly, not only did Orwell work for the BBC, but his wife, Eileen, through the Ministry of Food, was also co-operating with the corporation. She, along with others, was charged with creating nutritious meals from some 'interesting' ingredients, not without a few clashes of personalities, although not necessarily from Eileen, but from her superiors, both at the BBC and the Ministry of Food. Orwell and Eileen suffered from ill health and eventually they both left, Orwell in November 1943. He was quite often confined to bed with chest problems, like bronchitis, which kept him away for two or three weeks at a time. This condition goes right back to childhood. 'Baby has a bad chest', or 'baby is ill again', was a common comment by his mother and was to culminate in his death from tuberculosis in January 1950. Eileen's health was also poor, she being very run down since the death of her beloved brother, Lawrence, also known as Eric, at Dunkirk in 1940. It was common knowledge that they both suffered from ill health, compounded by being heavy smokers. Eileen continued to work until November 1944, five months after they had adopted a baby boy christened Richard. Orwell had dearly wanted to be a father and, in the absence of a baby of their own, had discovered that a patient of Dr Gwen O'Shaughnessy, Eileen's sister-in-law, was having a child that could not be kept and made arrangements for his adoption, a solution that delighted Orwell and Eileen in equal measure.

But what was Orwell's contribution to the BBC and the propaganda war? It must be considered within the context of Mr Bateman's analysis of how the BBC and the War Cabinet approached the subject of giving factual information and while presenting it in its best possible light without resorting to downright lies, an approach that would surely have seen Orwell 'running for the hills'. He always felt that his contribution to the war was of little importance in the wider context of what needed to be achieved in overcoming Nazi aggression. However, Mr Bateman has looked at the evidence and has written a factual account of the pathway that the BBC created from the early beginnings through to the end of the war, with all the problems it created and subsequently overcame as more and more experience was gained. Mr Bateman's book is another serious and valued addition to the collection of works that have been written about the corporation over many years and it will no doubt stand the test of time.

Richard Blair

INTRODUCTION

MEMORIES OF THE RADIO FRONT BY DIONE VENABLES

My father was, like so many of his generation, an inveterate wireless geek. On 14 November 1922, the 2LO Wireless Station in Marconi House, London, began broadcasting to the nation for one hour each day. Pa was in Geneva, Switzerland, at that time, designing the first electronic interpretation system for a host of language translators at the League of Nations building. They had been trying to interpret the speeches of the initial twenty-two nations struggling to communicate together to save the world in their own languages. Pa dreamed up a perfect solution, but he missed the 14 November broadcast when the wireless 'hams' in the United Kingdom were glued to their transmitters and receivers, awaiting the voice of Arthur Burrows. Out of the crackly static, at 5.33 p.m. came that distant but firm voice announcing '2LO Marconi House, London calling ...' And so the BBC was born, and with it this fascinating device called the wireless (soon to be renamed 'the radio') came into the lives of those geeks – and eventually into vast swathes of homes, from great mansions to two-room working men's houses.

My own first awareness of the wireless must have been at a very early age because home to me was always a place where cables and aerials were festooned everywhere, apart from the kitchen and bedrooms, and my mother was often required to sit at the piano and sing into the microphone at three o'clock in the morning so that some crackly American ham halfway across the world could pick up music as well as speech. I remember the first time that I really took in the importance of our wireless was on 1 September 1939, when Prime Minister Neville Chamberlain announced that Hitler had launched an offensive into Poland at daybreak that day; two days later the United Kingdom had declared war on Germany to defend her allies. My sister June and I were called into the living room that morning where our parents were sitting close together, bent forward to catch every word of the prime minister's sad, thin voice. Our mother was in tears and Pa had his arm round her shoulders, not far off tears himself. We thought that someone important must have died – and, of course, those first Polish deaths were to be the start of what escalated into a murderous conflict.

The radio was to become a device of supreme importance to the war areas, and to those countries that were not at war, but fearful for their peoples' safety. It featured in every aspect of the increasingly mechanised process of battle, on the land, in the ships at sea and under the sea, and in the air. In 1943 Forces Broadcasting expanded and, under the aegis of the BBC, became BFBS (British Forces Broadcasting Service), providing news, entertainment and even connections between servicemen and their families. Communication became refined and daily more portable as war correspondents took radios into active war sectors and broadcast back to the BBC the events of battles as they were happening.

My war was, like that of so many others, an eventful one when, first, our flat was bombed early one evening while we were visiting our cousins just five minutes' walk away. The loss of Pa's extensive radio equipment was mourned (by him) more deeply than the rest of our possessions!

The second 'event', and June and I had a harrowing escape when our parents decided to send us to an aunt in Canada so that, with the invasion impending, Pa's two precious daughters would not face the horror of that dreaded invasion and what pillaging German troops would do to innocent young girls. We were booked to sail from Liverpool on 13 September 1940, and our luggage went ahead and was stowed aboard. The night before we were due to travel to Liverpool our parents spent hour after hour talking. By dawn they had decided that they could not bear to be parted from us, so we would not set sail for Montreal after all but would remain together to face whatever was ahead. I bade a sorrowful farewell to my beloved panda and an aggressive-looking doll with silver teeth that had been packed in my trunk, and it was with absolute horror that, nine days later, a bulletin was released to say that the vessel we were to have travelled in, *City of Benares*, although in the centre of a convoy, had been torpedoed in the mid-Atlantic. Of the ninety evacuee children on board, only seventeen survived. I was not quite 11 on that day and it took many years, even into young adulthood, to persuade myself that two innocent children who had taken our places had not been killed because of us.

The third major event was when my mother and I were buried under the house we were staying in, outside Beckenham, when a flying bomb (affectionately known as a doodle bug) landed in the garden, blowing down all but one wall of the house. By that time, my father and sister were both at Bletchley Park – Pa's knowledge of radio waves was being put to very good use.

Without Britain's ever-advancing knowledge of radio frequencies used to break the German cipher systems, we are told that the Second World War would have taken two years longer to be resolved. Following the end of the conflict in 1945, the Bletchley Park 'boffins', as we called those who are today referred to as nerds, set to and produced Colossus, the room-sized first programmable computer. The BBC, having proved its worth and staying power throughout the war, despite having been bombed twice, set about employing the brightest of the young servicemen as they were demobbed from their fighting roles. Broadcasting icons such as Alvar Liddell, Bruce Belfrage, John Snagge, Audrey Russell and Marjorie Anderson trained up a host of new voices, and the BBC's leap into television took radio into uncharted but exciting waters.

My growing up years were seriously defined by our constant love affair with our radio. The programme *Workers' Playtime* was created in 1941 in order to lighten the mood of those who were working at full tilt in factories throughout the United Kingdom, making armaments and essential goods. Men between the ages of 17 and 45 who were not eligible for call-up were required to be factory workers, firemen, ARP wardens and anything else to which they could be put to good use. Single women aged 20–30 were also required to volunteer, but by 1943 nearly 90 per cent of women were doing some kind of war work. My mother had a part-time job in the London Censorship, checking letters to block out information that might be useful to the enemy. Having a very good singing voice, she used to sing along to programmes such as *Music While You Work*, *Variety Bandbox* and *Workers' Playtime*, in which we were introduced to singers and entertainers such as Vera Lynn, Charlie Chester, and Elsie and Doris Waters, who were incidentally the sisters of actor Jack Warner.

During the school term we would gather around the wireless at 7.30 on Sunday evenings to listen out for the first strains of 'Serenade', which heralded violinist Albert Sandler and the Palm Court Orchestra. These musical interludes became part of the fabric of being at war and making the best of it! There were so many hard-working artistes keeping our spirits up, so that the mention of, say, Sandy MacPherson at the BBC Theatre organ, immediately conjures up the sound of 'Happy Days Are Here Again' (seriously inappropriate at the time) and the imagined image of the mighty Wurlitzer organ, rising from the orchestra pit with flashing lights and majestic presence, with the little Canadian organist thundering cheerful cadences into every home in Britain. *Workers' Playtime* was broadcast from a different factory every weekday, and it was a delight to hear the roars of approval from hundreds of hard-working munitions workers, taking a much-needed half hour away from their work benches, one day from 'somewhere in Wales', another day from 'up in hill country'. The radio enabled the BBC to create a new kind of humour, less subtle but more relaxed than the humour we enjoy today, and in this way we came to know very well comedians such as Tommy Handley, Arthur Askey, Jimmy Edwards, Vic Oliver, Bebe Daniels and Ben Lyon. Oh, I could go on for pages because they allowed me to howl with laughter all through my tenth year to my sixteenth, during which both Great Britain and yours truly had some pretty hairy experiences.

One of our greatest sources of amusement was the daily broadcast of Lord Haw-Haw, the American-born Briton William Joyce, whom Germany thought would be just the right man to undermine the British stiff upper lip. His daily broadcasts from Hamburg sneered at the certain terror of British citizens caused by the utter devastation being rained on London and our major ports and cities by the Luftwaffe, but his total lack of understanding of the attitude of the British population simply made his ridiculous assertions a source of constant mirth. At the end of the war in Europe, William Joyce was captured, tried and, in January 1946, hanged. He was 39 at the time. The ability of the people of these islands to be able to smile, if not laugh, through those terrible months, when we were all quite certain that we were to be invaded by the vicious and demented German dictator Adolf Hitler and his armies, was remarkable. Hitler's storm troopers were trained to kill, and to destroy the very fabric of which Great Britain was made, so it has to be another of the many miracles that actually kept us afloat – and at arm's length from Axis invasion.

At the centre of everything in nearly every household was the wireless, the beating heart of our world. The wireless permitted our King to broadcast messages of hope, and our charismatic Prime Minister Churchill to strengthen the backbone of the nation with stirring speeches such as the one he gave in Parliament on 13 May 1940: 'We shall fight on the beaches, we shall fight on the landing grounds, we shall fight in the fields ...', and I can remember all too well how thin we became as food grew more scarce by the week and had to be rigidly rationed.

As time rolled by, the war spread across the world and the United States of America came to join us, and with them came their reference to the 'radio', as they called it, which became such a strong connection between the people of our two nations. The radio gave us mesmeric war correspondents such as Ed Murrow, Walter Cronkite, Edward Ward and Richard Dimbleby, who incidentally became the BBC's first war correspondent, and their voices became as familiar to us as those of our parents. And at the end of that terrible conflict, the announcement of 'peace in our time' was lauded with the raised voices of the people young and old. Every radio was turned up to join singers such as Vera Lynn, and the songs that we all sang along with were never to be forgotten, however sentimental or silly the words were.

Remember the forces' sweetheart Vera Lynn with: 'There'll be bluebirds over, the white cliffs of Dover; Tomorrow, just you wait and see ...' I suppose those never-seen 'bluebirds over' was all that lyricist Nat Burton could dream up to rhyme with 'Dover', but who cared – it was all part of the euphoria. Anne Shelton, Vera Lynn, Tony Bennett, Gracie Fields all sang their hearts out from our Pye wireless sets, and you may be sure that not one child of those years still alive today has forgotten any of the lyrics. The song that stays the clearest in my memory from that day was that of a young singer, whose name I cannot find, but who we were told was in a wheelchair and I can still hear that very clear youthful voice, trembling with the emotion around her as she sang from Piccadilly Circus:

When the lights go on again, all over the world; And our boys are home again, all over the world ...

On VE Day, 8 May 1945, I was scrambling along the steep roof ridge of my best friend's house and we were festooning red, white and blue bunting all along the roof and around the chimney stacks. We were 14 years old, bursting with excitement, and in the house below three radios in three different rooms were turned on full blast. The sounds of the nation's joy filtered up to us, so we sat astride the long roof ridge and joined in with that anonymous young singer: 'When the lights go on again, all over the world ...'

It was so very good to be singing with the rest of our world on the Radio Front.

Dione Venables, March 2021

WHEN RADIO CAME OF AGE

The first official public broadcast that Dione describes in her remarkable introduction was transmitted at a time when barely one in 1,200 people in Britain possessed a radio licence. Year-on-year radio ownership continued to rise and by September 1939 almost three-quarters of UK households possessed a set, with most of the remainder having access to one. For the first time in British history, virtually the entire population, including British subjects in the dominions, could experience the same event simultaneously. Not only was the BBC able to bring major sporting events to the listening public, it was able to bring royalty to the people and take the people to royal occasions. The coronation of George VI in May 1937 was broadcast to a potential audience of over 2 billion people.[1]

The level of coverage that the BBC had achieved by the late 1930s was a timely milestone, for it was at this point that the radio became the medium by which people in Britain, and British subjects scattered throughout the many regions of the British Empire, would learn that they were again at war. The BBC later reflected with a measure of pride that, on 3 September 1939, those in Singapore could hear that the British Government's ultimatum to Hitler had expired at the same time as those in London.[2] Thereafter began the first war in which radio would play a significant role, in more ways than anyone could possibly have imagined of a medium not too distant from its infancy. As the war progressed, the BBC evolved rapidly from being a predominantly *home* organisation to a predominantly *overseas* organisation; at its twenty-first birthday celebrations in 1943, it was widely acknowledged that the BBC effectively came of age at a time when its purpose was primarily devoted to war.

Throughout the century of broadcasting that this and other books will seek to commemorate, the BBC has generally endeavoured to be truthful, objective and tread the fine line of impartiality, alongside its stated purpose to inform, educate and entertain. Such standards were considered sacred when the BBC transitioned from a private company into a public service corporation on 1 January 1927. When the first director general, John Reith, had applied to become head of the fledgling company in 1922, he had very little idea what broadcasting was, nor any awareness of the potential power within the medium of radio. Reith successfully negotiated a significant measure of independence for the BBC – a hard-won argument that held firm until the General Strike of 1926, when he was strong-armed by Whitehall into denying striking workers and their unions a voice over the airwaves. The broadcasting company was the sole conduit of news, and was told to dispel rumours, doubt and uncertainty, and to boost morale whenever possible, inviting accusations from opposition MPs and unions that it was effectively influencing public opinion.

Reith had reservations about the corporation being used as a mouthpiece of government, but knew only too well that Whitehall had the legal right to commandeer the BBC any time it chose, and to broadcast whatever message it wanted. The Trade Union Congress was also sufficiently aware of the fragility of the BBC's limited independence, and warned its striking members that the corporation was 'just another tool in the hands of the Government'. Despite an insistence from Prime Minister Stanley Baldwin that the corporation had not been coerced into compliance, and that 'the power of broadcasting had triumphantly showed itself in a searching test', the BBC was rapidly becoming viewed as an instrument of political power.[3] The corporation was savagely criticised by opposition MPs in the aftermath of the strike, including Labour leader Ramsay MacDonald, who had made repeated requests to broadcast a speech, only to be rebuffed on each occasion. The mantle of impartiality slipped again in 1931 over accusations of political bias following coverage of the general election. This time a grossly unfair imbalance of broadcasting time allotted to each of the main parties enabled a coalition government dominated by Tories to achieve a landslide victory – described by Labour leader Clement Attlee as 'the most unscrupulous in my recollection'.* Propaganda might have been a dirty word at the time, yet there were people who knew how to exploit the potential of broadcasting, without recourse to the murky world of lies and deception.

When Reith resigned from the BBC in June 1938, it was acknowledged that he had given the corporation integrity; people still talk of 'Reithian principles', and staff at Broadcasting House often joke that 'his ghost still stalks the corridors'. As director general, Reith never sat down on the job; he always stood and had an especially tall 'desk' made for this purpose. Hence, his subsequent replacement, Sir Frederick Ogilvie, cannot *literally* be said to have taken over Reith's seat; however, the hot seat was about to get considerably hotter. In September 1939 the BBC was placed on a 'war footing' and, despite retaining its freedom to create and schedule programmes, it was required to seek advice from all manner of external government bodies. Even though censorship of programmes would still be carried out at source, the BBC's new Home Service would be monitored under the watchful eye of the Ministry of Information (MOI), and its news bulletins by an independent Press and Censorship Bureau. The corporation would also be required to support the government as an instrument of both domestic and overseas propaganda. This would require European and Overseas Service editors to engage with other more secretive bodies dedicated to enemy-directed propaganda, beginning with the Department of Propaganda into Enemy and Enemy-Occupied Countries, split between Electra House (Department EH) and Woburn Abbey, and then in August 1941 by the Political Warfare Executive (PWE). On top of this, with the constant threat of air raids and lack of available space, the corporation would become fragmented, with departments scattered among different regions of the country.

---

* The BBC's decision to treat the three elements of the coalition as being separate and therefore entitled to their full allotted broadcasting rights had proved decisive. The government was also accused of having exploited the gold crisis to gain additional broadcasting time under the guise of 'financial emergency', thereby affording its ministers an almost complete monopoly of broadcasts at a critical point in the election campaign.

Regrettably, the new director general had little interest in propaganda, and was indifferent to its potential usefulness as a weapon of war. Shortly after taking up his position, Ogilvie informed the assistant director of programme planning, Harman Grisewood, that he believed the Germans to be 'a very sentimental people' and that the best thing we could do was to treat them to a rendition of Beatrice Harrison playing her cello to the sound of a singing nightingale.[*] Fortunately, as recruitment intensified at the corporation in response to the demands of war, the BBC was able to utilise the exceptional talents of people who recognised the potential of radio to become a valuable instrument of national and international propaganda. Here was a medium able to reach large numbers of people simultaneously, both at home and across international borders, virtually uncontrolled. In contrast to the written word, the direct and personal approach associated with broadcasting could more effectively appeal to the emotions of the listener. The ability of radio to infiltrate enemy-held territory and to transcend the borders of vulnerable nations extended the reach of international propaganda significantly in the 1930s, enabling governments to disseminate their views to overseas audiences directly. Hitler, Stalin and Mussolini all recognised the propaganda potential of radio, and made massive use of it in influencing both home audiences and populations abroad by establishing foreign-language programmes. These were typically aimed at showcasing the supremacy of their ideologies over western democracy.[**]

In contrast, successive interwar British governments remained sceptical or suspicious about the use of radio propaganda, and only later when the realisation set in that everything that was said across the airwaves had the potential to either damage morale or undermine military forces did the issue of censoring broadcasts appear on the political agenda. Among a small minority of backbench dissenters was Winston Churchill, who initially believed in the propaganda potential of

[*] The senior British diplomat Sir Robert Vansittart believed this 'sentimental' label
    was a mistaken impression, rather they were 'an emotional people' – a trait which
    'can produce tears and savagery'. (Vansittart, p.37)

[**] The Soviets had been propaganda conscious since the October Revolution and
    began broadcasting in English, French and German in October 1929.
    (Tangye-Lean, p.212)

radio and wanted the government to take over the BBC before Prime Minister Stanley Baldwin blocked all attempts to strip the corporation of its independence. As things stood, few in government realised that the comparatively liberal radio laws that the Baldwin Government initiated had rendered Britain particularly vulnerable to psychological warfare. As early as December 1930, workers in Britain were targeted by an appeal broadcast in English from Moscow with the aim of inciting British workers to revolt against their leaders.[4]* This was an early warning for a government committed to supporting the BBC's independent status.

Baldwin eventually came around to the view that 'in wartime, propaganda was a necessary evil and must be taken seriously' – a view not shared by everyone in Parliament. 'Propaganda' was still a deeply disparaged concept meaning lies, exaggeration, thought manipulation: all things that were considered to be 'the stuff of totalitarian regimes' and not something that British broadcasting should seek to emulate. 'Britons do not want to be told what to think or feel, or to become that mutton-headed herd of sheep that Hitler believes the German nation has always been, and always will be,' complained Harold Nicolson at the MOI. 'Whereas the totalitarian method is essentially a short-term smash-and-grab raid upon the emotions of the uneducated, the democratic method should be long term, seeking gradually to fortify the intelligence of the individual.'[5]

As late as 1944, the BBC still referred to such practices as 'publicity' rather than stoop to using the 'awful word' that the British Government had tried to ban from diplomatic vocabulary when the original MOI was disbanded after the First World War.[6] Such an attitude resulted in Britain significantly lagging behind her potential enemy on the eve of war, with Germany broadcasting thirty-six foreign-language programmes compared with Britain's ten.[7]

Such an attitude illustrates the striking difference between how propaganda was being viewed by different systems of government during the interwar period. Countries already employing propaganda as a weapon of state, such as Germany and the Soviet Union, had adopted it

---

* This was a departure from an undertaking given by the Soviet Government in regard to propaganda, prompting Britain's ambassador to Moscow to protest to the Soviet Government.

as a tool for the exclusive use of a single political party. In democracies that typically contained two political parties with a degree of mutual respect for one another, this couldn't ordinarily happen, for to violently attack the other's propaganda would be viewed as a slight on the true spirit of democracy. Initially there were concerns about the tone of political propaganda in wartime Britain, especially so when the Tory peer Lord Macmillan was named as the new Minister of Information, leading Labour leader Clement Attlee to suspect that the new MOI was 'just another arm of the Conservative propaganda machine'.[8]* Attlee need not have concerned himself while Chamberlain held the reins of government, for even as late as January 1940, Macmillan's successor, the former BBC Director General John Reith, was still seeking to understand what the Chamberlain War Cabinet regarded as being 'the principles and objectives of wartime propaganda'.[9]

Meanwhile, by February 1939 members on both sides of the House had taken note of the considerable activity on the part of various foreign governments in the field of radio propaganda. Ministers were urged 'to pay more attention to publicity, and to render moral and financial support to schemes which will make certain of the effective presentation of British news abroad'. By 1939, the total government expenditure on news services and publicity for foreign consumption was less than £500,000 – a fantastically small amount of money to be spent on something that could be of immeasurable importance, according to one honorable member: 'If done correctly far less money would need to be spent on destroyers and bombers.'[10]**

In contemporary study, it has become commonplace to split propaganda activities into 'white' undisguised propaganda, where no attempt is made to deceive, and 'black' deceptive or covert propaganda. Grey propaganda typically leaves the recipient guessing the identity of the source. Because the BBC tried to stick rigidly to its principles of honesty and accuracy, its propaganda broadcasts typically remained

* The striking differences between the propaganda methods of different governments was highlighted by F. Bartlett in a paper titled *Political Propaganda*. (1940, p.16)

** One editor in New Zealand commented, 'One Churchill speech is as good as a new battleship.' (Briggs, 1970, p.10) within safe limits that rarely strayed into darker territory, as 'black' stations typically came under the control of Department EH and eventually the PWE. However, in the heat of conflict, the government had its own specific propaganda aims and endeavoured to shield the public from bad news by censoring the BBC, by providing false information, by obstructing reporters and by encouraging the 'softening up' of certain news items. This course of action might have occasionally been good for home front morale, but each time it happened it effectively handed the propaganda initiative to the enemy.[*]

In the first instance, it was incumbent on the BBC to help the public bear the strain of war, both as an efficient means of disseminating vital information, and as an effective filter between the grim realities of war and the anxious listener. When disaster occurred, or when situations became particularly grave, Whitehall drip fed information to the BBC in a calculated manner, and exerted pressure on the corporation to compile its news bulletins in a manner least likely to damage public morale or create anxiety. Such an approach created friction between the BBC and government ministers, especially at times when huge numbers of people were tuning in to the German broadcasts. With a seemingly irresistible appeal, William Joyce (Lord Haw-Haw) became Britain's first radio personality, sending millions of listeners running to their radio sets at the first sound of 'Germany calling' direct from Hamburg. Despite government pressure, the BBC refused to dignify Haw-Haw's propaganda by issuing rebuttals, believing it would undermine its reputation as a trusted news source.

By the time of Dunkirk, the BBC had searched in vain for its own radio personality in an effort to implore the listening public to stay tuned at a peak time. After trying several uninspiring presenters, they offered the chance to the popular novelist and playwright J.B. Priestley. Little did they know that once the Yorkshireman got into his straight-talking, common-sense stride, his broadcasts would provoke a controversy that brought the political impartiality of the corporation into disrepute.

---

[*] During the Norway campaign, the BBC was given false news by the government regarding military movements in an effort to deceive the German High Command. The Germans were not deceived, but the public were and the BBC's reputation nosedived, taking many months to recover.

Despite the official censors' reluctance to interfere, the MOI eventually slung him off the air, to the immense disappointment of his 11 million-plus listeners, who were probably still smarting the next time they visited the ballot box. Meanwhile, Britain had inadvertently discovered its most effective antidote to Haw-Haw in the person of the incoming Prime Minister Winston Churchill, whose speeches were arguably the greatest morale-boosting propaganda the BBC ever broadcast.

Another arm of the BBC's home propaganda illustrates the ability of radio to raise morale through entertainment at a time of deep anguish – many listeners had either lost or been separated from loved ones, including their children. When the country found itself under serious threat of invasion, the radio became an effective counsellor and a steadying influence upon the listening public, who were facing the possibility of falling into the hands of the Nazis. The merits of the BBC's wartime variety programming is an exhaustive subject that is often mired in sentimentality and nostalgia, with limited regard for either its propaganda value or the often punishing schedule to which top-line artistes adhered. Such nostalgic reflection often presents a past recreated for entertainment purposes free from the horror of war, and can easily result in a distorted or lopsided view of history. BBC Variety utilised its premier artists in an effort to achieve its morale-boosting potential in different ways. Neither Tommy Handley nor (Dame) Vera Lynn are revered for their propaganda value, and yet their positive impact upon the morale of the listening public and British troops has enshrined the names of both in the history of British wartime entertainment.

Handley was a comedian made for the radio who elicited a good many of his laughs at the expense of the enemy. His topical comedy show *ITMA* became a sensation to the extent that over 40 per cent of the entire population were listening in to what was essentially very good morale-boosting propaganda. Handley committed himself to an exhaustive and punishing schedule that almost certainly resulted in his premature death. Similarly, 'forces sweetheart' Vera Lynn is seldom regarded as an instrument of the BBC's propaganda machine; her programme *Sincerely Yours* attracted over 16 million listeners, and yet for all its good intentions the show and its presenter came under fire in 1942 over the question of the perceived emasculating effect that Lynn and her 'sentimental songs' were allegedly having on the British troops.

In the second instance, the BBC effectively became the fourth arm of warfare as it facilitated efforts to win hearts and minds in war-affected areas, and in other potentially vulnerable regions around the world. Attitudes changed, and the realisation that propaganda was no less a weapon than a bullet took hold as the corporation extended its overseas reach significantly. By 1943, forty-eight languages were being broadcast, and there was never a time when the BBC transmitters fell silent. With a combined total of 133 hours of broadcasting a day, it sought to raise the morale of ordinary people living under occupation by countering enemy lies with truthfulness, and through facilitating contact between exiled government representatives and their oppressed populations.

The corporation also provided assistance in the form of skilled personnel to 'black' stations dedicated towards inflicting a programme of psychological warfare on enemy subjects and soldiers alike, and by aiding and assisting in the creation of resistance groups that evolved and emerged from the shadows inside the conquered nations. The spirit of resistance in occupied Europe owed much to the BBC, firstly as a force of inspiration and empowerment, and secondly through providing operational assistance. Britain's solitary public broadcasting service, which barely two decades earlier seldom did anything more daring than broadcast a cellist playing with a nightingale, suddenly found itself transmitting coded messages that could mean life or death for large numbers of people.

In the absence of any forward planning, the BBC's overseas radio propaganda effort relied almost exclusively on improvisation, and yet the corporation very effectively established itself as 'the voice of Britain'. Its biggest worry was the risks associated with directing inflammatory propaganda to those who could not be helped militarily. For a listener in Nazi-controlled Europe to be discovered tuning into the BBC's European Service could mean a death sentence, but listen they did, and subsequently reproduced the programme content in clandestine newspapers to extend the message further. On occasions, so successful was the BBC's radio propaganda that the Nazis were compelled to confiscate all known radio receiving equipment, even if it meant abandoning their own propaganda strategy. The corporation also went to great lengths to broadcast carefully weighted programmes to the farthest regions of the globe, especially to India at a particularly delicate point in the history of the country. Populations needed to be convinced that they would be far worse off under Hitler – despite Gandhi having accused War Cabinet emissary Stafford Cripps of attempting to bribe India 'with a blank cheque on a failing bank'.

Slowly, but surely, Britain's radio propaganda found ways to make a difference to people's lives; it really was a case of cometh the hour, cometh the men. Much of the story of the BBC's European Propaganda Campaign is contained in twenty-two boxes of directives residing in the Churchill Archive Centre in Cambridge – a collection containing enough revelations of interest to fill half a dozen volumes. The vast majority of these directives were issued under the name of Noel Newsome, recruited from the *Daily Telegraph,* first as European news editor, then as director of the European Service. Newsome became a key figure in the organisation, described by Asa Briggs as 'the most industrious, lively and imaginative of all the department's wartime recruits'.[11] Newsome had the full backing of the director of the Foreign Division of the Ministry of Information, and eventually European Service controller, (Sir) Ivone Kirkpatrick. He afforded Newsome a generous measure of freedom from the strict control of government bodies, including the Political Warfare Executive. Backed by the support and advice of Minister of Information Brendan Bracken, this essentially became the 'dream team', a highly efficient triumvirate that ensured the BBC would deliver propaganda within acceptable limits of truth in the firm belief that the protection of its reputation was sacrosanct.

Carefully controlled propaganda was a serious business in the days when all hopes for the conquered nations rested on Britain's shoulders to stand firm and continue the struggle. However, if Britain was to emerge victorious, American listeners would have to be won over. By September 1940, it became an absolute necessity that the resilience of a people under siege from relentless aerial bombardment was broadcast right into the homes of American listeners. Since 1937 the European director of CBS, Ed Murrow, had been based in London, and having been asked to assemble his own team of news reporters to cover the war, he immediately became inspired by the efforts of the BBC's wartime reporters to bring more realism into their reports. After much deliberation between Murrow and the MOI, the potency of radio propaganda was significantly enhanced with the presence of the actual sound of events taking place – be it guns or bombs, or even the simple sound of ordinary people hurrying to the air-raid shelter. For someone who was not even an employee of the BBC, Murrow became a familiar and highly influential figure at Broadcasting House. His influence certainly rubbed off on Lawrence Gilliam in the Drama Department, who recognised how the same enhancements could benefit the counter-propaganda element within the BBC's ever-increasing feature programmes. Occasionally, this kind of realism could backfire, particularly when the BBC was accused of over-dramatising real life and death events for the benefit of the listener.

The full story of the BBC's wartime propaganda activities does not lend itself to a strict chronological analysis. Domestic 'white' propaganda is more easily evaluated in such a manner; however, the study of overseas propaganda requires one to examine each dedicated service individually, as the propaganda was generally tailored for a specific audience. It was impossible for the BBC to 'speak with one voice' as listeners could comprise German factory workers, French or other European citizens living under occupation, or even native people in the dominions of the British Empire. Added to this, the corporation came under increasing pressure to allow the London-based exiled governments of conquered nations 'free time' on its transmitters, not only to maintain contact with their peoples under occupation, but also to counter the relentless tide of Nazi radio propaganda to which their populations were being exposed. This privilege was eventually conceded to those governments who had requested 'free time' when it was deemed appropriate; however, the resulting services have been largely ignored in previous BBC histories, beyond a cursory mention.

The BBC's overseas propaganda operation was also complicated by the fact that Britain had no coherent propaganda policy during the first year of war. When Churchill decided to place all responsibility for 'black' propaganda in the hands of Hugh Dalton at the Special Operations Executive (SOE), it marked the beginning of fourteen months of continual inter-departmental squabbling that seriously delayed all progress. The fog of conflict eventually gave rise to a revolution of reorganisation in both the BBC and in government departments dedicated to propaganda. It became a complicated process of political sparring that the researcher is compelled to unravel, prior to examining how the BBC arranged its broadcasts to the individual countries. Similarly, at home, the ever-changing nature of total war also precipitated round after round of organisational changes at the corporation, the details of which would also fill another good-sized volume. Committees came and went; Ministers of Information came and went; and departments were scattered so far and wide that there was seldom a time when the BBC as a unified corporation could sit back and draw breath.

We begin our focus during the weeks and months dominated by the anticipation of war, when the corporation drew up plans that would involve reorganising itself in accordance with wartime requirements. Beneath a slew of advice from government sources, the BBC was compelled to consider how it could be most effective towards supporting Britain's war effort.

2

RADIO PREPARES FOR WAR

The Second World War differed from all previous conflicts in the sense that there was a degree of forward planning in the full realisation that it would be total. The concept of 'total war' can be interpreted in many ways; typically we imagine the entire military force along with the industrial manpower of a nation being hurled at the enemy, with disruption and destruction at home being wrought on a colossal scale. For the writer and broadcaster J.B. Priestley, total war was 'right inside the home itself, emptying the clothes cupboards and the larder, screaming its threats through the radio at the hearth, burning and bombing its way from roof to cellar'.[1] For the historian Arthur Marwick, the concept of total war added up to 'a colossal psychological experience', with the cumulative effect amounting to real and enduring social change.[2]

For Britain to effectively counter total war, able-bodied persons at all levels of society would have to be incorporated into the war effort, and direct radio appeals would become the ideal medium for the purpose. Government ministers would need to talk directly to the public to get their messages and appeals across. Volunteers would be needed across a range of Civil Defence positions if casualty rates were to be kept to a minimum, while other volunteers would be required to help defend the island from possible invasion. In times of emergency, the widespread popularity of radio facilitated critical opportunities to launch nationwide appeals instantaneously. When the British Expeditionary Force found itself in the situation of its greatest peril on the beaches at Dunkirk, would it have been possible to save so many of those men without the desperate radio appeals for experienced maritime personnel?

As in the last war, bodies had to be created to monitor the content of all media outlets to ensure as best they could that nothing damaging could leak out. War had come a long way from the days when they were fought by professional armies in far-off lands – when life at home in the mother country just carried on as normal – and gone were the days when the press enjoyed full freedom to submit war reports, unmolested by any censorship departments.

During the Great War of 1914–18, home front propaganda was rigid to the extent that the carnage on the battlefields of France and Belgium was not allowed to be reported. Little wonder that very few people realised that, every time the front lines moved in newspaper illustrations, the tiny gains or losses had come at the cost of thousands of lives. The government had introduced the Defence of the Realm Act four days into the war, giving the authorities unlimited power to stifle criticism of the war effort. In his book *The First Casualty,* Phillip Knightley claims that during the First World War 'more deliberate lies were told than in any other period of history, as the whole apparatus of the state went into action to suppress the truth'.[3] Lord Kitchener had banned reporters from the front line at the outbreak of war, and those who did try to embed themselves were captured and warned that they would be shot if they tried to return.[4] Five reporters were eventually afforded access but their reports were heavily censored. British blunders and German victories went unreported, and even the Battle of the Somme, in which Allied troop casualties numbered over 600,000, went largely unreported, with the disastrous first day being described as a victory. Journalists admitted to feeling ashamed at the lies written and could only console themselves with the thought that they were sparing the families of men at the front from the horrors that their husbands and sons were facing.[*] Only later did the public learn the full facts, including the high casualty rates, the effects of shell shock and the widespread use of poison gas. Little wonder that in the minds of the plain citizen 'wartime propaganda' meant lies and deception disseminated by governments to suppress the truth. Such public mistrust would inevitably carry over into the later conflict.

---

[*] Leading journalists of the day William Beach Thomas, Phillip Gibbs and Hamilton Fyfe accepted knighthoods after the war. Fyfe regarded the award as a bribe to keep quiet about the inefficiency and corruption he had witnessed.

Lessons learned during the First World War conditioned the trends for the future of front-line warfare in terms of much wider use of radio technology, in particular the ability to address large numbers of soldiers up and down the line from a single transmitter. However, the same cannot be said for the innovation of radio technology in the domestic sense, especially for the purposes of political warfare in the event of any future conflict. The original Ministry of Information, formed in February 1918 under the leadership of Lord Beaverbrook, was dissolved immediately after the war on the assumption of a lasting peace. There was no appetite within the British Government to retain a department dedicated to propaganda in peacetime, and very little money was invested towards extending the reach of BBC radio transmissions overseas. In the early days of public broadcasting, the infant 'company' was not allowed to broadcast its own news bulletins, and was restricted to dictating agency reports only after 7 p.m., as it was felt that they could not be afforded an unfair advantage over the newspapers. In January 1927, after extensive negotiations the newly founded 'corporation' was finally afforded the right to air a single news bulletin after 6 p.m. There were also limitations in place regarding what the BBC was allowed to report, and not until March 1928 was the corporation granted permission to report on more controversial subjects such as politics or industrial unrest. Reports had to be strictly objective, and under no circumstances was the BBC allowed to give an opinion.

Not until the beginning of the 1930s did the BBC begin to upgrade its news reporting operations, mainly through increased staff levels and the installation of tape machines at its Savoy Hill facility. It was still unable to provide reports free from government interference, on one occasion being forced to replace a bulletin with piano music to protect the reputation of a prominent Cabinet minister. The BBC started recruiting journalists as early as May 1932, and by December of the same year had begun transmitting news bulletins and outside broadcasts overseas on its new Empire Service. A flashpoint occurred after Hitler had been appointed Chancellor of Germany in 1933, when the man deemed to be the BBC's first foreign correspondent, Vernon Bartlett, presented a talk on the subject of Germany's decision to leave the League of Nations in November of that year. Members of the British Government, including Prime Minister Ramsay MacDonald, complained that the talk had not been sufficiently anti-German. Bartlett had, by his own admission, 'said a mouthful' and admitted that his over-emotional broadcast had been irregular. Ministers began to question whether it should be in the power of the BBC 'to create a panic whenever one of their officials is so overcome with deep and sincere emotion, that he has not time to reflect whether the broadcasting of his sentiments will injure or improve international relations'.[5] The implication here was that too much foreign news was being interspersed with opinions by regular announcers, who it was felt had acquired significant authority through their familiarity with the listener.

Despite enjoying a large measure of public support, Bartlett's contract was not renewed, and regardless of the ever-increasing volatility of international relations in Europe in the late 1930s, the BBC remained astonishingly unconcerned with providing commentaries on international affairs right up until the Munich Crisis of September 1938. Similarly, it remained lukewarm to the idea of radio as an ideal new propaganda instrument, a medium that was already being used for political purposes throughout much of Europe. By 1938, thirteen European national broadcasting systems were state-owned, nine were government monopolies, four were directly operated by governments and only three were privately owned.[6] In Britain the only measure of control exercised by the Home Office was the establishment of the Wireless Telegraphy Act of 1904 stating that no person could establish a wireless telegraph station without a licence from the Post Office.

In Continental Europe, the nation states that had fallen under the rule of single-party dictatorships were way ahead of the game in harnessing radio for their own ends. In Germany, the Nazi Party had been quick to realise the potential of radio as an instrument of propaganda and political manoeuvring – an appreciation that radio had the power to change the nature of warfare. Adolf Hitler had been acutely aware of the value of propaganda from the earliest days of his political career, and lamented in *Mein Kampf* upon Germany's failure to utilise propaganda as effectively as the British had done in the First World War. He saw in radio a conduit whereby information could be fed to bring about 'the psychological dislocation of the enemy' – essentially to destroy the enemy from within. Hitler arguably became the greatest propagandist of the twentieth century, and made full use of the microphone from the moment he came to power in 1933.* He advocated disseminating 'big lies' that couldn't possibly be disbelieved, and immediately set up the Ministry of Enlightenment and Propaganda (*Volksaufklärung und Propaganda*), which set radio at the centre of the party's aim to control German life. At its head, Dr Joseph Goebbels believed implicitly in radio as 'the most modern and the most important instrument of mass influence that exists anywhere' and he would employ the medium in the process of modelling his ministry on the principles of Britain's First World War propaganda, which he regarded as 'the perfect prototype'.[7] Previously, the *Reichs-Rundfunk-Gesellschaft* (RGG) was the German equivalent to the BBC, and, having been part owned by nine regional entities, was originally endowed with a considerable level of autonomy, before Goebbels successfully acquired 100 per cent of the shares to the benefit of his Propaganda Ministry. Thereafter he commissioned thousands of cheap radios to be manufactured with the aim that every home in Germany should have one. Known as 'Goebbels Schnauze' (snout), or 'the People's Receiver', the radios were manufactured with just two valves and were unreceptive to short-wave broadcasts, with only German and Austrian stations appearing on the dial.

Right from the beginning, Goebbels firmly believed that it was possible to 'make public opinion', and achieved this partly through lies and deceit, and partly by ensuring that nothing critical or contrary to the party line could ever find a voice on the airwaves. Goebbels appointed Eugen Hadamovsky as his chief programme director, a man who shared his conviction that radio 'was the most powerful and the most revolutionary weapon we possess in the struggle for the new Third Reich'. Hadamovsky set about his task with zeal, instantly terminating the employment of anyone who was known to be politically impure, and endorsing a view of broadcasting as being the chief instrument of German propaganda. In a speech to officials following the 'radio purge' of 1933, he announced that all employees with an anti-National Socialist bias had been dismissed, before declaring to prolonged laughter and cheers that 'only one had behaved like a gentleman and hanged himself'.[8] Speaking at the International Radio Show in Berlin on

---

* It is notable that Hitler's interest in radio diminished as the war progressed.

18 August 1933, Goebbels conceded 'it would not have been possible for us to take power, or to use it in the ways we have without radio'. In the course of all its future dealings up until 1945, Goebbels' ministry would utilise radio propaganda as an effective political action. Typically its methods would involve inserting just enough of the truth to make the listener believe the questionable and often ridiculous bulk of what was being said over the airwaves. In June 1939, Goebbels would openly brag, 'we have created the Reich by propaganda'.

Whereas the Nazis viewed radio as a political weapon before all else, the British Government remained slow in realising the propaganda potential within the medium of broadcasting. While Hitler regularly delivered fiery oratories over the ether, Chamberlain's rare broadcasts were like fireside chats over tea and biscuits. There was very little censorship either, as programme scripts generally passed through the hands of the BBC's own censors, who focused more on decency than anything else. Considering how Vernon Bartlett had been treated for 'not being beastly enough to the Germans', correspondents typically avoided passing judgement on the conduct of nations or foreign leaders. On the rare occasions that programmes were broadcast on the subject of Nazi Germany, the corporation appeared to chronicle Hitler's success with mild enthusiasm. In a BBC recording from Germany following the Saar Plebiscite in 1935, the commentator bragged that 'microphones had been hung from the windows treating listeners to the sound of rejoicing German crowds'. In the same year it had dedicated an edition of its monthly magazine, *The Listener*, to H. Powys Greenwood's take on 'The Race Idol of Nazi Germany'. Greenwood had taken part in a 'torchlight procession' with Hitler's 1,500-strong Brownshirts all 'Heil Hitlering along the way for about three miles'. The march was intended to culminate in a salute to Dr Goebbels beneath the propaganda minister's balcony, in an event that he described as being 'rather fun'.[9] Even more astonishing was a comment attributed to BBC Director General John Reith at a party in the German Embassy hosted by the Reich Minister for Foreign Affairs, Joachim von Ribbentrop, at the time of the Anschluss: 'I told Ribbentrop to tell Hitler that the BBC was not Anti-Nazi, and I invited him to have my opposite number come over to visit and put up the flag for him.'[10] Presumably Reith meant to raise the swastika above Broadcasting House!

Among the BBC's more positive achievements in the run-up to war was the setting up of a facility for listening to radio broadcasts in other countries. The BBC Monitoring Service, originally based at Wood Norton in Worcestershire, began in 1939 as a way of countering the propaganda of German and Italian broadcasters and was ramped up significantly when war began with the formation of the Monitoring Service Information Bureau at the request of Whitehall. For those on the front line of the BBC's propaganda war, the Monitoring Service would be the most valuable source of information towards turning the enemy's false claims back upon itself. By 1941 over 400 monitors of various nationalities were listening in for twenty-four hours a day, requiring over a million spoken words to be carefully assessed and condensed into a single document to be scrutinised for inconsistencies by the various Overseas Service directors.[11] Additionally, every promise contained in the Nazi broadcasts would be catalogued for retrieval at a later date, by which time the promise would have gone unfulfilled. Later in the war, the value of the service's contribution towards forearming the newsroom with the weapons of counter-propaganda was incalculable. Monitors were able to successfully intercept official German communications to friendly newspapers and radio stations in all enemy-occupied countries. These transmissions were typically broadcast at dictation speed on a frequency not usually used for broadcasting, allowing monitors to study the content and provide a response before the statement was published. When the Germans began to send them in code, monitoring service engineers soon managed to crack them, including weekly commentaries by Goebbels himself. This led the propaganda minister to suspect that there must be a spy in his ministry. The Monitoring Service relocated to Caversham in Berkshire in April 1943, where the reception improved significantly, making it possible to monitor further stations previously unheard.

Despite the BBC looking optimistically towards the future with enthusiastic features on its approaching summer season of programmes, by the spring of 1939 it was becoming ever clearer that war was coming. The Military Training Act of May 1939 was Britain's first act of peacetime conscription: confirmation that key figures in government did not expect to be at peace for much longer. Ministers would utilise the services of the BBC to accelerate preparations for a war in which the civil population could not be regarded as non-combatants. During the First World War, not only had the public been shielded from the horrors of mechanised warfare, they had also been taken by surprise by the all-new danger from air raids – firstly from the giant Zeppelin airships, and then from Gotha bombers. There were no purpose-built air-raid shelters (unless you designed and built them yourself!), meaning civilians had to rely on underground stations, cellars and basements for protection. Over 1,400 civilians had fallen victim to these raids in the summer of 1917, a morale-dampening strategy that had put those 'keeping the home fires burning' very much in harm's way. In the coming war, experts over-pessimistically predicted that casualty rates could be counted in their hundreds of thousands during the opening phase – envisioning a Nazi bombing fleet primed and ready for action from day one.

The government first used the services of the BBC in preparing the population for air raids at the beginning of 1938, when the Home Office began to broadcast publicity and explanations on the subject of air-raid precautions (ARP). With ever-increasing access to the microphone at this time, ministers were able to supplement information previously issued in the form of leaflets and booklets with the aim of priming the population for the coming emergencies. Much of the early government communication appeared to be aimed at advising people on some sensible measures to take should there actually be a war, but at the same time inducing people to stay calm. Other broadcasts and publications urged responsible people to get involved at an early stage – to join up with the volunteer services and become leaders, rather than bystanders. The BBC was also urged to forewarn and educate the public of the potential gravity of air raids, with reference to more recent events. This included enlightening listeners to the horrific reports of air raids during the Spanish Civil War in the mid-1930s, a time when the Luftwaffe Commander-in-Chief Hermann Göring had unleashed his young, trigger-happy fighter pilots of the Condor Legion onto the stricken areas loyal to the Republic, in particular the Basque region where the town of Guernica was totally obliterated. Chilling images captured through the lens of the acclaimed photojournalist Robert Capa showed people running for their lives.

In June 1938 the BBC recruited war correspondent John Langdon-Davies for a special broadcast in which he read extracts from the log of the municipal authorities in Barcelona in June 1938. The programme included eyewitness accounts from those affected by the air raids of 16, 17 and 18 March that year in which an estimated 3,000 people had been killed and over 25,000 injured. It might have scared a large number of listeners half to death, but the BBC described it as 'a valuable contribution to the ARP series of programmes that will warn listeners what it is like to be involved in a modern air raid'. In Britain, the government was determined that the people of London would not be as exposed or taken by surprise in the same way as those in Barcelona had been. The first air-raid shelters were delivered and erected in gardens over six months before war was declared.

Aside from broadcasting a slew of good advice on what people should do to keep themselves and their families safe, other BBC broadcasts throughout 1938 and early in 1939 engaged eminent speakers to talk in defence of the government's policy of appeasement. Talks were broadcast with such titles as *The Way of Peace* by Sir Alfred Zimmerman and *The Force of Compromise* by MP Harold Macmillan – carefully scripted programmes that lent an impression of the corporation 'buying into' government policy. In reality, as the former historian of the BBC Jean Seaton has suggested, the corporation might have echoed appeasement, but was secretly preparing for war.[12] Agreement had already been reached between Reith and the Post Office that the Board of Governors would be out of commission whenever war broke out. Less secretive were the programmes incorporating ARP instruction that were ramped up significantly following the Nazi annexation of Austria on 12 March 1938. A broadcast by Home Secretary Samuel Hoare two days later was titled *The Citizen and Air Raids*, and then a week later it was the turn of the London County Council leader Herbert Morrison to broadcast *London's Part in Air Raid Precautions*. These were followed in May by *How the ARP is Getting On* (Hoare) and, in June, *ARP – the London Auxiliary Fire Service* (Morrison), which included comments from the leader of the service, the aptly named Commander Firebrace.

Figures appear to indicate that people took the government broadcasts seriously, as appeals for ARP wardens seemed to grow impressively with each phase of the deepening crisis. By mid-1938 around 200,000 had been recruited, a figure that rocketed to 700,000 following the Munich Crisis of September that year. This figure continued to grow to a staggering 1.5 million volunteers by the beginning of the war. A broadcast appealing for recruits to join the Women's Voluntary Service by the Marchioness of Reading was equally successful – setting another valuable arm of the ARP service on the path to over a million volunteers. The BBC also assisted in the creation of a huge army of fireguards in major cities throughout Britain. The effectiveness of radio in rallying people to the cause is reflected in figures indicating that, by September 1939, almost 2½ million Britons had signed up for either paid or unpaid work in preparation for war – a figure well in excess of projected targets.[13]

It is noticeable from this time that the BBC's feature programmes also increased, many of which generated a form of official 'white propaganda' intended to stimulate or encourage feelings of national unity. The corporation's feature output grew rapidly from only five programmes in 1933 to over 200 in 1938, incorporating what Jeanette Ann-Thomas in her study of BBC features describes as 'a steady stream of morale features drawing on the traditions and history of the nation'.[14] From February 1938, the corporation embraced countless opportunities to showcase the military might of the British Empire, beginning with *The Inauguration of the Singapore Naval Base*, and thereafter seemed to be on hand to deliver outside broadcasts from the dockside wherever and whenever a battleship or destroyer was being launched. In June, it delivered a special broadcast from Gibraltar, featuring the Ceremony of the Keys by the 1st Battalion, King's Own Yorkshire Light Infantry. In September it was the turn of the RAF: *Life of an Airman* stressed 'life in the Air Force is not all work' and was calculated to entice new recruits into the service.

The idea of citizen soldiers did not enter the government's thinking at the beginning of 1939, despite clear recognition that a critical target would be the industrial heartlands of the enemy. Destroy industrial production and you severely restrict your enemy's ability to fight, was the war strategist's view. With much vital war industry situated in large cities, Samuel Hoare had hoped he could enter into a treaty with the enemy by which the city centres would only be bombed when those who worked therein had gone home.[15] Another chief worry among most of the nations of Europe concerned the likely use of poison gas, which had caused over a million casualties in the

First World War, resulting in at least 100,000 deaths. The acclaimed science fiction writer H.G. Wells had predicted in *The Shape of Things to Come* that the next 'great war' would be fought using enormous gas bombs. So terrified were the leaders that no fewer than thirty-one of them signed the Geneva Protocol in 1925 forbidding the use of poison gas, and yet at the time war was declared all thirty-one of them were busy experimenting with increasingly deadly gases.[16] The Home Office had been busy priming the population for the possibility of gas attacks as early as July 1935, when it began issuing information leaflets and booklets in anticipation of such an emergency. Not until July 1939 did the government begin instructing people to listen to the radio with paper and pencil in hand and to take note of what they were being told in relation to ARP. This was the earliest confirmation that, in wartime, government broadcasts would take precedence over regular BBC schedules. A measure of public assistance towards interpreting so many new government regulations would be largely invested in the BBC – an indication that the importance of the microphone was gradually, if a little belatedly, being recognised.

With the prospect of peace becoming more unlikely by the day, it should have been a blessing that the founding of another Ministry of Information to operate in conjunction with the BBC had been long in the planning stage. The new ministry, based at Senate House, would come into effect on the day war was declared, with its stated responsibilities being to oversee national propaganda, to maintain public morale at home and to influence public opinion abroad. This would include monitoring all press and radio transmissions to ensure that nothing potentially damaging to the nation's war effort was ever aired. In practice it would take a long time for the new ministry to become effective – mainly because it had been primed to expect immediate death and destruction on a grand scale, rather than a war in which nothing of major significance happened over many long months. The decision to create the new ministry had drawn heavily on the words of the former Prime Minister Stanley Baldwin, who spoke with authoritativeness in Parliament about how the First World War had demonstrated an absolute need for propaganda. Baldwin asserted that 'propaganda was a necessary evil of modern warfare', a point reinforced in a report by the Ullswater Committee into the future of broadcasting in 1936. The committee's recommendation that in times of national emergency the BBC would have to come under full government control would have been music to the ears of Winston Churchill, who had designs on utilising the service solely for propaganda purposes from the beginning.* His views were placated further by the setting up of the Joint Broadcasting Committee in the spring of 1939 for the purpose of creating and disseminating constructive propaganda programmes to enemy countries for clandestine distribution. The director of the new committee, Hilda Matheson, struggled to develop any rapport with the BBC's European Service personnel, who resented the interference of this additional body, particularly when war became real and transmitter time was increasingly more valuable.

The initiative begun in 1937 by Tom Harrison called Mass Observation serves as a useful indicator of what many people thought about the radio broadcasts and the information they were being fed in the run-up to war. The diary entries tend to suggest that most people took the public information broadcasts seriously, including the advice about the precautions to be taken when the expected air raids began – particularly on how they should protect their homes. Other information broadcast via the MOI successfully induced people to stick within the moral parameter of what was considered proper and decent in wartime, as nobody wanted to be viewed as extravagant, greedy or hedonistic in times of great hardship and selflessness, and least of all utter those careless words that might put home soldiers or civilians in danger. It is also noticeable that people had to deal with frightening rumours on an almost daily basis, and although there is not much indication that the more outrageous ones were being taken seriously, such rumours played on the minds of participants to the extent that they were regularly recorded in their diaries. Frustration over not knowing what to believe became a constant irritation among members of the public anxious to know what was going on, especially those with loved ones on active service overseas.

Regrettably, there is also evidence to suggest that some people took the pre-war advice they were being given a little too seriously. A BBC broadcast on 26 August 1939, accompanied by a pamphlet titled *Advice*

---

* In 1935 the Committee of Imperial Defence had also made the case for the government to take over the BBC in the event of war.

to *Animal Owners*, urged people to have their animals destroyed if they could not relocate them somewhere in the countryside. It was made clear to owners that pets would not be allowed in public shelters, and it is estimated that a fifth of London's cats and dogs (around 750,000 animals) were destroyed in preparation for food shortages before war broke out. Through the power of radio, people were effectively shamed into believing it would be inappropriate to keep an animal during a period of severe shortages, and were led to take action that they would long regret.

Despite some encouraging early signs, the constantly renewed appeals for evacuation of children from London being continually broadcast over the airwaves received a disappointing response, as though people simply refused to believe the bombing would happen until they started raining down. Mothers and fathers were suspended in a state of anxiety about what to do for the best; despite observations that some mothers took advantage of the opportunity, very few wanted to be parted from their children, and neither did they want to put them in serious danger. After six months of Phoney War, further appeals were made on the radio for parents not to bring their children home when so many were beginning to wonder why they had been so hasty in sending them away in the first place. Many parents had sent their charges away to the Kent coast on the promise of a long holiday, but they were essentially putting them right in the bombers' path, or even the likely entry point of any sea borne invasion. Parents soon began to ask themselves 'what exactly are we trying to protect them from?' for there were no invaders coming over the hill, and no sign of any air raids. By January 1940, it was estimated that almost 60 per cent of those who had been evacuated at the beginning of the war had returned home again, despite government broadcasts warning them not to.[17]

When the situation became more serious in mid-1940, a new wave of evacuation appeals were broadcast, leading people to seriously worry over whether the BBC's evacuation reports were effectively telling the enemy which stations were likely to be crowded. A different kind of mindset was apparent by this time, when the likelihood of invasion or air bombardment was imminent: 'If we're going to get killed – let's all be killed together.'[18] Another common complaint that was overheard and reported by the MOI was that 'the kids of rich parents were able to get away early' owing to overseas evacuation information only being receivable on the more expensive radio sets. When top-level discussions about the possible postponement of the government's Children's Overseas Reception Boards Scheme (CORBS) were reported over the airwaves, people began complaining that 'now that the rich children have all been got away, the scheme is dropped'.[19] In the light of true revelations, such cynicism was wide of the mark, as there were many among the better-off who selflessly volunteered to help administer the evacuation effort in deprived areas, and this included ensuring that *all* children were considered for overseas schemes.[*]

Aside from its constant appeals to anguished parents undecided about what to do for the best, the BBC also formed a strategy to provide continuity of education during the days of mass evacuation. These plans were put into effect within two days of war being declared, when programmes intended to amuse and interest the evacuees were transmitted, including broadcasts aimed towards helping them adjust to their new surroundings. It was recognised that schoolchildren often took an insatiable interest in war, and to placate them a weekly talk on current affairs and a daily five-minute news commentary was included, which became a great success.[20] Later in the war the corporation arranged programmes for children whose schools had been bombed. Figures published to illustrate the value of school broadcasting in wartime show that the number of schools using the BBC service rose from 8,500 in 1939 to around 11,000 in 1940, indicating that school broadcasting reached a new pinnacle in wartime.[21] A special royal broadcast aimed at boosting the confidence of evacuees was aired on *Children's Hour* on 13 October 1940, when Princess Elizabeth, with her sister Princess Margaret by her side, sent a message of encouragement and sympathy to the children. The broadcast also went down well with adult listeners, of whom a staggering 18 million had tuned in to hear the royal statement. The BBC would strive to do whatever it could to facilitate morale-boosting contact between worried parents and their children with such features as *Hello Children* and *Children Calling Home*,

---

[*] Dione Venables clearly remembers her mother's concern over the East End charity where she volunteered, which included some twenty primary schools, and her relief at the setting up of an overseas evacuation scheme for state schools.

which began on Christmas Day 1940 and often caused much emotional upset among corporation staff.

All of that was to come, for in the meantime the corporation had drawn up its plans in line with government requirements in advance of the coming emergency. Little did senior department heads realise that, following the dreaded announcement that Britain was again at war, it would be almost another year before the kind of war they had envisaged would begin to take a terrible toll on the listening public – a situation that resulted in a significant measure of unfair criticism being directed towards the corporation.

3

NOT THE WAR WE EXPECTED

rom the moment Hitler focused his guns on Poland, few people in Britain wanted to be too far from a radio. When the tanks finally breached the Polish border on 1 September 1939, people typically kept the set permanently on, 'listening with half an ear', and even in rural Cornwall people congregated in groups around the rustic cottages of those who possessed radio sets.[1] Believing that war was now inevitable, the Secretary of State for the Home Department, Samuel Hoare, stated Whitehall's somewhat ambiguous position in relation to the BBC:

> the government would not take over the corporation, but would encourage close liaison between the Ministry of Information and the BBC, with definite regulations as to how the work would be carried out.[2]

On the morning of 3 September, after being told several times to 'stand by for an announcement', there followed frustrating delays filled with irritating peals of bells as though Britain were already celebrating victory. Nobody was in any doubt about what was to follow, and when Prime Minister Neville Chamberlain finally delivered the address, the despairing listener typically found solace in a period of quiet reflection. One diarist for Mass Observation recalled that 'no one said a word. We sat there in silence until the National Anthem was played, then, still in silence each got up and went to their own room.'[3]

Inside Broadcasting House, the war footing that had long been prepared began when all pre-arranged programmes came off the air without warning, while corporation staff studied the contents of sealed instructions that they were now permitted to open. A new transmission system was to be introduced for the purpose of avoiding giving assistance to enemy aircraft – a measure that resulted in the eight pre-war stations being reduced to a single Home Service, with the former regional services providing a contributory function. The new service would air each day from 7 a.m. until 12.15 a.m., with bulletins and communications being intensified daily as it was widely suspected by people inside government 'that London would be reduced to rubble within minutes of war being declared'.[4] Top-level meetings had already taken place within the Home Publicity Division in which the likelihood of an overwhelming bombing campaign being launched immediately by the Luftwaffe was discussed.[*] Those fears seemed to be confirmed when an air-raid siren sounded just minutes after Chamberlain's announcement, and even though the mystery warning had turned out to be a false alarm, soon-to-be war correspondent Godfrey Talbot remembered that the wailing siren 'gave everybody that sinking feeling that war was finally here'. It would be almost another year before any bombs would fall; although when King George VI spoke to the nation on the six o'clock bulletin, his speech included a chilling reminder that 'the war would not be confined to the battlefield'.

While the BBC retained its autonomy to schedule programmes, the MOI would exercise considerable influence and control over the corporation's earliest war-related broadcasts. This arrangement was not revised until 1941, when responsibility for home news and talks was restored to the governors of the BBC. In the meantime, the proposed new order of things did not get off to the best of starts for the new ministry when, within a day of war being declared, its leaders were incensed that the War Office had bypassed the new protocol and given information about the appointment of Generals Ironside and Lord Gort to lead the British Expeditionary Force directly to the BBC. Over the next two days both the Air Ministry and the Admiralty did the very same thing, and just a few days later, things went from bad to worse when a series of blunders occurred that resulted in the removal of the ministry's responsibility for censoring news broadcasts. An official broadcast from Paris on 11 September had wrongly stated that British

---

*   The acclaimed military historian and strategist Sir Basil Liddell Hart had earlier prophesised 250,000 air-raid casualties during the first week.

troops were engaged in offensive action against German forces, leading the MOI to conclude that there was little point in continuing to withhold news that the British Expeditionary Force was in France, and it released a statement to that effect to the assembled press. Anxious to make the morning editions, journalists submitted drafts of the press agency report that included the false information about armed combat, to which the War Office expressed considerable alarm and swiftly reimposed the ban. In the ensuing chaos, the MOI had to make a plea for retrospective self-censorship, while Scotland Yard were required to seize newspapers, erect roadblocks in Fleet Street and raid newspaper offices. Following a storm of protest in the popular press, from 9 October responsibility for issuing and censoring news was thereafter transferred to a separate department under Sir Walter Monckton called the Press and Censorship Bureau, and was not reinstated under the MOI again until April 1940. Opposition leaders thought this was a daft idea and questioned the decision to put in charge of news distribution the man who was responsible for killing it.

For the public at large, wartime radio rapidly became interwoven with daily life as the primary medium of communication. A memorandum to the director of Home Publicity recommended that the language of the BBC's wartime output must be kept simple because the vast majority of people had left school at just 14 years of age.[5] Now that they were officially at war, government ministers noticeably altered their language when referring to the Nazi hierarchy in news bulletins. Men who up until yesterday had been Mr Hitler, Mr Ribbentrop and Doctor Goebbels were now just Hitler, Ribbentrop and Goebbels.* There was also a deep sense of anger among the general public following the failure of 'appeasement' and diplomacy in general, and Broadcasting House was urged to consider programmes that might help to reunite the country in the interest of the common cause.

With the task of fighting the war and ultimately paying for it inevitably falling greatly upon the shoulders of the plain citizen, the one thing that still stuck in the throat among the veterans of the previous war was that the promised 'land fit for heroes' had not materialised. They would not be forsaken again in the same manner, for unlike in 1914 when working-

---

* This was despite a BBC directive to retain the titles.

class education was still in its infancy, the ordinary working man was much better informed by 1939, particularly if he was an active participant in the trade union movement, or even a regular student of the National Council of Labour Colleges. The colleges were the intellectual arm of the Labour Party and the main organ of working-class education before the war, and in the summer of 1939 they published a book with the title *Why War? A handbook for those who will take part in the Second World War*. The embattled MOI, whose major function was now dedicated to what its minister called 'that unattractive word propaganda', had already begun to detect a measure of complacency among some working men, believing they had no idea what a Nazi victory would mean. It was noted that their high level of 'war anger' was not necessarily being directed at Germany.[6]

The government used the media services to explain away the failure of its diplomatic efforts to avoid war. Chamberlain believed he had acted in accordance with the mood of the British public, which he felt had been overwhelmingly opposed to another war. The claim has been made that he hid behind public opinion, with the result that no attempt was ever made to stiffen public resolve towards standing up to Hitler.[*] In an effort to cut the crestfallen prime minister some slack, the MOI published additional booklets, including *How Hitler Made the War*, in an effort to illuminate the culpability of the Nazi leaders. The publication was supported by a number of 'enlightening broadcasts' from the BBC that were not well received, for it was difficult to justify war against the background of a failed policy of appeasement. Opinion among the public had previously been divided over the Munich Crisis, while the government itself had been torn apart following the outcome. Duff Cooper had resigned as First Lord of the Admiralty, having seized a pro-appeasement MP by the throat, while Harold Macmillan took great delight in burning an effigy of Chamberlain on Guy Fawkes Night.[7] Not only has history looked unkindly upon Chamberlain's part in 'serving Hitler his victuals course by course', as Churchill had put it, he was further criticised for continuing to speak out against a policy of accelerated rearmament. Despite a measure of superficial support

---

[*] An opinion poll in July 1939 found that 76 per cent of Britons believed Britain should honour her obligations over Poland. (Bouverie, p.339)

from the BBC, 'appeasement' had ended in failure, and few took pity on the man who believed he could make deals with dictators – one contributor to Mass Observation reported comments that he should be 'put up against the wall and shot!'[8] Much worse criticism would follow in the months ahead for the beleaguered prime minister. The humiliating retreat from Norway in early May 1940 would cost him his job, and the subsequent disaster at Dunkirk would further expose how under-equipped and ill prepared the armed forces were following his assurances that the BEF would be of sufficient strength to counter the Nazi invader. In its report of 15 June, the MOI reported 'talk of lynching Chamberlain and the old gang if things got bad'.[9]

In the meantime, little did the government know that Hitler had specifically forbidden bombing attacks on Britain during the first six months of 'Phoney' or 'Bore War'. All of the hardships inflicted on the public during much of the first year – be it disruption, restriction, or inconvenience – were not inflicted by the enemy but by the British Government. The lack of news departed significantly from expected forecasts; the BBC scheduled up to ten news bulletins a day and finished up with nothing to report – even Richard Dimbleby's broadcasts from France with the BEF seemed devoid of anything of real interest. With virtually all other leisure activities closed down, the radio was the sole means of entertainment and served up an endless mixture of gramophone records and organ recitals. In between music there were often-repeated announcements that led to the creation of the age-old perception of the BBC 'fussing away like an aged spinster offering all manner of advice', earning itself the everlasting nickname 'Auntie'. Referring to the insufferable dullness of the new radio schedule, Labour's deputy leader Arthur Greenwood accused the government and the BBC of being 'determined to make everyone's life as miserable as possible', and later warned the government that if the news is dry, the entertainment mediocre and the music of a low standard, the listener just turns the dial to get a foreign broadcast.[10]

Criticism of the new Home Service was not confined to Whitehall either. Within two days of war being declared and four days after the Home Service had replaced the normal BBC schedules, regular listeners also started to complain about the dullness of the new service. Within the first fortnight of its existence, listeners were 'treated' to no fewer than forty-five sessions of organ music by the hapless Sandy MacPherson. Listeners complained sarcastically that they would rather face the German guns than any more of MacPherson.* Very soon it was not uncommon to hear listeners in queues openly admitting that they preferred the French and German services better – this at a time when the government was seriously worried about the popularity of Lord Haw-Haw's propaganda broadcasts from Germany. The listening public were far more amused by Haw-Haw (William Joyce), regardless of his claims that Britain's food queues were a mile long, the barracks were in open mutiny, the munition workers were on strike, and nor did they tire of hearing for the umpteenth time that HMS *Ark Royal* had disappeared.

It wasn't necessarily the information that attracted listeners in their thousands, rather his personality, and in particular his accent that, to the government's displeasure, too many people found irresistible. It was all the more galling for ministers to hear Joyce's sneering remarks in the full knowledge that he had already been on the security radar through his involvement with the British Union of Fascists. When the Home Office finally issued a warrant for his detention, to the immense embarrassment of his pursuers, Joyce and his wife were already in Germany, having slipped through the net a week earlier. As a fluent German speaker, Joyce courted an introduction to officials in Goebbels' Propaganda Ministry and was immediately offered a job as an announcer on the Nazi-controlled radio service's British broadcasting section. Joyce designed his broadcasts specifically to please the Nazi hierarchy, and quickly emerged as the leading radio propagandist at the station. Through him the Germans held a firm grip on the propaganda initiative, and what was worse, because it was radio propaganda, it could not be censored by the British in the same way as reports appearing in the daily newspapers. In an effort to understand the extent of his popularity in Britain, the MOI asked the BBC to ascertain the listening figures, which by January 1940 did not make for comfortable reading. It was estimated that one-sixth, some 6 million, of the adult population were regular listeners, and another 18 million were occasional listeners.[11] Mass Observation

---

* Sadly, MacPherson's organ and much of his music was destroyed when a bomb hit the BBC's St George's Hall in September 1940. The BBC decided not to report it. (Baade, 2013)

studies also showed that in the early stages of the war people were more inclined to believe the German broadcasts than their own, for unlike in Nazi Germany, it was not a crime to listen to enemy propaganda in Britain, as manufacturers actively promoted sets that could pick up foreign stations. In February 1940, the BBC finally acknowledged Haw-Haw's existence on air in an effort to shame listeners as 'unpatriotic' and 'of playing directly into the hands of Goebbels'.

Having no means to prevent Haw-Haw's broadcasts, much heated discussion took place between Whitehall and the BBC over how best to neutralise him. The corporation's head of Drama, Val Gielgud, was shoved into the front line to answer government criticism, and conceded that the BBC had planned for the wrong war – the war the government itself had feared of mass destruction and death, rather than the long months of not much happening. Nobody in government could argue with him, as it was those in office who had masterminded the BBC's response to the state of emergency that it thought would happen any day. The search for a rival to counter Joyce would eventually light the fuse for an additional source of irritation for the government (something I will return to); however, it would take a change of prime minister for the most effective man for the job to come to the fore. Chamberlain would suffer a no-confidence vote in May 1940 and resign from office, leaving the man who replaced him, Winston Churchill, to emerge as an unlikely master of the medium of radio. Only after his legendary speeches that followed the disaster at Dunkirk, did Haw-Haw come to realise that he now had a formidable opponent in the person of the new British prime minister.

In the meantime, there was some relief for fans of the BBC's regular football commentaries when, after having voided the season just eighteen days after war was declared, the Football Association temporarily re-formed the leagues on a regional basis. Despite the fact that a total of 784 footballers had signed up for the war effort, the loss of football was very soon deemed to have a negative influence on morale for soldiers, civilians and radio listeners alike. Even though stadiums were limited to an 8,000 capacity, the MOI were mindful that such relaxation of safety measures could give rise to complacency. Further discussion on more direct home propaganda resulted in all-round agreement that ministers should broadcast at weekly or fortnightly intervals for half an hour, 'to summarise the current position for the benefit of the listening public'. This arrangement irritated opposition leaders, who were frequently 'bumped off the air' to make way. In a letter to the director general, Frederick Ogilvie, London Council leader Herbert Morrison pressed him to come clean about the BBC having become a mere government organ, 'just so we know where we are'.

A key directive issued during the first weeks of war was that there should be 'sustained propaganda on the Home Front', and that the Ministry of Information should prioritise this consideration.[12] At Broadcasting House, Programme Controller Basil Nicolls and Talks Director Richard Maconachie were given joint responsibility for Home Service propaganda – despite both men being suspicious of propaganda and equally determined that the corporation should not become an agency for it.[13] The Home Broadcasting Board, established in October 1939 for the purpose of 'controlling programme policy', also deemed that any propaganda representing 'a perversion of the truth' was not considered to be 'in accordance with BBC policy'. The first attempt at formulating a propaganda policy occurred shortly before former BBC Director General John Reith replaced Lord Macmillan at the Ministry of Information in January 1940. Reith's first task was to amend and improve a working guide drafted by his predecessor titled *The Principles and Objectives of British Wartime Propaganda* for the attention of the War Cabinet. The substance of the document was all encompassing and was drafted to concord with the French position on the same issue. Surprisingly, Reith's revision made no mention of radio propaganda; rather, it focused on spelling out what was at stake and how victory would be achieved. Its opening message was blunt: 'This is your war; the people's war, and defeat would mean the end of life as we understand it in Western Europe.'[14] The War Cabinet agreed in principle, but did not care much for his 'war by the people, for the people' approach and asked him to amend it. Furthermore, the Cabinet was adamant that the document should receive no publicity, 'as it was the essence of propaganda that it should not be recognised as such'.[15]

For all Reith's efforts, it would be some considerable time before any form of propaganda operation was formalised as official policy. His next move was to pay a visit to his successor at Broadcasting House, Frederick Ogilvie, with an insistence that more must be done on the home front, rather than just continue an ever-increasing round of government advice features. In response, the Home Service began a series of eight broadcasts between December 1939 and May 1940 called *Voice of the Nazi* by the philosopher W.A. Sinclair on the subject of Nazi propaganda. In a determined effort to educate the British public towards knowing their enemy and the 'Nazi tricks' to watch out for, Sinclair put all anger and emotion aside in a process of discussing Nazi aims and methods as calmly and scientifically as possible. In the second talk broadcast on 26 December, Sinclair told how Goebbels' propaganda succeeded in making ordinary decent Germans believe that 'the British are so cruel and bloodthirsty, that Englishmen out east who want to hunt crocodiles are in the habit of tying up little native boys beside a river and using them as bait'. The story was repeatedly published in German newspapers, along with claims that 'the cannibals of New Guinea were being called up to join the British Army', and that 'the inhabitants of London had to be calmed by an insistence that they were only being used to construct fortifications'. Sinclair wanted listeners to understand that plain common sense was not enough when it came to resisting Nazi propaganda. What people needed was an understanding of the Nazi method of propaganda: 'Unlike a bomb, if you understand the propaganda and how or why it is done, it will have no effect on you.' In Goebbels' propaganda there was always that small element of truth to lead the listener on, 'like a card player letting the opponent win, before swindling him'. Summing up, it was the aim of the Nazi leaders to do or say anything that would benefit Germany; regardless of whether it was a lie or not, the tone of the Nazi voice would always change in accordance with whatever suits 'but the mind behind it is always the same'. Listeners would be afforded further opportunities to get to know their enemy when a four-part series was aired following Japan's entry into the war, called *Japan Wants the Earth.*[*]

Throughout the period of Phoney War, the BBC broadcast many programmes that fostered the spirit of community ethos required to bind the nation together as one. *Home Front* aired on the Home Service between September 1939 and May 1940, focusing on such subjects as *Children in Billets*, *Keeping the Home Fires Burning* (featuring a Welsh

* First broadcast on 4 May 1942.

mining community), *Harvest of the Sea* and *Women in War*. Other features also reflected current events in the news, such as *The Spirit of Poland*, *The Empire's Answer* and *All France is Here*. Another regular feature followed the Leversuch family through the trials of obtaining the essentials for effective ARP. It is noticeable that *Home Front* often followed big audience shows in an effort to reach many millions of listeners. These were also times of scarcity, and the BBC was urged to assist in tackling the problems of a lack of quantity and quality of available food, which the MOI recognised as being a potentially significant drain on morale. The corporation successfully addressed this anxiety with *The Kitchen Front*, which effectively kept housewives in touch with the policies of the Ministry of Food, and gave advice on the best way of using the limited supplies. It is estimated that the BBC's wartime broadcasts on the subject of food amounted to just under 1,200 programmes.[16] Other broadcasts supplemented the government's Dig for Victory campaign that led to over 1.4 million people turning their lawns into allotments for growing vegetables. The campaign was later supported by the programme *Radio Allotment*, broadcast live every week from an undisclosed location in London. The BBC also had its very own radio doctor in wartime who, besides providing the public with valuable information towards maintaining good health, gave regular talks on subjects of concern that included Britain's declining birth rate.

Val Gielgud also reassessed his priorities in wartime, believing that drama features had the potential to become a unique propaganda tool, and sought to link Home Service feature programmes to the national war effort.[17] The ability of wartime drama programmes to showcase 'white' counter-propaganda material in a much more entertaining fashion emerged as a significant advancement in the broadcasting technique of wartime propaganda. Lawrence Gilliam oversaw the development of the BBC's feature programmes at the beginning of the war, and it was he who recognised the possibilities for incorporating realism into propaganda features. His nine-part series *Shadow of the Swastika*, commissioned by the MOI in 1939, documented the rise of Nazism, in what was regarded as a major breakthrough in the power of factual documentary for propaganda purposes. The sound effects included cheering crowds, loudspeakers, marching feet and accompanying music – all combined to enhance the effect of realism. Even though the feature contained fictional dialogue, it was occasionally juxtaposed with the real voices of Hitler and Chamberlain, and was presented by the BBC as authentic and based on real-life events. Material used in the series was provided directly by the MOI, with the emphasis on veracity being further reiterated in the published version of the scripts.[18] Grace Wyndham Goldie commented in the November issue of The Listener that Shadow of the Swastika was the programme of the moment, 'presenting to the world a clear indictment of the Nazi party, and the first deliberate propaganda we have ever had in dramatic form from broadcasting'.[19] Despite a measure of criticism from listeners over the 'BBC's latest propagandist offering', its Research Department calculated that the number of listeners to the Shadow of the Swastika broadcasts peaked at around 12 million – at that time the largest ever audience for a feature programme.[20]

Any satisfaction Reith was able derive from the success of the MOI-funded feature was short-lived when he was sidelined into the Ministry of Transport by Churchill, to be replaced by a reluctant Duff Cooper, who had previously resigned from government over the Munich Agreement. These constant changes of Ministers of Information – Macmillan to Reith, Reith to Cooper – all in the first ten months of its existence, added to the disorganisation and misunderstandings that tarnished the ministry in its early years. Reith had resolved to remedy the situation before he was axed, and thereafter remained critical of Churchill during the remainder of his short time in government. His diary records his bitterness when he learned that Duff Cooper was given control of enemy propaganda and the BBC: 'Churchill has done everything for him that Chamberlain wouldn't do for me.'[21]

Cooper's appointment almost immediately became a poison chalice when somebody at the BBC's Drama Department believed there might be some positive propaganda value in dramatising the story of one of the earliest military conflicts of the war. The Battle of Narvik, fought off the Norwegian coast between 9 April and 8 June 1940, aimed to secure an ice-free harbour for the transportation of Swedish iron ore; the operation had failed despite the Germans suffering heavy losses in the naval war, and led directly to the change of government previously mentioned. The BBC's reporting of the events was a hugely controversial matter that I will return to; however, what the government had not expected was the largely inaccurate re-enactment of the failed enterprise presented for home propaganda purposes, especially in the light of the casualties British forces had suffered in trying to hold back the German Army. MPs were incensed at the broadcast, during which impersonations of both living and dead persons had been given over the air in an attempt to reconstruct personal conversations and orders given by men who had lost their lives in action. Commander Sir Archibald South described the programme as 'a revolting innovation which ought to be stopped at once'.[22] The widow of an officer who had lost his life leading the attack on Narvik wrote a letter to *The Times* to the effect that, had the BBC told the story simply and correctly, it would have contained all the drama necessary, and no one would have listened to it with greater pride than her, 'but to impersonate the voices of the living and dead is unpardonable'. Another letter described the programme as 'a vulgarly sensational attempt at a dramatisation of a wonderful exploit and one which can only have caused distaste and distress to many'. Gielgud replied to the letters, regretting what had happened, but the damage had been done – especially when it emerged that a certain chief stoker named as a survivor had, in fact, been killed in the battle.[23] The harm done to the BBC was exacerbated further twelve hours later when the same broadcast went out on the Empire Service – despite an undertaking from Cooper that such broadcasts would not be repeated. Again, there were calls for the BBC to be brought under the direct control of a Minister of the Crown. Cooper attempted to explain the error away by referring to the magnitude of the task of the BBC: 'stuff going out to every quarter of the globe listened to by many millions of people 24 hours a day with barely any complaint'. He reiterated that he had no intention of taking over the administration of the BBC and would not be responsible in any way for its entertainment schedule.[24]

There would be no repeat of this form of drama documentary following the events in northern France at the end of May 1940. By that time the Home Office would have far bigger problems to address, and would require the help of the BBC in meeting the challenge of preparing the nation for possible invasion. The rapid advance of the German forces throughout Western Europe had pushed the imminent threat of invasion high up the agenda by the time Churchill assumed the office of prime minister, and it became the dominant subject throughout the early weeks of his premiership. Such a horrific prospect was something that Britain did not have any recent history of and, even then, the country had not covered itself in glory when it had happened – especially so in 1667 during the Anglo-Dutch naval wars when a Dutch incursion up the River Medway in Kent resulted in wild rumours and misinformation followed by widespread panic and confusion.* By the summer of 1940, the government was anxious that the lessons of nearly 300 years ago ought to have been learned. Unfortunately, despite people being continually warned over the radio to stay calm and not to listen to rumours, in the days that followed the fall of France, the Ministry of Information forwarded a memorandum imploring the government to broadcast a statement dispelling rumours that it was about to flee to Canada.[25]

Churchill was going nowhere, and had already decided that a Home Defence Executive should be put in place; proclaiming that 'every male of fighting age should be issued with a rifle'. On the evening of 14 May, the Secretary of State for War, Anthony Eden, broadcast an appeal over the BBC inviting men who were either too old or too young to fight to join the all-new Local Defence Volunteers with the promise of a uniform and arms. The response to Eden's broadcast was phenomenal, although at the time, the idea of a citizen's army repelling a German invasion was nothing more than fantasy. When France capitulated on 19 June, many London Defence Volunteers were still improvising with wooden poles or even golf clubs, and little had improved by late August when units, including a factory platoon of 400 men, were still without rifles and uniforms.** Despite around 680,000 rifles and millions of rounds of ammunition having arrived from the United States and Canada, the weapons were taking a frustratingly long time to reach the

---

* Strategic locations such as Chatham, Gravesend, and Dover were all reported as being burnt to the ground (they weren't), and much alarm was triggered by false reports that invasion forces were landing at Portsmouth, Plymouth and Dartmouth. Trade came to a standstill, the Port of London was closed and King Charles II fled the capital. The famous diarist Samuel Pepys – himself an officer of the Admiralty – viewed the whole spectacle as a 'dishonour never to be wiped out', and having also fled London he buried his life savings of 1,300 guineas in the ground and was never able to find it again.

** In mid-September, George Orwell recorded that his LDV platoon had one rifle for every six men. (Davison, 2009, p.281)

various platoons. The MOI noted that people would only begin to take the volunteers seriously when they were seen in uniform.[26] Following the broadcast of Churchill's 'Fight them on the beaches' speech, people were heard scoffing over how this could be possible when the LDV had such inadequate material provisions.[27]

This lack of preparation owed much to the fact that the previous government had failed to realise that the general population would no longer be those formerly passive civilians – an oversight that angered J.B. Priestley, who made his feelings known in a BBC broadcast on 8 September 1940:

> I think it was a pity that in the earlier months of this war that the authorities were so emphatic that we were civilians, a helpless passive lot, so many skins to save, so much weight of tax-paying stuff to be huddled out of harm's way. We see now, when the enemy bombers come roaring at us at all hours, and it's our nerve versus his; that we're not really civilians any longer but a mixed lot of soldiers – machine-minding soldiers, milkmen and postmen soldiers, housewife and mother soldiers – and what a gallant corps that is – and even broadcasting soldiers.

The idea of the British people holding their nerve under heavy bombardment, and even fighting back against the Nazi onslaught, contrasted sharply with previous government information imploring people to stay calm and do as they were told. Cynicism about government advice was commonplace, and people were regularly overheard making their feelings known, before new laws were introduced to compel them to keep their radical or subversive opinions to themselves. Such measures became more compelling by the middle of 1940; an Emergency Planning Committee was formed to co-ordinate special measures to be taken on the home front, while the MOI was charged with countering widespread uneasiness among the public. The War Cabinet invited the ministry to prepare a publicity campaign including a series of written instructions and broadcasts explaining the steps that should be taken in the event of an invasion. Differences of opinion arose when the ministry wanted to 'rouse the public' by including instructions for anyone behind enemy lines to 'do everything in your power to render [the German troops'] position difficult', to which the War Cabinet responded by highlighting how French forces had been unable to stop the flood of refugees leaving Paris, making it more difficult to counter enemy action during the Battle of France. The resulting leaflet, *If the Invader Comes*, bore the hallmarks of compromise. Its tone oscillated between confident assertions that any invading force would be 'driven out' and dire warnings that 'If you run away you will be machine gunned from the air'. After it was released on 18 June 1940, 15 million copies of the leaflet – one for every household – were distributed during the next three days. The campaign was supplemented by a four-part BBC radio drama of the same name, and was praised by listeners for giving a clear and concise account of what to expect.

By the middle of June, the MOI was again raising concerns about defeatist talk among the public. First there were reports of working-class women putting it about that they had 'nothing to fear from Hitler', and would probably be 'better off', and 'suppose we do lose, what difference would it make?' The ministry felt compelled to release a pamphlet titled *What Would Happen if Hitler Won?* and encouraged the BBC to give more airtime to speakers who could continue to educate the British public towards not only knowing their enemy, but also understanding the consequences of defeat. The BBC's 'pep talks' to try to counter this attitude were not well received, and people also complained that its new interval signal was like 'the tick of doom'. Later in the war the BBC was commissioned to produce a drama to show the public what would happen if Hitler won. *I James Blunt*, broadcast in June 1942, brought the consequences of the Germanisation of Britain to the radio listener in which the miserable prospect for the conquered was deftly portrayed. Described by George Orwell as 'a good flesh creeper', the feature was directed at 'complacent optimists and wishful thinkers with no conception of what life would be like if we lost'. Following the fall of France, the 'complacent optimist' became a much rarer breed. Despite the calming advice being given out by the BBC's radio doctor, some practitioners reported a number of wealthy patients asking for poison prescriptions to take if the Germans came.[28] It was a time of intense fear as people began to imagine the sight of hordes of Germans suddenly arriving; one lady recollected that she stored aspirin tablets with the intention of euthanising her child in such a scenario.[29]

At this moment of great peril, the BBC had to do more than simply call its listeners to prayer in *Lift Up Your Hearts* every weekday morning, and was specifically tasked by the MOI to warn the public of the danger of loose talk. A specially commissioned play by G.R. Rainier, *Information to the Enemy*, was first aired in June 1940, and again in the following year, to illustrate just how easily careless talk might be pieced together by the enemy. Later in the war the same theme would be addressed in the BBC's radio version of the film *Next of Kin* – a broadcast that received high praise among MPs as superb home-front propaganda. In a determined effort to raise morale in the face of the invasion threat, a new series of broadcasts was announced in June called *Marching On*: 'Day by day the nation is marching on to ultimate victory, outstanding events of the past two weeks will be vividly presented in dramatic form in the first edition of a radio newsreel.'[30] *Marching On* was to be broadcast alternately, week by week, with another feature called *Go to It*, described as 'a progress report on Britain's industrial war drive' and beginning with a talk on aircraft production from the new Minister of Supply, Herbert Morrison.[31] On 25 June it broadcast another feature, *Spitfires over Britain*, about the work of a home defence squadron of RAF Fighter Command. Listeners were also kept up to date with current developments by a fifteen-minute *War Commentary* broadcast every evening.

Evidence suggests that most people appreciated regular government information, uplifting broadcasts and news bulletins that they could trust. However, there were those who avoided the radio and had very little interest in the perilous position that they were in. The observations of acclaimed political writer George Orwell on the behaviour of ordinary people in wartime Britain are particularly revealing. On the evening of 27 May 1940, at a time when the BEF was hemmed in at Dunkirk and Britain could potentially have been invaded at any moment, Orwell went with his wife to the local pub to hear the evening news. The barmaid had no intention of turning the radio on, and when she finally relented, he observed that nobody else in the room bothered to listen. On another occasion she told him, 'We don't turn on the radio because the punters don't want the piano playing to be interrupted.' Orwell commented, 'You have all the time the sensation that you are kicking against an impenetrable wall of stupidity!'[32] A few days later he drifted among the usual Sunday crowds in the city and reported that he saw no indication in any face, or in anything that he could overhear, that 'the people grasped that they were likely to be invaded.'[33] An opinion poll conducted by the Home Intelligence Division discovered that the *If the Invader Comes* initiative had not been taken seriously by around 20 per cent of the population, mainly because they viewed the threat of invasion as 'a joke'. A non-official report by Mass Observation was even more critical. It thought that the tone of the leaflet was 'out of touch with common sense', and treated the public as 'blithering idiots'.[34]

It was at this time that rumours and fictitious tales began emerging on a daily basis: 'could it be possible that hundreds of German parachutists had already landed in Britain dressed as nuns?'[35] Some of the behavioural characteristics of the general public in wartime Britain provide some interesting precursors to the modern era, particularly throughout the early months of the war when the country was awash with fake news (spread by gossip, rather than social media). Reliable information about what was really happening was difficult to obtain – especially when radio listeners suspected they might be better informed if they tuned into the German broadcasts. Stories of spies and fifth columnists were also rife, along with tales of bombing raids that never happened, and the exact date and the manner in which Hitler planned to invade Britain. In February 1940, the former producer from the BBC's fledgling television service, Mary Adams, was asked to set up the Home Intelligence Department at the MOI. A key component of its remit was to detect false rumours that were likely to damage morale, so that the ministry could officially rebuff them over the airwaves. Some people did manage to remain upbeat and turn a deaf ear to the rumour mill, attributing their cheerfulness to a deliberate avoidance of the BBC news bulletins and the 'gloomy promenade music' or 'Elgar symphonies' that always seemed to follow.[36] News bulletins were not something the BBC had been overly concerned with throughout much of its pre-war existence, but now in wartime, especially when things started to happen, the importance of disseminating the news was suddenly of critical importance. By the time the war was being fought out in the skies over the English Channel, the BBC had opportunistically, almost by accident, eclipsed the written press with its up-to-the-moment reports. News coverage in Britain would never be the same again.

4

STRIKING THE RIGHT CHORD

WARTIME NEWS

During a Parliamentary debate on the dissemination of news in February 1939, one honourable member warned the BBC against replying to subsidised propaganda with more subsidised propaganda: 'It is said that every poison has its antidote, but the antidote in this case is not another poison but a wholesome diet of straight news to build up the patient's powers of resistance.'[1] This was sound advice that some might argue should have been directed towards the government and the Ministry of Defence, rather than the BBC. In Germany, Dr Goebbels had long been adamant that news policy was a 'weapon of war', and now, in Britain, the government had finally realised that the careful control of news broadcasts would become a critical factor in the propaganda war. This would mean that the measure of independence previously enjoyed by the BBC newsroom when compiling bulletins would gradually be subject to much tighter censorship. The corporation would also be continually urged by Whitehall to expand its news operation significantly as the conflict spread into the farther regions of the world. At the beginning of the war, sixty-three news bulletins in English and ninety-two in foreign languages were being broadcast each week on the Home and Overseas Service. By March 1943, these figures had risen to 149 and 771 respectively. Over the same period, the number of languages being broadcast rose from ten to forty-six, while staff numbers increased from 4,300 to over 11,000, with the result that revenue expenditure more than doubled from £3.5 million to over £7.5 million.[2]

In many ways, the BBC's wartime news operation was analogous with that of any newspaper, in that it reported news agency material and sent out correspondents to unfolding events or major incidents.[*] The corporation typically received guidance from the MOI at daily meetings, press conferences and in notes passed to editors, and submitted its material for censorship under the current rules. Broadcasts concerning military matters would be read out over the telephone to the Military Intelligence Section of the War Office, who would make an on-the-spot decision to either reject or allow the broadcast to go ahead. News items reporting sensitive war information were usually referred to the individual service departments concerned in each case, 'so as to provide an additional and more elaborate check on accuracy and slant'.[3] The MOI's guidance to the BBC rested on one simple policy: 'to tell the truth, nothing but the truth, as distrust breeds fear much more than knowledge of the reverse'.[4] This did not always work in practice when the war became 'real', and the ministry was compelled to reword its policy directives at various stages of the war.[**]

In other ways, delivering news bulletins over the radio differed significantly from ordinary press reporting. Broadcasting news was a new art, meaning announcers had to be trained to lead the listener through the story step by step until he or she had a clear picture of the events in mind. Bulletins had to be clearer and more precise than the printed word, in which ambiguous passages could be re-read. There was also considerable pressure on the BBC news department during wartime, especially as news often arrived seconds before a bulletin was aired, and had to be subedited, dictated and censored before being slipped onto the announcer's desk mid-broadcast.

During the first months of war, the almost total news blackout of whatever might be happening on the Continent smacked of the bad old days of the First World War when the public were kept completely in the dark. Even though everyone knew the BEF was in France,

---

[*] News agencies used were typically Reuters, the Press Association, Exchange Telegraph and Central News.

[**] In a directive of March 1940, the MOI proposed a more pragmatic approach to propaganda, beginning with the assertion, 'The truth is what is believed to be the truth'. (McLaine, p.28)

the BBC's news desk often had little to report beyond a selection of maritime issues, of which the First Lord of the Admiralty, Winston Churchill, was quick to vent his displeasure at the downbeat nature of the bulletins. In December 1939 he composed a memorandum for his War Cabinet colleagues headed with the comment: 'I circulate the following specimen of cheerful chats about naval matters by the BBC.'[5] The bulletin in question focused on the significant loss of life following a collision between two vessels, before relaying news on the fate of six other vessels including two Norwegian steamers, a Greek steamer and a small Swedish boat. The First Lord clearly did not think the BBC needed to ram every minor setback down the throats of listeners; at a meeting of the War Council that month he 'deplored the unrivalled pessimism of the BBC' for typically opening with 'long accounts of ships having been sunk'. His views were supported by a note from the Commander-in-Chief of the Royal Navy, who criticised 'the demoralising effect of the broadcasts'.[6] Churchill continued his attack by stating that such reports were having a highly prejudicial effect on public morale and insisted that shipping losses should only be broadcast weekly.[7]

Despite Churchill's protestations, little else improved in the following months beyond the revised procedure for reporting maritime incidents. At a meeting of the Supreme War Council on 28 March 1940, Prime Minister Chamberlain had been inveighing against the BBC's reporting of an untrue German account of an attack on a convoy the previous evening when Churchill interrupted, 'While you are putting pressure on neutral countries, would it not be a good plan if you were to put some pressure on the BBC?' Oliver Stanley, the Secretary of State for War, asked if it was 'fair to regard the BBC as neutral'.[8] By this time, the war was not so phoney any more, and the listening public were suddenly much hungrier for news – especially when rumours of military setbacks were in the air. The BBC's reporting on military matters was dependent on what information the military intelligence authorities were prepared to concede, while shipping losses involving significant fatalities were typically subjected to a D-Notice (Defence and Security Advisory Note), which denoted 'an official request not to publish for reasons of national security'.

The damage caused by the BBC's restricted access to news was first highlighted after an air raid on the British fleet at Scapa Flow on 16 March 1940, after which the Germans had been allowed to gain a significant propaganda advantage. The German Zeesen propaganda station had broadcast heavily exaggerated details of the raid on British and US wavelengths around six and a half hours after the raid had finished, while the BBC was forced to sit on the story for another six hours to allow the Admiralty to release its own account. The BBC complained that such censorship and late release of news was damaging its effectiveness and undermining the confidence of the public in the integrity and accuracy of its news sources – not to mention encouraging listeners to switch to German stations for more up-to-date bulletins.[9] The *Evening Standard* took up the case in its editorial of 20 March, insisting that 'the old saying that a lie gets halfway round the world before the truth has time to get its boots on' should be hung up in the office of every government department.

A short while later, the BBC found support for their case from across the Atlantic when CBS reporter Drew Middleton condemned how news of events in Norway was being handled: in particular, how the facts of the Allied defeat had been concealed from the press until, without warning, it was told that the troops were pulling out. European News Editor Noel Newsome was much more direct in his criticism of the War Office. After false information had been fed to the BBC in the Norway debacle, he accused ministers of attempting to use its news broadcasts as a means of military deception. Newsome complained bitterly to anyone with influence that an unsuccessful attempt to use the BBC's European news service as a 'blind tool' to deceive the German High Command had severely damaged its reputation for truthfulness.[10]

These criticisms, plus an MOI report of 18 May that indicated 'people want all the news – even if it is bad', would go largely ignored for some considerable time.[11] The events that concluded with the mass evacuation of the BEF from northern France were not reported in the press until the operation was almost over, and this was not because there were no pressmen on hand to report it. In *Dunkirk: The Necessary Myth*, Nicholas Harman wrote of the 'willing and patriotic co-operation' of the press and the BBC with the military and government 'to create a myth whose poetic strength sustained the morale of the nation'.[12] This is an effective summing up of what happened. Operation Dynamo had been in progress for five days and three-quarters of the BEF had departed from the French coast before listeners of the BBC news heard anything about it. When the evacuation commenced on the evening of 26 May, the only people who knew about it, aside from government members and the military, were the relevant railway authorities and the Women's Voluntary Service, who provided comfort and refreshments to the exhausted soldiers. The few journalists who picked up on the story were ordered to keep it dark (which they did), and it has since been discovered that key members of the government were not told, including Harold Nicolson at the MOI.[13] Those pressmen who had made it back to Britain aboard rescue ships were summoned to a meeting with the director of military intelligence for the BEF, Major General Mason-MacFarlane, on 28 May. He had already chosen the words he wanted them to report:

> I'm afraid there is going to be a considerable shock for the British public. It is your duty to act as shock-absorbers, so I have prepared, with my counterpart at the War Office, a statement which can be published, subject to censorship.

Mason-MacFarlane left the press in no doubt that the British Expeditionary Force was surrounded and its soldiers were unlikely to all get away safely, and thereafter instructed the reporters to blame the French:

> It is now no secret that on several fronts, the French failed to withstand the assault. The result of these failures was disastrous from the point of view of the BEF, and led directly to the critical situation with which it is now faced.[14]

The official view was that the Allied High Command had been outmanoeuvred and the armies of the French outfought – not the BEF. For the anxious listeners at home, the first indication that things were not going well was a remark broadcast on 14 May from French Premier Reynaud that 'only a miracle can save France', coupled with the well-publicised dismissal of several French generals. Two weeks of uncertainty followed, and listeners still had no idea that the British Expeditionary Force was hemmed in at Dunkirk by the invading German Army. The MOI reported that the public were no doubt aware of another deliberate policy of restricting news but agreed that 'the slackening of news has a definite advantage at the present time'. By 28 May, people were openly anxious about the fate of the BEF. Some press reports indicated that they were 'trapped', while other headlines specified that they were 'fighting their way out'.[15] Listeners got their first clue regarding the gravity of the situation when a BBC broadcast on 29 May appealed for men with the relevant knowledge and seafaring experience to come forward. One listener still remembers an announcer breaking into *Children's Hour* to appeal to 'anyone who has a boat capable of crossing the English Channel to take it now to the coast of France to bring back some soldiers'.[16]

When the BBC was finally allowed to broadcast news of the evacuation, the corporation was effectively bound by the official Ministry of Information statement:

> All night and all day men of the undefeated British Expeditionary Force have been coming home from France. They have not come back in triumph; they have come back in glory.

The report ended on the note that they were anxious to be back in France soon 'to have a real crack at Jerry'. BBC Correspondent Bernard Stubbs described the scenes as the evacuated soldiers arrived back in Dover. His words had to be chosen carefully if the report was to make it beyond the censorship office, and it was finally broadcast on 31 May. He began by focusing on the selfless bravery of the crews of ships coming to and fro across the Channel under the fierce onslaught of the enemy's bombers. Describing the soldiers who filled the decks as 'tired, battle-stained and blood-stained' was probably about as far as Stubbs was allowed to go. From then on, his report was decidedly upbeat, with a little help from the censor:

> The most amazing thing was that practically every man was reasonably cheerful, and most of them managed a smile. Even when a man was obviously on the verge of collapse from sheer fatigue, you could still see in his eyes that his spirit was irrepressible ... and that is a thing that all the bombs in Germany will never crush.*[17]

---

* Shortly after filing his Dunkirk report, Stubbs joined the Royal Naval Volunteer Reserve and was killed a year later.

Initially, the correspondents had been allowed to speak to the soldiers as they debarked from the rescuing vessels, but on 1 June, this was strictly forbidden by the military, and even Mason-MacFarlane was banned from addressing the public. The BBC's reports were unrecognisable to the men who had been trapped, and away from the microphone their verdict on the disaster was so much more damning, as many remembered feeling lost for words, demoralised and humiliated. Others, having had just a few months with a rifle and no proper field training, could not believe how well prepared and equipped the Germans were. Some men reported feeling shame and exhaustion after 'having driven up so jauntily and now, like whipped dogs, we were scurrying back with our tails between our legs'.[18]

This was also the first occasion that the press had been left hamstrung, as the BBC exclusively broadcast details of the British defeat. Some of the last retreating soldiers were able to listen in to the BBC news broadcasts and were surprised to learn that they were making 'a strategic withdrawal'. Others were even more shocked to discover from the BBC that the army was in 'dire peril' – leading them to reassess their faith in the commanders who had not warned them of the dangers ahead. Even the director of statistics at the War Office was compelled to admit that the Dunkirk episode was far worse than was ever realised in Fleet Street, or on the BBC broadcasts. There were reports of men, on getting back to England, throwing their rifles and equipment out of the railway carriage windows. Some sent for their wives with their civilian clothes, changed into these and walked home.[19]

Between them, the BBC, followed by the press had, through the use of any number of unsupported allegations, managed to make a humiliating military defeat seem like a victory. In his 2013 book *Propaganda, Power and Persuasion*, David Welch suggested that the government assumed 'the limited capacity of the public to absorb bad news', and deliberately excluded material from dissemination – effectively distorting reality.[20] Throughout the whole Dunkirk episode, the BBC had been an obedient servant of government as though they were filling a blank canvas. In the days following the evacuation, the corporation determined that Dunkirk would be a turning point in the propaganda war, and never again would they tell a deliberate untruth. Positivity could still be maintained without reversing the key facts about which side had suffered the most casualties, or who had lost the most aircraft – at one time they had claimed thirty-seven enemy planes had been shot down when the true figure had been half that number.[21] The BBC also felt its credibility could be further restored by enacting a policy of 'bad news first' – no matter how bad the defeat or the disaster – and only then would future victories be believed.

The public knew the corporation had been kept in the dark over Dunkirk, while a Listener Research Survey revealed that people actually had more confidence in the BBC than they had two months earlier.[22] It rests as a testimony to the power of propaganda that, rather than demoralising the population further, the Dunkirk episode turned out to be a huge boost; in its Home Intelligence briefings the MOI reported 'extreme elation', stating that public morale had 'stiffened'.[23] Rather than bemoan the apparent military failings, the people focused on the glorious role played by the small rescue boats; it was as though the nation was united as one, 'having been galvanised into a new energy', wrote Bruce Lockhart. In a broadcast delivered shortly after the evacuation, the playwright and broadcaster J.B. Priestley magnified 'the miracle of Dunkirk' when he spoke of the little paddle steamers that made an excursion into hell and came back glorious: a masterful epitaph that enshrined the episode forever in history as an image of the little seaside 'Belles and Queens' chugging into the heart of the inferno.[24] The BBC would exploit the propaganda potential of Dunkirk on every anniversary of the evacuation throughout the remainder of the war, and never fail to refer specifically to the 'little ships that sailed through hell to rescue an army'.[25]

In the weeks following Dunkirk, public morale was reported as being 'too good', and that people were failing to realise the significance to the extent that it overshadowed their fear of invasion and air raids. Concerns were also raised about returning soldiers in packed pubs contradicting the BBC's reports of the RAF exploits at Dunkirk to anyone prepared to listen, not to mention rumours of soldiers 'jeering at RAF personnel'.[26] As much as everyone else seemed to be exalting the successful evacuation, June 1940 was not the time to be basking in the 'glorious miracle of Dunkirk'. While the BBC and the MOI, under the direction of the Home Office, attempted to prepare the public for the likelihood of invasion, an important change at the BBC at this time was to begin the habit of naming the person reading the news. Many listeners viewed it as nothing more than exhibitionism, without realising it was important for the public to become familiar with 'a name tacked onto a voice', as the BBC had described it.[27] The fear was that if the Germans invaded, the first thing they would seize was the radio station and begin broadcasting their own propaganda, including false news. Listeners also began complaining about the tone of voice used by the BBC announcers – particularly the change of tone that so obviously indicated that bad news was coming, and then another change of tone prior to indicating 'the stupidity of the enemy'.[28] Bulletins were also condensed to be no longer than twenty minutes after it was agreed that far more concentration was required to listen to the news than to read it.

The government again came under fire in June 1940 when the public suspected it of withholding news in connection with the imminent fall of France. George Orwell felt he knew what was going on:

In the middle of a fearful battle in which I suppose thousands of men are being killed every day, one has the impression that there is no news.

As to the truthfulness of news, however, there is probably more suppression of news than downright lying.[29]

When France finally capitulated, bulletins gave prominence to pockets of French forces 'fighting on', before killing any sense of optimism it might have created with more depressing Elgar symphonies. A few days later, the news of a German bombing of the Channel Islands on 28 June, in which forty-four civilians were killed, was withheld for two days, by which time the islands had been occupied unopposed. Despite a fresh determination to stick to the truth, the one thing that the corporation could not control was the continued withholding of news, a policy that enraged the public, who typically directed their anger towards the government rather than the BBC. This policy of shielding the public from the full facts of 'bad news' would continue with every major setback throughout the war, right up until the Allied invasion of Europe in 1944. Whenever such incidents occurred, the corporation's news correspondents were left feeling demoralised and frustrated. Frank Gillard's report of the disastrous assault at Dieppe in 1942, when more than 3,000 Canadian troops were killed, wounded or captured, was heavily censored, to his lifelong disgust. The public similarly hated any misplaced positive spin attached to events – 'if we retreat, let's admit it', complained one disgruntled listener.[30] Even the men at the front began to decry the 'softening up' tactics imposed on the BBC to prepare listeners for bad news. The most inexplicable example was a radio broadcast prior to the fall of Tobruk in July 1942 announcing that 'Tobruk was no longer of any strategic importance and was likely to fall' – an astonishing, morale-sapping statement that would also have been heard by the enemy. The defenders of Tobruk were outraged, and began ridiculing future broadcasts thereafter.*

By the beginning of July 1940, the BBC had become the primary source of news, as newspaper sizes dwindled down to a mere six pages – including advertisements and financial columns.[31] This didn't stop news of major incidents continuing to be suppressed as a matter of policy. On 25 July it was discovered that the government had enacted a D-Notice to withhold news on the sinking of the troop evacuation vessel RMS *Lancastria* over a month previously following Operation Ariel on 17 June. This incident invited more widespread criticism from listeners, who complained that 'the great mass of the people should not be treated like children'.[32] Estimates on the loss of life ranged from 3,000 to 5,800. Thereafter, even more people began tuning in to Lord Haw-Haw's broadcasts, if only to discover more current information about shipping losses.[33]

This lesson appears to have been learned by the time of the horrific incident involving the evacuation ship SS *City of Benares* relayed by Dione Venables in her introduction to this book. On the evening of 17 September, a German U-boat fired three torpedoes at the Canada-bound vessel, of which the third one struck the stern, causing her to sink within thirty minutes. Out of the ninety evacuees, seventy-three had either drowned in the Atlantic or died of exposure on lifeboats, leading to bitter criticism of the barbaric actions of the Germans.** Within five days of the sinking, the government had informed the next of kin of all those who had perished, and allowed the BBC to broadcast

---

* General Klopper was reported to have said, 'I cannot carry on if the BBC is allowed to make these statements.' (Mitchelhill-Green, *Tobruk 1942*)

** Out of a passenger list of 407 on board, 87 children and 175 adults lost their lives following the sinking.

details of the tragedy. Meanwhile, the German propagandists dismissed the incident as 'looking like good propaganda', a remark that so enraged Noel Newsome at the European news desk that he insisted the comment must be quoted in all languages: 'It will be shown to the world that this is one of the foulest calumnies ever uttered.'[34] The level of anger and indignation the public felt over the torpedoing led to bitter demands for immediate reprisals – effectively deflecting interest in air raids for a number of days. The overseas evacuation scheme, already the subject of much criticism, was subsequently abandoned as a result.

With the imminent danger of invasion came an obvious need to provide more up-to-the-moment news reports, and yet the BBC was still being hampered by its own rules of reportage. From the beginning, the news department had effectively restricted its own development in terms of live broadcasting of news owing to its system of self-imposed censorship, whereby all material to be broadcast had to be written down and checked prior to transmission. The news department needed to bring more immediacy to its reporting, which was not always an easy thing to do in the shock, excitement and horror of total war. Recordings often took place within the sound of bombs crashing all around – on one occasion Charles Gardner was about to speak into the microphone when a Heinkel dropped a 500lb bomb so close that the equipment was blown into the air. In the meantime, it was the same Charles Gardner who inadvertently discovered that 'greater immediacy' when he parked his recording van on the cliffs of Dover on the afternoon of 14 July 1940. All previous issues that might have brought the BBC into disrepute on the basis of decency paled into insignificance when compared with what was about to happen in the skies over the English Channel. Gardner, who had been afforded the luxury of a live link-up, suddenly found himself commentating on a dogfight between RAF and Luftwaffe dive-bombers happening right before his eyes. He proceeded to grasp the opportunity of bringing the daring of Britain's young fighter pilots into living rooms around the world; his enthusiastic excitement was transmitted to his audience as though he were commentating on a major sporting occasion:

There's one going down in flames. Somebody's hit a German and he's coming down with a long streak – coming down completely out of control – a long streak of smoke – and now a man's bailed out by parachute. The pilot's bailed out by parachute. He's a Junkers 87, and he's going slap into the sea – and there he goes – SMASH! A terrific column of water and there was a Junkers 87. Only one man got out by parachute. So presumably there was only a crew of one in it.[35]

The public reaction to the broadcasts was mixed. A good many letters in praise of the broadcast were published in *The Radio Times* issue of 26 July 1940:

> A thousand thanks for the most exciting recording I have heard yet. I was knitting a pullover for the RAF – the knitting had to go down. I enjoyed every bit of it. My only child is in the RAF. Oh, how proud we are of our lovely sons – God bless them.
>
> May I suggest more broadcasts of this description be given, as I feel it acts as a tonic to hear of the wonderful show the RAF put up against the rogues – and boy did they scatter!

Remaining true to the spirit of impartiality, the BBC also published letters that were highly critical of the broadcast:

> I must protest against the manner of Charles Gardner's recording of the air battle over the English Channel. Coming immediately after the Prime Minister's broadcast, it filled me with indignation. It was as if he was light-heartedly describing a mixture of a running commentary on a boxing match and horse race. Has he no thought for the feelings of the relatives of our brave men engaged?

Worse was to come when the official report of the incident was released. The first Junkers 87, from which Gardner describes the pilot bailing out, was in fact a 615 Squadron Hurricane flown by Pilot Officer Michael Mudie, who was picked up by the Royal Navy but died the next day of his injuries. Regardless of the controversy, the MOI reported that the majority of people approved of the live commentary, and that among those who didn't were people complaining that his 'callous Oxford accent' had made it worse.[36] Gardner might have felt bitter over the reaction to his broadcast and left the BBC to serve in the RAF himself later that year.

Despite the controversy surrounding the transmission, there would be broadcasters following in his wake who appreciated, and were inspired by, Gardner's pioneering work in the field of outside broadcasting. To the displeasure of Civil Defence workers, Gardner appears to have started a trend as crowds remained in the open during air raids to watch and cheer dogfights going on overhead. The MOI reported that Civil Defence leaders 'deprecated the condoning of this attitude and behaviour by the BBC', who had earlier reported on miners standing on slag heaps cheering the RAF as battles raged in the skies overhead.

The propaganda war between Britain and Germany during the Battle of Britain was intense, with both sides guilty of over-exaggerating enemy aircraft losses and under-reporting home losses. It was the BBC reports that tended to be believed, for morale had risen sharply on the back of the 'legendary few', and it was felt that the BBC should continue to make full capital out of the propaganda value of the heroics of the young fighter pilots. Ever since the Narvik controversy, the policy of BBC radio feature programmes had changed; the department noticeably distanced itself from any future dramatisation of real-life battles. When it finally relented, it was careful to make sure that the content conformed to the actual government version of events. An hour-long feature for the BBC Home Service, *The Battle of Britain*, first broadcast on 8 May 1941, was based directly on the official Air Ministry publication of the same name. Originally intended as a propaganda pamphlet, it had become an international bestseller with 4.8 million copies sold in Britain alone by the end of 1941. Further editions (including an illustrated version for children) were published in twenty-four languages by 1942. The BBC's version, written and produced by Cecil McGiven, was similarly popular, and by public demand was broadcast again on Friday, 8 August 1941 on the Home Service. It was later rebroadcast with the introduction of a German and Italian announcer reading misinformation bulletins on the air raids, highlighting the difference between the propaganda circulated by the Axis powers and the official Air Ministry version as presented in the feature.

By September 1940, the cost to the RAF of repelling the Luftwaffe's attempts to gain mastery of the skies had reduced it to a near perilous position. Over a quarter of its fighter pilots had been either killed or maimed by that stage of the battle, and more aircraft had been lost than people had been led to believe. Had the Germans known that the RAF could only have held out against concentrated attacks on its airfields for barely a few more weeks, they might have persevered with the attacks. Instead, Fighter Command were given an unexpected reprieve when the Germans moved from a strategy of trying to destroy the RAF as a prerequisite to invasion to an all-out bombing campaign directed at the capital. This, they believed, would stretch Fighter Command's resources to the limit, and thus open up the possibility of the final annihilation of the fighter aircraft they had so far failed to dominate in the skies over the English Channel. It was at this point that the accuracy of news reporting took another turn when the thing that the people had been most dreading – air raids on civilian targets – was suddenly upon them. Large numbers of people would be killed outright or hospitalised for months after being buried beneath tons of rubble. Churchill was anxious that the results of enemy bombing raids should not be the subject matter of sensationalist headlines. In a note to the Minister of Information in June 1940, he instructed that the BBC 'should be asked to handle air raids in a cool way, and on a diminishing tone of public interest. The public should be accustomed to treat air raids as a matter of ordinary routine.' The note continued with an insistence that there should be no emphasis on shattered houses, and that there should be focus on how well the essential services were operating in the emergency.[37]

One of the earliest incidents of civilians being bombed occurred in Croydon on 18 August, when bombs intended for the aerodrome had fallen on a nearby housing estate, resulting in much loss of life. This was something BBC reporters had been unprepared for, leading the public to vent their disapproval of the 'highbrow and patronising manner' in which news readers had casually announced details of the raid. Many listeners complained that they wanted to hear more accounts from people who were affected, rather than details relayed from carefully prepared scripts, and shortly afterwards the MOI condemned the broadcast as 'bad propaganda'.[38] The reporting of air raids was heavily censored when the frequency of the raids increased in September 1940. The BBC's newsroom at the MOI fell into a regular routine: a bell would typically ring three times just before 8 a.m., an indication that a carefully prepared communiqué from either the Air Ministry or the

Ministry of Home Security concerning the night's air raids would be read out to BBC and press agency representatives.[39] By March 1941, the MOI had begun to take a different view of how the BBC should treat air raids. Mary Adams, the head of its Intelligence Division, asked the BBC to clamp down on any broadcast advocating heroism or making generalisations about public morale, as it was deemed that inaccurate and overly propagandistic reports of people 'smiling through it' or of 'carrying on with a sense of pride' would more likely damage morale and possibly invite another raid. The corporation was also told not to minimise the destruction caused by the raids, and to avoid giving out news that 'factories had resumed working'.

Occasionally, the MOI was caught in the middle of what the Air Ministry was ordering and what the listening public were demanding. Duff Cooper got into a furious row with the former over the issue of the naming of bombed cities and towns – especially after the failure of the BBC to report on the bombing of Birmingham in November 1940, which created much anger among the population. Cooper felt that to deliberately prevent the rest of the country from knowing the full facts about air raids was having a damaging effect on morale. The relentless struggle to get control of news would eventually grind Cooper down to the point that he would ask Churchill to release him from his role as Minister of Information. Meanwhile, German radio flooded the airwaves with lies about 'mass panic' in the capital and Londoners 'taking flight', as people had done in other heavily bombed cities in Europe. It also became essential that the British people were presented with a view of the enemy as 'getting as good as they were giving'. This enabled correspondents Richard Dimbleby and Wynford Vaughan Thomas to distinguish their reputations by providing reports from Lancaster bombers of actual bombing raids over Berlin. Unfortunately, the BBC governors forbade live recordings of such raids, and because the Air Ministry delayed the release of the reports, the Germans often scored propaganda points by reporting on retaliatory raids first.[40]

With little or no comfort to offer the terrified listener during these dark times, the BBC decided to air a live recording of Big Ben at the hour of nine every night before the news as a mark of unity for the national cause. It was felt that the people needed 'a minute for consecration to the land they love, and the success of its cause'. As difficult as the Blitz was to report, there was a certain propaganda value in the resilience with which Londoners and civilians in other major cities were facing up to the horror of air raids. With Britain effectively now standing alone, Churchill placed all hopes for Britain's salvation on the United States entering the war – something that the majority of the American people were set against. Towards the end of June 1940, discussions had begun between the Foreign Office and the MOI on arrangements for broadcasting propaganda to America. When the War Cabinet convened on 28 July, it was agreed that the time had come to take more proactive steps towards 'making the British point of view more widely known in America, especially so to counteract the slew of German propaganda'.[41] The BBC's ever-expanding network of news bulletins and commentaries delivered through its Overseas Services would be critical in this respect. America would have to be 'won over' and the BBC, in collaboration with the American broadcasting services, in particular CBS, would play a significant role in disseminating the right kind of propaganda for the purpose.

5

COURTING AMERICA WITH 'THE MURROW BOYS'

While broadcasting in Britain was the monopoly of the BBC, the United States had developed in a radically different direction with free enterprise providing a range of commercial broadcasting stations. Although a broadcasting team from the Canadian Broadcasting Corporation (CBC) had been in London since December 1939, the American radio stations did not rebroadcast any of the material put out by the CBC in the first half of 1940, and the BBC's Empire Service contained no programme aimed primarily at American audiences. With rival transmissions from Germany and Italy already targeting public opinion in the neutral US, the BBC took steps to ramp up broadcasts to North America in the summer of 1940 in a bid to attract American listeners. A new nightly half-hour programme called *Radio Newsreel*, featuring political commentaries, eyewitness accounts and short talks was launched, became a vital conduit of truth for Americans. One listener in Massachusetts praised the BBC for 'bringing truth to many people who have, in the past, been too often under the spell of the false Nazi propaganda'.[1] Also featured was the popular series of talks *Britain Speaks* by the author and playwright J.B. Priestley, which first appeared on the Empire Service, enabling his distinctive down-to-earth manner to become hugely popular on both sides of the Atlantic. Letters received by the BBC from North America praised Priestley for 'placating our anxieties with his unruffled calmness'. 'His talks are like a tonic – we have not felt afraid or discouraged since.'[2]

The success of the new service relied heavily on programmes being rebroadcast on short wave to all parts by American and Canadian stations. The service had very quickly become a hit in the US, with *Time* magazine describing it as 'a vast improvement over the stodgy stuff the BBC used to short wave to North America'. In spring 1941 it began broadcasting a serial play six times a week called *Front-Line Family* – the day-to-day story of a London family in wartime that was broadcast in a format known to be familiar and popular among Americans. By that time the CBC network was broadcasting two BBC news bulletins a day, and alongside *Britain Speaks* were other topical programmes such as *Questions of the Hour*, *With the Troops in England* and *Off the Record*. Other programmes for French listeners in Quebec included *The French Newsletter* and *Les Voix Français* (*French Voices*). As time went on, few Americans needed to listen on short wave because the service was rebroadcast by many domestic networks. By the time of the Allied invasion of Europe in June 1944, 725 out of 914 radio stations in the US carried BBC war reports, and by early 1945 it was estimated that more than 15 million people in the US listened to at least one BBC programme a week.

Despite the increases in radio broadcasts to the US, the question of who was actually representing British interests on the other side of the Atlantic was still a sensitive issue. In October 1940, MPs in Parliament had questioned the granting of an exit visa to the science-fiction writer H.G. Wells for the purpose of carrying on a lecture tour in the United States. MPs were reminded that Wells openly expressed radical opinions about the British monarchy being 'a medieval and useless institution', a view of Christianity as 'a senseless, Judaic superstition', and a firm belief that the whole structure of society was rotten. It hadn't helped either when, at the time of the Munich Crisis, Wells was openly referring to Hitler as a 'certifiable lunatic'. Earl Winterton warned MPs during a Commons debate that Wells would 'use all the publicity and power which he possesses to denigrate his country abroad and, of all places, in the United States, where in the hour of our greatest peril we enjoy more real sympathy with our unity and moral strength than ever before in our history'.[3] The honourable member was proved right when Wells was reported to have given a series of radio interviews condemning 'sly and second-rate politicians making ambiguous, non-committal speeches'. Thereafter, he criticised Lord Halifax as being 'the quintessence of everything that an

Englishman should not be', and launched a stinging attack on the religious ideals of Lord Gort VC, who had led the BEF on its ill-fated campaign in northern France. Winterton insisted it had been a 'dangerous mistake' to have allowed a man like Wells to air his views in America.

The honourable members need not have worried too much about whatever influence the ageing Wells possessed among 130 million Americans. The triumph of the Battle of Britain, followed by the besieging of London by aerial bombardment, was being reported for American listeners with exceptional brilliance by the legendary CBS broadcaster Edward R. Murrow and his team of accomplices. In 1937, when 'Ed' Murrow first arrived in London as the European director of CBS, the company did not intend for him to do any broadcasts himself; his specified task was to organise programmes using the studios and transmitters of the BBC. During the Battle of Britain, Murrow became inspired by the drama that Charles Gardner had injected into his July 1940 broadcast of the dogfight from Dover, and marvelled at 'the ability of the Sound Engineer and reporter to compile a dramatic mix of ambient sound and narration'. When the aerial bombing campaign over London began in September 1940, Murrow believed he could apply the same dramatic effects to his reports on how Londoners were bearing the strain of the Blitz and succeeded spectacularly, to the benefit of Churchill's US-directed propaganda ambitions. He set about assembling a team of journalists around him that became known as 'the Murrow Boys' and among them was Eric Sevareid, who he described as 'a literary artist trying to awaken American listeners to the urgency of the issue before them'.

The afternoon of 7 September 1940 found Murrow lying in a field on the outskirts of London as an orderly formation of close on 350 Heinkel and Dornier bombers, supported by over 600 fighter aircraft, cast a dark shadow over the capital. A short while later, the dull crump of falling bombs followed, and the East End Docklands was very soon engulfed in a vast plume of smoke accompanied by huge flames rising above the Thames. As darkness fell, the night raiders arrived, and the still-blazing fires guided the 250-strong bomber force to its target. By morning 430 people would be dead and around 1,600 seriously injured. Murrow described how 'the fires up the river had turned the moon blood red', and how the smoke drifting down 'had formed a canopy over the Thames'. He referred to the gun bursts working all around him as being like 'fireflies in a southern summer night' and watched the Germans sending in their planes in twos and threes, passing overhead followed by 'huge pear-shaped bursts of flame' rising up into the smoke. Murrow was effectively describing the first planned bombing raid over London in a dramatically instantaneous fashion, rich with metaphors that went way beyond mere facts. His broadcasts, or 'radio essays' as they were often called, conveyed an immediate here-and-now experience of Britain under siege inside the homes of a listening audience thousands of miles away.

The raid Murrow described was just the beginning of a relentless bombing campaign that continued every night for the next two months.* Subsequently, his apparent fearlessness and proximity to the scene he was describing became the key factors in the effectiveness of his broadcasts. It was a real-time, audible experience of terror and aggression that represented a threat to all of mankind; Murrow wanted Americans to stand in his shoes and to appreciate the fear and the horror as he stood within that cauldron of gunfire and bomb bursts. In his book, *Forgotten Art of Radio Storytelling*, Jeff Porter wrote that 'Murrow's sheer daring became an inseparable part of his broadcasting persona'.[4] The technique of incorporating the authentic sounds of war into his broadcasts was not always permitted, as the British censors forbade location-specific broadcasts for fear of betraying geographical information to the enemy. Murrow had to use all his persuasive energy to get his broadcasts past the censorship officers at the BBC and the MOI, who eventually cleared him in August 1940 for live outside broadcasting. First up would be a joint venture between the BBC and CBS, titled *London After Dark*, featuring eyewitness accounts of air raids with the Murrow Boys – Larry LeSueur, Eric Sevareid and Vincent Sheean – broadcasting from around the capital, including rooftop recordings from undisclosed locations. J.B. Priestley was brought in to conclude the programme from Whitehall.

Typically, 'the sound of war' was an integral part of the broadcasts. Murrow would describe the scene and momentarily pause to allow listeners to hear the sounds of the air-raid siren and the 'screaming

---

* By the time Hitler called a halt to the raids in May 1941, over 40,000 people had been killed, and almost a million houses destroyed or severely damaged in the capital alone.

ambulances'; on one occasion he placed his microphone on the pavement so American listeners could hear the sound of Londoners shuffling into the Underground stations for shelter. Murrow's motivation was to capture the reality and the deeper meaning of the Blitz over London, effectively 'putting America's ear to the pavement'. Both *London After Dark* and its sister programme *London Carries On* not only found a regular slot on CBC and NBC, but also across a whole network of mutual broadcasting systems. Noel Newsome made good use of Murrow's broadcasts on the European network, believing them to be vital propaganda on account of Murrow's status as a neutral observer. Reflecting on what had been achieved in an article he wrote for the BBC just prior to D-Day, Murrow conceded that some of the most important propaganda broadcasts to America had been delivered from what was formerly a caterer's storeroom in the basement of Broadcasting House:

> The air was filled with the smell of boiling cabbage from the nearby canteen, at other times permeated with the smell of disinfectant and often littered with the bodies of sleeping colleagues; from here we tried to tell America something of Britain and the war.[5]

Newsreaders typically worked 'forty-eight hours on' then 'seventy-two off' with two three-hour sleep breaks, during which they were still on duty. Visitors to Murrow's underground den included royalty, Cabinet ministers and those among 'the high and mighty' who wanted to talk to the US. This had been the nerve centre of the *Round London* live recordings during the Blitz that no newspaper could possibly compete with.

Murrow could always sense a good propaganda opportunity, and with Eric Sevareid's literary talent at his disposal, he had all the tools to make it count. In October 1940, just before Sevareid was due to return to America, Murrow put him in front of the microphone and asked him to summarise what he had seen. Sevareid talked about France 'dying in her coma' and about other European cities 'broken in spirit', with the exception of London. Londoners would in years to come speak with the same pride as the armed services who had fought against the Nazis, in that they had been 'citizens of London'.[6] When Sevareid arrived back in the US, he met countless people who had been moved to tears by his broadcast, and he knew for sure that he had hit his target. Another

American who saw the indefatigability of the London public was the outgoing US ambassador to Britain, Joseph Kennedy, who returned home just a fortnight before the November election in 1940. Despite having had a tepid relationship with Franklin D. Roosevelt and openly aligning himself against any policy of providing aid to the British war effort, the Democrat sided with his man and helped the incumbent president to a 55 per cent victory in the popular vote. The BBC's overseas propagandists were careful not to permit any note of exultance to creep in when announcing the result, nor to describe the loser, Wendell Willkie, as 'Hitler's Man'.*[7] They need not have worried when, in open defiance of his colleague's advice, Roosevelt set in motion the Lend-Lease policy that was essentially a blank cheque to Britain and her allies, dressed up as an act to promote the defence of the United States. The act enabled the president to provide whatever materials, oil, or food the Allies required, including warships, aircraft and other military hardware. By the time the agreement ended in September 1945, over $50.1 billion ($575 billion today) worth of supplies had been shipped.[8]

The Murrow Boys played no mean part in the BBC's propaganda campaign towards America, and the corporation supplemented their efforts with several carefully scripted commentaries and talks. On 31 October 1941, the programme *Atlantic Convoy* invited listeners aboard SS *Elizabethan* to share with them the dangers of the supply voyages to and from America. Murrow was then invited to present the first talk in the 1941 four-part series *USA*, first broadcast on 13 January, during which he described the perilous conditions under which he and his team from CBS had worked. Having further endeared himself to British listeners, he returned to the US for a spell of leave in the autumn of that year, where crowds of fans and reporters met his ship. He was as famous as any reporter had ever been and was given a banquet at the Waldorf Astoria with 1,100 guests and millions more listening via a national radio broadcast. After being presented with a congratulatory telegram from President Roosevelt, the poet Archibald MacLeish told him, 'You burned the city of London in our houses and we felt the flames that burned it.'[9]

---

* Willkie had originally favoured a policy of intervention. Only during the final weeks of electioneering when his campaign stalled did he become more isolationist, and accused Roosevelt of being a 'war-monger'.

Murrow had made his mark as a significant player in the war effort, having made the perilous position of Londoners appear a lot less irrelevant.

Such was Murrow's importance in winning over the Americans that Churchill considered him to be a personal friend, and he was invited to join the reception party when Roosevelt's closest advisor, Harry Hopkins, visited London in December 1940. It can be argued that Murrow was given far greater freedom than British broadcasters, especially as switch censors (those who were entrusted with cutting the broadcast if it deviated from the agreed script or was considered damaging to the war effort) were instructed to use their switches only as a last resort. It was felt that nothing could be more disastrous to the interests of the country than the deliberate cutting off of America's most effective speaker in the middle of his commentary. On a return visit to England shortly before his death in 1965, Murrow reflected that he 'had left his youth there and too much of his heart'. Eric Sevareid later recalled that 'England in that thrilling and terrible summer of 1940 was our Camelot'.[10]

On 7 December, a few days after Hopkins' visit, Noel Newsome, the recently appointed director of the BBC's European Service, sat at his desk checking through the day's mostly uneventful up-and-coming evening bulletins. At around 7.15 p.m., a copy boy appeared with a Reuters newsflash stating that Japanese planes had bombed Pearl Harbor. 'I nearly hit the ceiling,' Newsome recalled, 'then I typed out the new lead to all the bulletins: "The war in the Pacific has begun. Japanese aircraft have bombed Pearl Harbor, Headquarters of the United States Pacific Fleet"'.[11]

In keeping with the required protocol, Newsome tracked down someone from the Foreign Office and read out his intended opening headline for all bulletins. The official was insistent that he should 'sit on it' for the time being in case the Americans regarded it as 'just an incident'. Newsome wasn't deterred, and immediately rang the European Service Controller Ivone Kirkpatrick who, despite being alarmed, agreed that he should run the story, and Newsome's unlikely scoop was thereafter picked up by the BBC Home Service. At Chequers that evening, Churchill tuned into the news bulletin and was suddenly shocked to hear unconfirmed reports that Japan had attacked the United States. Ignoring the advice of his own US ambassador to await confirmation, he telephoned Roosevelt directly, and after hearing the president lament to him 'that we are now all in this together', he replaced the receiver firmly convinced that Britain 'had won after all'. Churchill saw very clearly that with 'the British Empire, the Soviet Union and now the United States bound together with every scrap of their life and strength' that there would be no other outcome. He thereafter retired to bed 'and slept the sleep of the saved and thankful' with the words of former ambassador to the US Edward Grey ringing in his ears: 'The United States is a gigantic boiler. Once a fire is lighted under it there is no limit to the power it can generate.'[12]

The entry of the United States into the war would be a huge boost for the morale of the nation, although it had come at a terrible cost of eighteen ships and 2,400 American lives. Newsome impressed upon his staff at the European Service that it was the biggest story of the war so far and needed 'the best handling we can possibly give it'. Churchill's statement that Britain now had four-fifths of the population of the globe on its side was quoted repeatedly, and the Germans were warned that the entry of America into the war made their doom certain. Emphasis was placed on the enormous war potential of the US in what had become 'a war of reserves that Germany could not possibly win in the long run'.[13]

Broadcasts to North America increased significantly after Pearl Harbor as thousands of Americans poured into Britain in advance of preparations for an invasion of Europe. The service eventually transferred to the basement of Peter Robinson's disused drapery store in Oxford Street, where new transatlantic programmes were produced with the aim of tightening the unity between the allies. New productions included *Britain to America, American in England, Stars and Stripes in Britain* and *Meet John Londoner*. Considering that transatlantic broadcasting was regarded as little more than an interesting stunt prior to the war, the BBC could look back favourably on its role in winning over public opinion in the United States, and thereafter facilitating US requirements to keep its citizens and armed forces informed and entertained.

While news coverage and the realism of aerial bombardment was being successfully transmitted into American homes, the suffering and loss in London and other big cities up and down the country was having a crushing effect on home front morale. It was never more important for the BBC to try to raise people's spirits, and to foster an 'all in this together' feeling among the British public. Fortunately, the corporation's wartime variety unit proved itself to be more than up to the job.

German Propaganda Minister Dr Joseph Goebbels examining the new 'People's Radio Receiver' at the Berlin Radio Exhibition on 5 August 1938, alongside the president of the Reich Broadcasting Chamber, Hans Krieger. The receiver was set to go on sale for 65 Reichmarks. (© Bundesarchiv)

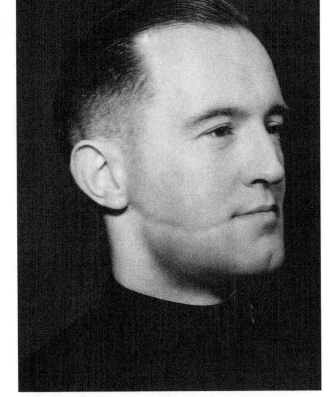

William Joyce (Lord Haw-Haw) in 1940. Through Joyce, the Nazis seized the early propaganda initiative. It wasn't so much the content of his broadcast that attracted British listeners in their millions, rather his accent and personality. (© Corbis Historical/ Getty Images)

The BBC refused to dignify Lord Haw-Haw with a response and presented an upbeat front, despite the immediate curtailment of its regional services. *Radio Times* Special Supplementary Edition, 4 September 1939. (© Immediate Media Co.)

have nothing to offer but blood, toil, tears and sweat.' Prime Minister Winston Churchill broadcasts to the nation on 13 May 1940. His speeches were probably the most effective radio propaganda the BBC ever broadcast. (© Keystone-France/Gamma-Keystone/Getty Images)

CBS journalist Edward R. Murrow in Oxford Street, London, in June 1941. Murrow and his accomplice very effectively described the horror of the London Blitz to American listeners while using the actua sound of events. (© CBS Photo Archive/Getty Images)

Sincerely Yours, Vera Lynn – a sentimental presentation. L–R: Howard Thomas (producer), Vera Lynn and Fred Hartley, photographed in November 1941. (© BBC Photo Library)

'It was the constant danger and worry that made people ready, or even anxious, to accept the craziness that was *ITMA*.' L–R: Tommy Handley, Sidney Keith (Sam Scram), Horace Percival (The Diver) and Jack Train (Funf and Colonel Chinstrap), photographed at rehearsals in November 1942. (© BBC Photo Library)

14 September 1940: J.B. Priestley rehearses his speech for broadcast on the Home Service. Priestley's *Postscripts* were hugely popular, but not everybody approved. (© Gerti Deutsch/Picture Post/Hulton Archive/Getty Images)

6

MAKE THE PEOPLE SMILE AGAIN

In his celebrated book *The People's War*, Angus Calder observed that during the Second World War 'morale' was a word that 'haunted politicians, civil servants and generals' alike.[1] Whether it stemmed from the depressing effects of increased security measures, fear of war, fear of invasion, or the terror of aerial bombardment, the debilitating effects of low morale were viewed as a potentially serious threat to the general war effort. The onus on the BBC to assist in the maintenance of public morale had previously been outlined in a report by a Home Defence Sub-Committee dated 11 January 1939, advising the corporation that 'the maintenance of morale should be their principal aim in times of war'.[2] When the new Ministry of Information came into effect, it was compelled by the War Cabinet to prepare a monthly statement that would outline 'an appreciation of public-morale; complete with recommendations'. It was emphasised regularly that BBC programmes should focus on keeping the public well informed about positive achievements or developments and encourage commentaries 'giving well-informed answers to criticism of the government's conduct of affairs'.[3]

This was all well and good, but the idea of listening to a procession of Cabinet ministers trying to put a positive spin on questionable decisions was unlikely to raise anybody's spirit. At the beginning of the war, when the corporation contracted into a single Home Service, it very quickly came under pressure from both houses and the public to improve the dull service. At a time when theatres and cinemas and other means of entertainment had all been closed indefinitely, the corporation was at once reminded that the public now relied solely on the BBC for their entertainment. With a postbag filled with complaints from listeners bemoaning the endless gramophone records and organ recitals, and in the face of demands from Whitehall to liven things up, the BBC got down to business to placate an audience hidden away behind blackout curtains. Gradually the tide of official government announcements receded, and out went dramatisations of such classics as *East Lynne* and *Murder in the Red Barn*; the people were finally beginning to get what they wanted in the form of morale-boosting, high-quality entertainment. There was a strong belief inside the BBC that variety had good propaganda value in letting people know that such entertainment was carrying on – regardless of the difficulties.[4]

The initial raft of criticism seems unfair when one considers the sheer scale of the upheaval involved in transferring the entire BBC Variety department to Bristol, particularly when the expectation was to hit the ground running. Few people in variety received any sealed instructions; they were simply told to listen for the code words 'this is London calling' and make their way to Bristol as swiftly as possible before the bombs began to fall. While other BBC units were transferred to other locations around the country, a procession of trains, buses, cars and lorries arrived in the West Country loaded with artistes, producers, musicians and engineers, all weighed down with the instruments and other essentials for their purpose. Nobody needed to hear the words, 'we shall be working under difficulties' spoken at the first departmental meeting shortly after arrival. Engineers had to reinstall all the hardware that had been stripped from the London studios into local halls and attend to any number of other complex details to get the show on the road. Multitasking was crucial to the swift turnaround with everyone doing everyone else's job, as well as their own. Phone lines, blackout materials and defence requirements of all kinds had to be attended to, and before broadcasts could begin, scripts had to be written, musical scores copied and numbers rehearsed. In the space of three days, the resources of live radio were reassembled, and on 6 September 1939, the first 'live' revue of the war was broadcast from BBC Variety's new Bristol headquarters; thereafter the department began producing shows at the rate of four a day.[5]

With the international situation no longer so delicate, comedians were released from the shackles of political correctness, meaning the Nazi leaders could now be regarded as fair game. 'You can make jokes about Hitler – provided they are good ones,' joked the Director of Variety John Watt at that 3 September meeting. Previously, representations of Hitler had been banned by the Lord Chamberlain's Office, and theatres were refused licences for plays that critically depicted events in Nazi Germany, over fears that they might become centres of anti-Nazi feeling.[6] In 1937, at the King's Theatre in Hammersmith, a British actor had been prosecuted and fined for his humorous caricature of Hitler. The leading Nazi newspaper *Der Angriff* criticised the lenient punishment for such impertinence and questioned the lackadaisical manner in which England approached her judicial responsibilities.[7]

The propaganda department at Electra House might well have been dissuaded from making fun of Hitler over concerns about driving the anti-Nazi element in occupied Europe towards him; yet there was no reason why the public at home could not have a good laugh at his expense. It was evident that the BBC was somewhat perplexed in the early months of war by a feeling that radio listeners had not been able to make sense of the 'hysterical screams of the Führer'.[8] Among the BBC's earliest attempts at mocking Hitler was the spoof parody *Adolf in Blunderland*, first broadcast as a drama on 6 October 1939. The programme told the story of Hitler's rise to power along the lines of Lewis Carroll's famous children's classic *Alice in Wonderland*. Reflecting on the programme a few years later, the BBC Yearbook of 1944 praised the broadcast for 'setting us all laughing in sheer relief' to hear the song within the production titled 'Tis the Voice of Hitler'. The book on which the broadcast was based by James Dyrenforth and Max Kesler did not simply mock Hitler, it also represented a stern critique of the international community, including Britain, for allowing Hitler to get to where he was. Although Dyrenforth and Kesler stuck very close to Carroll's original plot, the key difference between the two was that, whereas Wonderland was no more than a dream world, the propaganda version parodied real events that would have made for uncomfortable listening among diplomats.

Parodying Hitler when nothing much else was happening kept listeners amused, but when the emergency became real in the form of mass bombing of civilians, the question of broadcasting became a much more serious issue. Firstly, it became essential that all 'white' propaganda, including variety, took on a 'we're all in this together' approach as all parts of the community were sharing a terrible burden. Secondly, the British public needed constantly to be fed on a diet of optimism, and both comedians and writers were expected to express this. As far as propaganda in variety was concerned, the broadcasting of conscious propaganda was deemed to be ineffectual and would only be permitted by the Home Service Board as an 'unenforced ingredient'.[9]

A key criteria for BBC Variety was entertainment value sufficient enough to 'relieve the strain and monotony' of those working in factories geared to the requirements of total war. Programmes such as *Workers' Playtime* were crucial in this respect, bringing well-known comedians and singers into factories across the country to deliver broadcasts from the heart of Britain's wartime industry. The programme was met with much enthusiasm from audiences of critical workers that could be anything from 400 to 5,000 strong. The Minister of Labour and National Service Ernest Bevin welcomed the programme, along with another special programme, *Music While You Work*, similarly devised for workers' entertainment. Bevin paid tribute to the BBC, describing it as 'a factory for entertainment and education and a vital service, representing a necessary link and contribution to production'.[10] The programmes succeeded because the BBC had carried out its own research to determine how best the broadcasts could boost production in Britain's war industries. It discovered that there were two half-hours (mid-morning and mid-afternoon) when boredom was at its greatest and the workers tended to slacken off and chat. It was also found that a daily production of dance music could step up production by 30 per cent, while *Music While You Work* produced marked increases in production when compared with other periods in the working day.[*11] The show's producer, Wynford Reynolds, promoted the catchphrase that through radio Britain could achieve 'victory through harmony'.

As much as the BBC bent over backwards to deliver the right kind of morale-boosting programmes to the armed forces and to factory workers, it also had to do more to raise the spirits of its fiercest critics, 'the fireside public'. Many were difficult to please, and some listeners even objected to what they perceived as constant propaganda being

---

* *Music While You Work* and *Workers' Playtime* both outlived the war, well into the 1960s.

directed into their living rooms – this from a listener writing to the BBC in early 1940:

> I think your comedians are stale, your singers are poor, your shows badly produced. You bring propaganda into everything you can. It is disgusting and not worthy of the English people. But, of course, this will not be published. Complaints never are![12]

And neither could the corporation please everybody with its musical productions. It was constantly accused of either 'pandering too much to the lowbrow' or being berated by listeners who were 'heartily sick of the way you favour highbrow music lovers'.[13] Few realised the BBC's music selection was not immune to the fortunes of war, as the immediate dropping of such favourites as 'Hang out the Washing on the Siegfried Line' following the fall of France effectively illustrates. The corporation rolled with the punches and ploughed on in its time-honoured quest to bring the people 'the best of everything', including comedy intended to mitigate the depressing effects of war. Things were made additionally difficult when so much time was being lost due to air raids. Soundproofing was not good at the Parish Hall studios in Bristol and, when the bombing campaigns started, programmes had to be pre-recorded in daylight hours. Cast members also had to take turns at being plane spotters, and when time was of the essence, writers began disregarding orders and remained inside working on scripts instead of sheltering. There was always a determination that 'the show must go on' and that the listeners should not go without their entertainment.*

No performer epitomised this spirit of determination more than the comedian Tommy Handley, a man who felt his responsibilities so deeply that, even as his health failed, he went on relentlessly, desperate to avoid letting down a public who relied on him for their weekly tonic of morale-boosting comedy. The great American writer John Steinbeck

---

* One Sunday during a heavy raid in Bristol, the orchestra could not be crammed into an emergency studio for a recording of the *Religious Postscript*. Instead, the microphone was placed under a table and, with bombs crashing all around, the postscript was delivered, accompanied by the sounds of a violinist playing on his knees. (*BBC at War*, p.11)

wrote in 1943 that when 'recognition of service to the nation in wartime comes to be considered, comedian Bob Hope should be high on the list'. The same can equally be said of Handley, who gained a hard-earned reputation as the man who made wartime Britain laugh. Handley and his comedy show *ITMA (It's That Man Again)* far exceeded its morale-boosting value, especially when it was discovered that people in occupied Europe were listening in on clandestine radio sets, just desperate to hear *real* laughter.

Handley was already a big name at the BBC before the war. His versatility had gained him a reputation as the corporation's 'handyman of comedy' and his cheery 'hello folks' lighted the gloom on the darkest of days. His success at the microphone in wartime was phenomenal, to the extent that he became arguably the greatest radio comedian the world has ever known. At the height of his fame, he enjoyed a prestige at the BBC that no other comic-artiste had achieved before, and probably has not enjoyed since. So highly was he regarded that when he died prematurely aged just 56 soon after the war, his funeral was on a scale typically reserved for royalty. Tearful mourners lined the streets six deep as the funeral procession passed by, while another 10,000 stood solemnly at the crematorium waiting for the arrival of the hearse. A few days later, a national memorial service was held at St Paul's Cathedral in celebration of Handley's life and was filled to capacity. Thousands listened outside through loudspeakers, causing traffic to be diverted. Naturally the service was also broadcast to Handley's millions of adoring fans on the BBC; his scriptwriter Ted Kavanagh called it 'a heartfelt tribute to a beloved jester, and also to the power of the microphone that brought his voice into every home in wartime Britain'.[14]

For all its success, the first series of *It's That Man Again* came close to being axed after just four programmes following the lukewarm reaction to its first run in the summer of 1939. At that time, it was no secret that the BBC's then flagship comedy show *Band Waggon* was on its final run and would come off the air before the year was out. Fronted by Arthur Askey, *Band Waggon* had made history as the first comedy team to air on radio on the same day at the same time every week. People made a regular date with it, and such was the success of the programme, the BBC was anxious to repeat the formula and turned to Handley, who agreed to front a new show. While radio listeners were in a constant state of anxiety over what might happen with international relations so finely balanced, Handley and his producer, Francis Worsley, teamed up with Kavanagh to work on a forty-five-minute comedy to begin broadcasting on the BBC Home Service on 12 July 1939. Worsley remembered that 'at that time we had been hearing a great deal of one Adolf Hitler continually bursting into the news with some territorial claim or other'.[15] Because of this, the familiar catchphrase of the moment was *It's That Man Again*.

The show featured Handley on board a spoof floating radio station as the 'link man' between a cast of characters that featured regularly on alternate shows. Worsley remembered that after the first show 'we did nothing more than repair to the local where we sipped our warm beer with an uneasy feeling that we had another flop on our hands'.[16] Things did not improve much as the team continued on through another three shows. The criticism the BBC dared to publish was cutting in the extreme:

> Why should the producers in the variety department assume that listeners are a body of half-wits? The puns served up in last night's *It's That Man Again* were an insult to anyone's intelligence! Even that studio audience couldn't laugh.[17]

The reactions recorded in the diaries of Mass Observation participants to the BBC's new radio comedy was much the same – singling out Handley for special treatment:

> Do I listen to Tommy Handley? Good Lord, No! I turn the set off as quickly as possible. Of all rotten comedians, Tommy Handley is the rottenest.[18]

> The Wireless was ghastly tonight. Tommy Handley! I ask you, if you had not heard him, would you have believed that anyone could be so terrible?[19]

Originally scheduled for a run of six fortnightly shows, the first series was cancelled after just four programmes when war was declared. To his relief, Handley was given a second crack of the whip in BBC Variety's new location in Bristol with a different cast of characters. There were no preliminary meetings between the team; the BBC simply strong-armed the corporation's requirements in a memo to producer

Francis Worsley. The programme length would be reduced to thirty minutes and would air for the first time on 19 September 1939. The team set to work immediately in the full knowledge that because the country was now at war, it was deemed permissible to make fun of Hitler and the Nazis, and because the show was to be shorter in length, it was felt that a snappier title would suffice. Wartime Britain had plunged everyone into a world of abbreviations that had broken out 'like a plague', according to Worsley. Handley came up with the abbreviated *ITMA* and, although the BBC never formally headlined the show as *ITMA* until 7 November, it stuck for the remainder of the programme's ten-year lifespan.

The first show of the new *ITMA* format began on schedule with Handley in command of the Ministry of Information, sent up as the 'Ministry of Aggravation':

> Hello Folks – its Mein Kampf again – sorry, I should say hello folks It's That Man Again. That was a Goebbled version – a bit doctored. I usually go all goosey when I can't follow my proper–ganda.[20]

Something very soon 'clicked' with the new crew, for within a short space of time *ITMA* became a firm favourite with listeners, mainly owing to the infectious cheeriness of Handley's voice at a time when everyone's life was in turmoil. With children being evacuated, husbands and sons being called up and orders coming in from so many new 'authorities', the show had a strange capacity to revive and rejuvenate people. Handley reasoned that if he could give people the feeling that half an hour of laughter every week was the one thing they could be sure of in an uncertain world, he would have achieved his goal.

Because Kavanagh was now writing in wartime, everything had to be passed by a censor and everyone included in the cast and crew had to be vetted by the MOI – the same arm of government that Handley was lampooning. The sudden success of *ITMA* was largely due to the satirising of passing events against a new background of war. This meant that constant topical references were critical to the continued success of the show, and scripts were always written surrounded by the latest newspapers, or within earshot of the BBC's latest news broadcasts, sometimes being edited just a couple of hours before the show was aired. Worsley and Kavanagh went to great lengths to get a feel for all areas of the war effort; this included visiting a Wellington bomber factory in Chester to pick up on the right slang phrases used.[21]

Worsley believed that it was the constant danger and worry that made people ready, or even anxious, to accept the 'craziness' that was *ITMA*. One listener wrote in to thank Handley for 'the sheer foolishness' of his comedy; 'no matter how tired or despondent I have felt, his programme has never finished without causing me to smile'.[22] People wanted to laugh again for real, and who better to laugh at than the enemy in form of the character of 'Funf'. He was written as the embodiment of all the current 'spy neurosis', despite him being a hopelessly ineffective spy. In Worsley's view, 'he crystallized the contempt tinged with unacknowledged fear with which the British people faced the new enemy'.[23] The character might only have been cast member Jack Train speaking into a glass tumbler, but Funf could be used to reduce either Adolf Hitler or the much-feared Gestapo to ridiculous caricature. By the autumn of 1941, an Italian version of Funf was created in the character of Signor So-So, and Kavanagh's script took great advantage of the perceived squabbles between the dictators when things went badly for the Axis powers in North Africa.

As popular as the show was, there were rumblings in Parliament that this type of propaganda was not in Britain's best interests. One MP complained in February 1942 of 'the constant laughing at, or ridiculing of Hitler without ever recognising that everything that the Prime Minister is to us, and everything that Mr. Roosevelt is to America, Hitler is to the overwhelming majority of the German people'.[24] Such criticism did not stall an invitation from the king and queen for the cast of *ITMA* to perform at Windsor Castle in April that year. By that time, Handley had decamped to the holiday resort of Foaming at the Mouth, with the show being temporarily renamed *It's That Sand Again*. So quick-fire was Handley's manner and so perfect was his timing, Kavanagh would need to write over a hundred potential laughs across eighteen and a half minutes of available dialogue – a rate of approximately a laugh every eleven seconds! According to Kavanagh, the essence of Handley was that he was more than just a radio comedian; listeners viewed him as a personal friend, even though very few of them had met him. 'He made them laugh during a period when laughter was precious, and stuck to them in all their troubles and, famous and successful though he was, he had always remained one of them.'[25] Former BBC Director General Sir William Haley believed Handley had 'that rare gift which few are born with, and most never acquire, of being able to broadcast sincerity. As you listened to him you felt the personality of an essentially friendly and good man.'[26] By the time of its fifth series, *ITMA* was commanding 16 million listeners a week, peaking at 43.3 per cent of the population.[27] Newspapers joked that 'if Hitler were to invade at 8.30 p.m. on a Thursday night he could catch Britain completely unawares'.[28]

Success did not seem to change Handley and he rarely missed a show, despite the stress and worry of total war. He regularly suffered from severe headaches, intolerable fatigue and hypertension, and rejected medical advice in the fear that his doctor would prescribe a rest from broadcasting. There was always another boys' club to open, factories to visit, hospitals to attend, speeches to deliver. Kavanagh remembered that in giving so much of himself to others 'he reached a state of mental and physical exhaustion which he was struggling vainly to overcome. His job was the hardest in the world. He also had to be funny in public as it was expected of him, and he didn't want to disappoint anyone.'[29] Handley died suddenly from a cerebral haemorrhage in 1949. He received no award, nor coveted one, and yet was arguably as much a war hero as the brave men that had fallen in battle.

The relative significance of Handley and *ITMA* is the extent to which it exemplifies the power of comedy as a medium of morale-boosting propaganda, not just at home, but also abroad. For the British, although the war was taken seriously, humour was a protective mantle that helped an otherwise terrified public get through the bombing campaigns and the threat of invasion. This was something that the BBC had actively encouraged, and Handley believed that he had earned the right to be funny in wartime 'just as listeners had earned the right to laugh at our nonsense'.[30] Even bomber crews were reported to borrow catchphrases from *ITMA* before unleashing their bombs on the enemy – a habit that also extended to air-raid victims upon being dug out of the rubble!* Harold Nicolson at the MOI went so far as to broadcast a talk on the superiority of English humour to that of the status-conscious

---

* Bombing crews typically uttered 'After you Claude,' while air-raid victims are known to have asked 'Can you do me now sir?'

Germans. The German intelligence authorities had become aware that there had been a significant amount of illicit listening during the times of *ITMA*'s broadcasts. It was thought that the programme was being used either for direct propaganda, or for coded messages to the European underground. The British Government was similarly worried about the possible subtle use of popular BBC variety programmes by fifth columnists, either on the staff, or as audience members, for passing information.[31] There were occasions when people who had escaped Nazi-controlled Europe approached Handley asking if a piece of music could be included, so that their families knew they had made it safely to Britain. After suitable investigation by the authorities, this was done whenever possible. It was also known that *ITMA*'s secret audience in occupied Europe was surprisingly large, despite the risks involved in listening to carefully turned-down illegal radio sets. Many of them could not understand a word of it – they just wanted to hear unrestrained laughter for the first time in years! One influential French newspaper paid a posthumous tribute to Handley:

> The good man let us enjoy laughter, loud, sounding, free, large, honest, childlike and strong: the laugh that is not a grin, no dissoluteness, no blasphemy: the laugh that illuminated our glory, relieved our sorrows and revived our courage.[32]

Handley would have been humbly satisfied that he had, if only for a moment, put smiles on faces throughout occupied Europe in the darkest of times.

Another entertainer in the employ of the BBC knew she was being subtly utilised for counter-propaganda purposes, and remained unfazed by the political storm that swept over her when things did not go to plan. (Dame) Vera Lynn was already a successful recording artist and stage performer in early 1940 when the BBC had been coming under increasing pressure to provide entertainment to lift the morale of the armed forces overseas. There were hundreds of thousands of British servicemen in northern Europe who seemed to be sitting on their hands in the bitterly cold winter, probably listening to the French commercial station Radio Fécamp, waiting for something to happen. When BBC Director General Frederick Ogilvie visited the BEF in France to speak to servicemen about their entertainment needs, many responded that they simply wanted 'something to cheer us up – something to keep us in touch with home'. These requests were mitigated on 7 January 1940 by the introduction of the *Forces Programme*, to be broadcast on an alternative wavelength.[33] The new service began as an experimental nightly service running from 6 p.m. until 12.15 a.m., and typically comprised musical presentations that featured dance bands, and remained free from drama, talks and religious instruction. On 18 February, the programme was extended to a full twelve-hour service, enabling it to include more variety including programmes specially broadcast for the forces such as the popular comedy show *Garrison Theatre*, as well as twice-weekly lessons in French, and updates on the ice hockey leagues for the Canadian forces. On 16 June, the service was extended further to begin at 6.15 a.m., and included the popular new sitcom series *Hi Gang*, which also enjoyed poking fun at the Nazi leaders and propagandists. Another programme, *Ack Ack Beer Beer*, was specifically aimed at anti-aircraft and barrage balloon personnel; motorists who had been required to remove radios from cars for security purposes were requested to kindly donate them to these units so that the men could listen in to their programme. Diarists at Mass Observation recorded that they preferred the programmes available on the Forces Service to those of the Home Service. Records made by the men themselves were sometimes included, along with popular concerts given to the men of the BEF featuring the likes of Gracie Fields, Maurice Chevalier – and eventually Vera Lynn.

'That there was something about my voice which appealed to servicemen began to reveal itself quite early in the war,' wrote Vera Lynn, upon remembering that her name had appeared at the top of a list of 'the favourite female vocalists among members of the Tank Corps'.[34] A short while later, Lynn's star had risen to greater heights when it was announced on 17 April 1940 that 'the plumber's daughter from East Ham – wide-eyed, open-faced Miss Vera Lynn had topped the British Expeditionary Force's singing popularity poll'. Thereafter, owing to publicity given to the poll by the *Daily Express*, a permanent link was established between Lynn and the armed forces.

It was during the London Blitz in the autumn of 1940 that Lynn first began her formal association with the BBC when she made regular appearances in *Starlight*, a fifteen-minute show featuring singers 'in an intimate setting'. She would arrive at the BBC's Overseas Entertainment studios in the underground Criterion Theatre before the bombs began to fall, and then sleep until her rehearsals for the 2.30 a.m. broadcast for the troops overseas were due to begin. The *Starlight* programme was typically rebroadcast several times. Lynn came around to the idea that the key ingredient in her appeal was an ability to sound sincere about what she was singing. Although she had not written the song, it was her belief that the words expressed what she herself would say in the context of the song, and its message always came across. The effect of the tenderness of the songs and the meaning she was able to enrich them with could have a powerful effect upon a young soldier many miles from home – effectively making him feel as though she were singing directly to him. Lynn may not have been fully conscious of this effect, for by her own admission she was working purely from 'the instinct of what lay within her emotional and technical range'. It was a range that satisfied her, and as a young girl she had rejected the idea of voice training, choosing instead to nurture the singing voice that she felt comfortable with, and thereafter excelled as a singer of sentimental lyrics because she believed in them.

Lynn also saw in radio the great unifying link between family members 'scattered by war'. She also viewed radio broadcasting as the natural outlet for her songs, and it was the 'songs that spoke for the ordinary people' that became her chosen means of expression. She had initially approached the BBC about the idea of a fifteen-minute request show especially for the troops, an idea that was met with much enthusiasm, only to be kicked into the long grass, where it remained for several months. She had all but given up on the idea until the day BBC producer Howard Thomas called her up and invited her to do a weekly half-hour show in the form of 'a letter to the troops' called *Sincerely Yours, Vera Lynn*. The sudden enthusiasm for Lynn's original idea lends support to the impression that the new programme was conceived as deliberate counter-propaganda in the face of what British troops were being exposed to overseas from foreign broadcasting stations. A sentimental song called 'Lili Marleen' had become a huge favourite with German soldiers at the front, and despite its German lyrics, had additionally found its way into the hearts of serving British troops. In her memoirs, Lynn referred to the effect that the song was having on the servicemen, as it was used to imply that their wives and girlfriends at home 'were up to all sorts of things in return for black market butter and meat while their men were away at the front'.[35] *Sincerely Yours* was conceived as a possible antidote to this form of morale-damaging propaganda.

The sudden rise in popularity of 'Lili Marleen' and how the song emerged as such a potent propaganda weapon on both sides is an interesting story. Based on a German soldier's poem, 'The Song of a Young Sentry' written by Hans Leip during the First World War, 'Lili Marleen' had somehow emerged as the embodiment of the sadness of separation brought on by war. A German soldier awaiting shipment to the front laments on the girlfriends he was leaving behind and remembers his evening trysts with a girl beneath a lantern outside the barracks. 'But that', the soldier says, 'was long ago': he's been killed in battle, and the lantern has forgotten him. 'Who will she be meeting there now?' he wonders. From the silence of the grave he will rise, and his ghost will be standing beneath the lantern, just as Lili Marleen once did. The long-forgotten musical score by Nerbert Schultze had re-emerged in 1941 when the German Station began using it to conclude nightly broadcasts to troops in North Africa from a powerful transmitter in occupied Belgrade, and continued doing so for around eighteen months. Despite German troops deluging singer Lale Andersen with mail addressed to 'Lili Marleen', Nazi Propaganda Minister Joseph Goebbels insisted that, rather than boost morale, the song made soldiers homesick and moved to have it banned.* Meanwhile, Andersen was also barred from performing and narrowly escaped being sent to a concentration camp after reportedly staging a fake suicide attempt.[36]

At the same time, British soldiers picked up the song from the German radio and either sang it in German, or improvised with different lyrics. Because there were strong suggestions that Lili was a prostitute rather than 'the girl next door', the MOI urged the BBC to commission a sanitised version; thereafter it fell to prolific songwriter Tommie Connor to write an official English composition. His song followed a story similar to the German version, with the girl now known as 'Lili Marlene', and was recorded by both Anne Shelton and Marlene Dietrich. With enthusiasm for the war in Germany noticeably on the wane,

---

* The Lale Andersen version was spelled 'Lili Marlen'.

Goebbels banned the song again in August 1944, but by this time the Allies had realised its morale-busting potential and had the version sung by Marlene Dietrich blasted out across the front lines to further depress the German troops. A version sung by cabaret star Luci Mannheim that went out on the German Service implied that the lamp post could be used to hang Hitler.[37]

Vera Lynn would eventually record her own version of 'Lili Marlene', but in the meantime she had readily agreed to the *Sincerely Yours* proposal – the *Radio Times* advertised the first show on 9 November 1941 on the Forces Service as being 'To the men of the forces: A letter in words and music from Vera Lynn, accompanied by Fred Hartley and his music. A sentimental presentation by Howard Thomas.' The show became an immediate success, with listening figures amounting to almost a quarter of the population – the largest ever audience for a forces programme at peak listening time on a Sunday night.[38] The flood of incoming mail from the serving men was enormous, and brought the lucky servicemen who were mentioned closer to their families. On such occasions, the sentimental songs really did come into their own, and every response suggested that the show had been uplifting and good for morale. Lynn saw in herself a simple message carrier between separated people, and merely conveyed what they would in all likelihood like to say to one another; she also visited mothers in hospitals to be present at the births of their babies while their husbands were serving overseas.* Letters were answered either on air or in person; photographs were signed and even small gifts of cigarettes were mailed off to the men on the front lines. Lynn always went the extra mile as a way of saying thank you to the men 'for what they were doing for us'. From the point of view of the troops, aside from her singing talent, Lynn's humble, warm-hearted broadcasting style fashioned the morale-boosting effect of a girl-next-door radio girlfriend.

Sincerely Yours ran for six weeks up until 14 December, and then, by popular demand, Lynn readjusted her theatre schedule to begin another six-week run beginning on 15 February 1942. As popular as the show became, it wasn't a particular favourite with the BBC Board

---

* The 'babies announcement' was eventually discontinued when the show became overwhelmed with messages from new mothers and district nurses.

of Governors; the oft-quoted missive '*Sincerely Yours* deplored but popularity noted' effectively illustrates this.[39] This comment was just the beginning of a gathering undercurrent of criticism that slowly began to be directed towards Howard Thomas's 'sentimental presentation'. Slow progress in the North Africa campaign, coupled with the disastrous loss of Singapore, had begun to give MPs and some influential retired military personnel the idea that sentimental music was producing sentimental soldiers who were not proving themselves in battle. The fact that both setbacks had resulted from a mixture of inexperience, unpreparedness and poor decision-making at a high level was brushed aside, as instead, an accusing finger was pointed at the programme and its much-loved presenter. The scale of the criticism resulted in the BBC forming what Lynn described as 'an Anti-Slush Committee' on what was deemed fit to broadcast to a nation at war. It was the British press who originally came up with the name 'Anti-Slush Committee' as an alternative name for the BBC's Dance Music Policy Committee (DMPC), who viewed themselves as cultural arbiters, entitled to discriminate between good and inferior music on the listeners' behalf. Decisions about what was deemed appropriate were made on moral, rather than aesthetic or intellectual grounds. Following a further disastrous military loss at Tobruk in North Africa, the 'Hawks' at the BBC seized the opportunity to stamp out songs that were deemed 'too sentimental', and from July 1942 effectively banned all 'sloppy lyrics, male crooners, and overly-sentimental female singers' from broadcasting. The alleged debilitating effect of these performance styles was deemed by the BBC to be the result of the singers and songs being 'anaemic and slushy in sentiment'.[40] While British generals licked the military wounds of their own making, *Sincerely Yours* was officially 'rested' from transmission.

The listening public were dismayed; one listener sent in a question to the experts on the regular *Brains Trust* programme asking, 'Is Vera Lynn harmful to morale?'[41] In the wider context of wartime entertainment and the fluctuating fortunes of war, the whole charade of railing against the 'negative effects of sentimental songs' was not only ludicrous, but reflected a profound lack of sensible judgement. On 19 October 1941, when the siege of Tobruk was holding firm, Lynn had appeared on the BBC's special tribute show dedicated to 'the gallant garrison of Tobruk' compiled as a special thank you to the imperial forces defending the stronghold. Additionally, a couple of months later, when the popularity of Sincerely Yours was at its highest, the British Eighth Army had scored a significant victory in the Western Desert campaign during the Allied effort to relieve the siege of Tobruk in Operation Crusader.

Lynn was far too much in demand for this setback to damage her career and carried on performing regardless, but her popular solo programme did not return for another eighteen months. This meant that, along with many other crooning and sentimental numbers, iconic wartime songs such as 'We'll Meet Again' and 'The White Cliffs of Dover' were not so frequently heard over the airwaves. Despite this, Lynn's songs had evolved into popular singalongs by this time, meaning their popularity was continually perpetuated by her adoring public, regardless of whether they were played on the radio or not. They were powerful morale-boosting songs, offering the sincere promise of the certainty of reunion between soldiers and their wives or girlfriends, their families or their friends on 'Some sunny day!' The BBC followed up its decision by taking the opportunity to assert its own culturally based principles by promoting an 'antidote' of 'virile, man-to-man songs', to the satisfaction of the hierarchy.[42] The resulting protests from servicemen were brushed aside, and one newspaper critic wrote of Sincerely Yours, 'the songs dripped with sentiment. After a while they dripped so much they were dropped.'[43]

The show returned again in 1944 when the war situation had turned and the Allies were in a much stronger position. Despite a minority of listeners still bemoaning the 'superabundance of crooners and singing sweethearts', Sincerely Yours continued to be as successful as it had been previously, unmolested by ageing military chiefs, or the BBC's 'culture hawks'.[44] As popular as the show became, it did not stop one speaker in Parliament from likening the BBC's female crooners to 'the caterwauling of an inebriated cockatoo'.[45] Such criticisms are an indication of just how out of touch people in higher authority were with Britain's changing culture, accelerated by war, and how blindly they misjudged the mood of the nation. The success of Vera Lynn with her sentimental songs, her selflessness and her affectionate words of encouragement highlights another key difference between this and previous wars, namely that broadcasting could enable the fighting man to have a daily morale-boosting link with home. A lot of men and women serving overseas expressed a wish to share the same programmes with their families at home in the interests of securing 'a community of spirit' between them and their homes. As a result, from 27 February 1944, the *Forces Programme* was replaced on the home wavelengths by the service for those serving overseas called the *General Forces Programme*.

The changing culture of entertainment was not the only change in the air in a nation ravaged by the 'winds of war' barely two decades on from the previous conflict. The fighting man wanted something more than victory in exchange for risking his life for king and country, and the BBC, to the displeasure of its overseers, would inadvertently find just the man to champion his cause.

7

CROSSING THE PROPAGANDA LINE

Since 1928, when the BBC had finally been permitted to broadcast talks on 'controversial subjects including politics', there was no shortage of MPs in Parliament who repeatedly emphasised the huge responsibility on the shoulders of those in charge at the corporation – not least the enormous power for political propaganda if they chose to use it. One keen observer of people and matters in Britain stated that, if only he were given control of the corporation, within less than twelve months he would make the whole country Conservative. Anything that smacked of left-wing or communist propaganda was typically seized upon. As far back as 1931 there had been outrage when a talk was given on the subject of the Soviet Union, described by one member in the House of Lords as 'one of the finest pieces of subtle propaganda that I have ever heard; leaving one with the impression that the Russian system as now carried on was the most admirable thing'.[1] It was not only the honourable gentleman accusing the BBC of trying to educate the British people towards socialism, as there were sections of the press making similar judgements in their editorials:

Widespread and legitimate anxiety is being caused in the public mind by a whole series of recent events, which cast grave suspicion on the political impartiality of the BBC. The function of the BBC is to provide entertainment and instruction, and not to disseminate political propaganda obnoxious to large sections of the community who pay for its amenities.[2]

Eyebrows had also been raised when, in its most recent editions of *The Listener*, advertisements had appeared appealing for the donation of funds for the Labour Party. Lord Gainford, BBC governor and former chairman, refuted any suggestions of bias, and reminded members of an agreement drawn up with the three main parties 'as to what we may and may not broadcast of a political character'.[3] The BBC was also committed to consulting the parties over anything to do with political matters that may be thought to trench upon that agreement. It is also evident that the corporation sought to exclude broadcasts from the more extreme political groups, denying both fascist and communist elements any opportunity to direct 'subversive' propaganda towards listeners. An uncomfortable episode had occurred in May 1935 when the Anglo-Irish poet and Communist Party member Cecil Day Lewis had been allowed to broadcast a talk on the connection between politics and literature.[4]

Because the BBC remained independent from government control, it was always likely to attract accusations of political bias. This was evident following the Munich Crisis, when its news editors were compelled to fight off accusations that they were following an anti-government line.[5] By the summer of 1939, the British Labour Party had adopted a position of 'patriotic opposition', and unwilling to lay itself open to further claims of political bias, the BBC afforded the party sufficient airtime to state its case. On the night of 3 July 1939, an appeal to the German people was broadcast on behalf of the National Council of Labour titled *Why Kill Each Other,* with summaries broadcast in German, French, Italian, Spanish and Portuguese. Additionally, the NCL had arranged broadcasts to German workers from secret radio stations on the Continent and distributed printed matter through its underground organisations. The amount of time afforded to Labour speakers during the early months of the war became a cause of irritation within the Chamberlain War Cabinet. The Secretary of State for War, Leslie Hore-Belisha, complained of the 'deleterious effect of the weekly broadcasts' that frequently amounted to 'attacks on the government by leaders of the Labour opposition'.[6]

On 10 May 1940, when Winston Churchill was confirmed as prime minister, much of the domestic in-fighting was quelled by the formation of a coalition government, initially incorporating a five-man War Cabinet consisting of members from both main parties bound together with a single purpose 'to wage war until victory is won'. With the situation becoming graver by the hour, the house united behind Churchill, who solemnly declared in his first speech as prime minister, on 19 May, that 'I have nothing to offer except blood, toil, tears and sweat'. This was the first of a series of speeches that intensified the resolve within the British people to resist and to wage total war with everything they had. Even the fact that radio enabled his rousing speeches to be heard in the farthest corners of the world did little to endear the BBC to Churchill, who had little time for the corporation (mainly because its activities were often beyond his control). He railed against those who championed its independence, and later downplayed its contribution to the war effort – his extensive six-volume collection of wartime memoirs barely gave it a mention. That said, there is a strong case for believing that Churchill needed radio broadcasting as much as the people needed him – especially as his fire and brimstone speeches became arguably the most powerful force of home and overseas propaganda that the BBC could offer. With France on her knees and in the near certain knowledge that Britain would soon be standing alone, Churchill listened to opinions and advice from those of all political creeds, before deciding he would make a bold statement in terms of 'fighting on' in the expectation that the speech would have an extensive global reach through the medium of radio. Churchill knew that Britain could not win without American assistance and drafted his famous post-Dunkirk 'Fight on the Beaches' speech under an assumption that it would be broadcast to his friends across the Atlantic – those on whom he placed all hope of delivering the 'Old World' from Nazi tyranny:

> Even if, which I do not for a moment believe, this island or a large part of it were subjugated and starving, then our Empire beyond the seas, armed and guarded by the British Fleet, would carry on the struggle, until, in God's good time, the New World, with all its power and might, steps forth to the rescue and the liberation of the old.[*]

---

[*] Churchill delivered his speech in Parliament on the afternoon of 4 June. It was not recorded for the BBC, although extracts from it were read out on the nine o'clock news and repeated the following day. It was intended that the prime minister would address the nation from Broadcasting House on 6 June, but this never happened. (Toye, p.54)

Churchill's morale-boosting speeches were broadcast repeatedly as far and wide as the facilities of the BBC could transmit them. However, the MOI had long been insisting that the corporation needed to come up with something more to dissuade home listeners from channel hopping onto the Nazi-controlled stations. A series of 'peak-time' Sunday evening *Postscripts* had not gotten off to the best of starts when the first speaker, Maurice Healy (a well-known barrister), had his contract terminated when the MOI complained that his broadcasts were 'divisive and tactless'. Additional speakers also failed to make any strong connection, especially among working-class listeners, leading the MOI to lament that the last thing the BBC needed at this perilous hour was yet another cultured, patronising accent – particularly while enemy propaganda was spreading that British policy was being exclusively directed by capitalists and imperialists. Typically, the stiffness of vocabulary enunciated by BBC broadcasters made it difficult to tap into working-class audiences. George Orwell described the voice of the BBC as being unlike anything spoken outside of Broadcasting House: 'The first sign that things are really happening in England will be the disappearance of that horrible, plummy voice from the radio.'[7]

The microphone was eventually given to the Bradford-born novelist and playwright J.B. Priestley, who it was felt would fit the bill in terms of accent, upbringing and outlook. With his warm Yorkshire accent and thinking man's viewpoint on current events, the BBC felt they had discovered their man to eclipse Lord Haw-Haw. Priestley's success as a playwright had brought him fame in the 1930s, and he was no stranger to the microphone. Over the course of the war he delivered no fewer than 225 talks for the BBC's Home and Overseas Services, and had been scheduled to broadcast on the day that war was declared.[8] While the population of bereft radio listeners vacillated between overwhelming emotions of anger and despair, Priestley had been contracted to read the first instalment of a serial called *Let the People Sing*, and groped his way through the blackout towards Broadcasting House, where he found himself among 'sandbags, bayonets and nurses in uniform'. He already knew he was on a hiding to nothing; his masterful delivery of the spoken word as he relayed his light-hearted tale on that infamous day was never likely to sweeten the bitterest of pills. Priestley readily admitted that he did not like radio, although he later conceded that when the nation found itself at war, 'the radio at last had come into its own'. At the moment of Britain's greatest peril following Dunkirk, Priestley was already broadcasting twice weekly to the United States, Canada and Australia in the hugely popular *Britain Speaks* on the Overseas Service, and felt that he had more to say to people in Britain other than simple recitations of his work. Priestley approached the BBC with his request, and with the corporation desperately searching for the right man to fit the requirements of the MOI, he seemed ideal to take over the Sunday night *Postscript*.

Lillian Duff had the job of looking after Priestley at the BBC and was entrusted with the duties of switch censor should he ever deviate from the agreed script. She realised immediately that the tone of reassurance in Priestley's broadcast might be exactly the kind of propaganda the MOI had been hoping for:

> In the BBC there was tremendous excitement about this exercise in propaganda (that wasn't propaganda), and yet I don't think anyone was prepared for the overwhelming response of the public to the *Postscripts*. They became essential listening on a Sunday evening. This was due, obviously, to the rare and happy fusion of writer, humanitarian and natural broadcaster in J.B. Priestley. I don't know who originally suggested he should do those broadcasts, but the idea was an inspired one.[9]

Duff became captivated by the magic of voice and language in Priestley's *Postscripts*. It absorbed her so completely that, as the person entrusted to avoid giving the gift of information to the enemy, she conceded that she would probably not have noticed any deviation from the script anyway. The first of Priestley's talks went out on Wednesday, 5 June 1940, and he was thereafter allotted the Sunday evening *Postscript* slot on the strength of his first broadcast. Priestley's opening talk, broadcast in the aftermath of Dunkirk, very effectively supplied the firm bed upon which all the heroics of the 'little ships' would lie in British maritime history for all eternity, illuminating their role in the evacuation as being a typically British epic of gallantry after what had begun as a miserable blunder.*

---

* Priestley never actually used the term 'little ships' in his broadcast.

He spoke of 'the fussy little pleasure steamers' or 'Shilling Sticks' and 'the Belles and Queens' used for ferrying holidaymakers and day-trippers around the bay; he 'called out' to the world of piers, sandcastles, palmists and sweaty promenades to 'sail into the inferno, to defy bombs, shells, magnetic mines, torpedoes, machine-gun fire – to rescue our soldiers'. Priestley's first *Postscript* was an extraordinarily powerful example of motivational and inspiring propaganda, especially his closing paragraph, which is worth quoting in full:

> Among those paddle steamers that will never return was one that I knew well, for it was the pride of our ferry service on the Isle of Wight – none other than the good ship 'Gracie Fields'. I tell you we were proud of the 'Gracie Fields', for she was the glittering Queen of our local line, and instead of taking an hour over her voyage, used to do it, churning like mad, in forty-five minutes. And now, never again will we board her at Cowes and go down into her dining room for a fine breakfast of bacon and eggs. She had paddled and churned away for ever. But now – look – this little steamer, like all her brave and battered sisters, is immortal. She'll go sailing proudly down the years in the epic of Dunkirk. And our great grandchildren, when they learn how we began this war by snatching glory out of defeat, and then swept on to victory, may also learn how the little holiday steamers made an excursion to hell and came back glorious.

Priestley's opening broadcast very effectively eulogised a view of the old order sacrificing itself for the cause of advancement into a better world. His *Postscripts* thereafter became immensely popular among listeners, particularly if judged by the size of the response that turned up in the BBC's postbag. At the end of the first season, around 1,600 letters had been received, of which very few were critical.[10] Unfortunately, owing to the severe paper shortage, the BBC had to scale down the size of its weekly publications, meaning that hardly any of the letters were ever published. One or two did make the similarly scaled-down listeners' letter page in the *Radio Times*:

> Priestley sees with the eyes of a poet the small, but great things of everyday life, which we in this world of turmoil are inclined to pass by.[11]

May I pay tribute to J.B. Priestley for his Sunday evening postscripts? There is always a wealth of understanding of 'this England' in his simple yet subtle talks. He is the typical Englishman who, almost more than anyone else, makes us feel that we must win.[12]

Priestley clearly displayed an ability to connect with listeners in a manner that they could understand regardless of class or intellect, leading the BBC to describe him in an editorial of 26 July as 'the voice of England'. In the press, the *Daily Mail* described Priestley's postscripts as 'a privilege to listen to', while the *Nottingham Guardian* insisted that the government immediately appoint him as director general of broadcasting.

If Priestley had previously enjoyed his mild celebrity status as a writer, he very soon began to dislike 'being celebrated in this gigantic, semi-hysterical scale' as a result of his *Postscripts*. He may indeed have felt irritated by his increased celebrity, but he was soon to discover that he was rapidly becoming a source of irritation himself. If the BBC had initially been excited by this 'new experiment in propaganda', they were very soon under fire from elite Tory representatives in government for allowing Priestley to deliver the wrong type of propaganda – moreover 'leftish' political propaganda. Many of his broadcasts employed a measure of radical common sense that often revealed more than just a hint of socialist thinking. As early as his third broadcast, Priestley had taken up the thread of the natural piety of simple sane men, rather than the intellectual who was 'apt to see things as the lunatic end of everything, before running away to America in the expectation that other people would look after his property until he got back'. The issue of private property over community was a grinding irritation for Priestley. He spoke of hundreds of working men living locally who all needed allotments to try to grow a bit more food, and houses that were also desperately required for billeting. Priestley felt that large houses should be used for such a purpose 'whether the owner had run off to America or not'.[13]

Priestley continued to become more controversial with every broadcast, such as his insistence on 23 June that Hitler would never have got this far if the world had not been half rotten. On 14 July, he struck out again at the establishment during a broadcast about a recent day trip to a deserted Margate: 'If we know that we can march forward, not merely to recover what we've lost, but to something better then we've known before.' This Margate he described 'was saddening and hateful; but its new silence and desolation should be thought of as a bridge leading us to a better England, in a nobler world'. By this time, the Tory press had begun to make its feelings about Priestley's broadcasts known, leading his listening public to openly express dismay at their suggestion that he should be censured. The MOI reported that Priestley was now regarded as 'the best broadcaster yet', with many of his listeners regretting that he should clash with *Hi Gang* on the Forces Programme.[14] The following Sunday he urged listeners to regard this war as simply a chapter in our changing history: 'the breakdown of one vast system and the building up of another and better one'. Priestley wanted people to stop thinking in terms of property and power, and begin thinking in terms of 'community and creation'. It was a view of war compelling the people to change habits of thought in relation to class and accept that we were all in the same boat – 'an ark in which we can all finally land in a better world'. Even his famous yarn about the steaming Bradford pie was told in a manner illuminating the need for greater equality and opportunity.

It was the betrayal of the heroes of the Great War that irked Priestley more than anything, a subject that frequently surfaced in his broadcasts. Britain had failed its gallant soldiers who returned home from the front in 1918, and he was adamant the same thing must not be allowed to happen again. On 28 July 1940, Priestley spoke of the young bomber pilot and his new wife living on the edge. 'What did we do for such young men at the end of the last war? I'll tell you what we did. We did nothing!' Such people staking their life on their country's freedom had, in return, been cast into the wind, as Priestley saw it, 'to take their chance in the world at the mercy of gangsters, tricksters and rogues – each let loose to do his damnedest'. He reminded listeners that the young heroes of the last war had simply 'fallen by the wayside in the scramble for jobs, with little or no assistance', and turning back to the RAF man, he asked again 'in return for their skill, devotion and self-sacrifice – what are we going to do?' Even among the RAF aces the war had fostered a new spirit of camaraderie and co-operation, and Priestley was never short of material that had been submitted to him to assist in reinforcing his message.

By the end of August 1940, Priestley had already begun to get a different type of letter – mostly from irate Tories telling him to 'get off the air before the government puts you where you belong'. Priestley even quoted the criticism in his broadcasts; listeners accused him of being a danger to national unity and of being more interested in ideas than working and fighting. Priestley responded by asking of the listener 'should we be fighting this war with a closed mind?' Additionally, Priestley never tired of championing the men and women spending ten to eleven hours a day doing war work in the factories, and rounded on the comfortable clique that criticised them. Time after time the *Postscripts* wound up in tribute to the ordinary British folk and 'what we can all achieve after this war'. As he saw it, 'the levelling aspect' of the current war represented an improvement on the last war when some people lived in comfortable security while others – mostly young men – were slaughtered in their thousands.

For Duff Cooper – recently installed at the MOI by Churchill with a remit to establish effective control over the BBC – there would have been nowhere to hide. Cooper had previously informed the War Cabinet in May 1940 that he had received an assurance from Director General Frederick Ogilvie that no political broadcast would be arranged without his approval.[15] However, whatever control Cooper believed he had secured had effectively been circumvented by Priestley, a situation made all the more difficult by listeners praising to the hilt this man who appeared to want a socialist revolution as much as victory. So popular was he that when the question of broadcasting a gas mask demonstration after the 9 p.m. news for maximum effect had arisen in Parliament, one member responded that it would be advisable to do it 'just before the Priestley broadcast'.[16]

Priestley had a key ally in government; the Minister for Labour, Ernest Bevin, felt that the prime minister's hostility towards setting down any clear war aims had cost them the opportunity of winning the sympathy of the masses. At a meeting of ministers at the Foreign Office in July 1940, Bevin bemoaned the fact that the 'Government always seemed to take the side of the capitalists' and that 'the feeling among the working class is that they are merely fighting for the capitalists'. As Bevin saw things, British propaganda should promote an economic policy that afforded the working class 'a place in the new world', for as things stood there was no hope for the masses in Europe 'even if we did win the war'. Could the appeal of the Soviet Union continue to be ignored when working-class morale was being so undermined by a lack of hope for the future?[17]

On 20 October 1940, Priestley came on air and announced that this would be the last of his *Postscripts* for some time, 'perhaps the last I will ever do'. He was quick to indicate that the decision had been his alone, and had not in any way been forced upon him by the BBC. Before signing off he rounded on 'stupid persons' who had frequently accused him of 'taking advantage of my position and bringing party politics into my talks'. Priestley was not a member of any political party and turned the table on his accusers as being the ones to put party before country by adopting a narrow political line. The Nazi propagandists took immediate advantage with the announcement that 'Duff Cooper had booted ace commentator Priestley off the airwaves for threatening to supplant him as Minister of Information'. The letters that poured into the BBC following his departure insisted that 'we shall have nothing finer or more inspiring' than Priestley's broadcasts. *Time* magazine reported that Priestley had left the BBC 'amid a hubbub of press excitement; silenced by pressure from Whitehall', while the *New Statesman* saw it as 'a national calamity which may matter more than Dakar'.[18]

Priestley continued his postscripts in the *News Chronicle* throughout the remainder of 1940, and continued his regular broadcasts to North America in *Britain Speaks* alongside Leslie Howard, complaining, 'I cannot make a good script for a programme shared by an actor fellow.' Priestley would arrive at 9 p.m. for a 2 a.m. broadcast, and habitually sulked if programme directors or minor officials didn't care to hang around with him prior to the broadcast. Meanwhile, after unsuccessfully trying a number of speakers in the *Postscripts* talks, the listening figures dipped alarmingly – especially after A.P. Herbert opened with a thinly veiled dig at his predecessor's 'restless mind' and 'musings upon his own new order of Europe'.[19] With the disgruntled public now venting its dissatisfaction, the corporation also found itself under fire from its own people in the autumn of 1940 when it asked its broadcasters to withdraw their support for the People's Convention, an organisation that was being used as a platform for the Communist Party to attack the government and promote a 'stop the war' campaign.

Having climbed down in the face of criticism from the composer Ralph Vaughan-Williams and the writer E.M. Forster among others, the BBC then decided to sack all conscientious objectors in December 1940, leading many listeners to believe that the corporation had launched its own political crusade. The ban was subsequently lifted within three months following a storm of protest.

At the beginning of 1941, the BBC received a home intelligence report indicating a high level of dissatisfaction among the public that Priestley's broadcasts had been stopped. With the agreement of the MOI and the Foreign Office, the corporation moved to woo Priestley back to the microphone for a second series of *Postscripts*, prompting the *Radio Times* of 24 January 1941 to emblazon its front page with the headline 'Priestley Returns!' Originally contracted for six broadcasts, the actual number would rest upon how much 'political bite' was included in the content. His opening broadcast on 26 January 1941 returned again to the familiar themes of 'peace aims' and 'social justice', and more of the 'aggressively democratic stuff' that would again lead him into troubled waters. Taking a typically broader view of the war, he launched an attack on the world that had allowed the rottenness of the enemy to flourish; 'a world in which men would close their eyes to torture and murder, so long as it suited their pocket and prestige'. It was a war of ideas as well as weapons, and demanded a 'short, clear creed acceptable to the common man that would bring the Nazi Empire of blood and terror crashing to its doom'. The Tory right were again outraged at the content of this opening broadcast. A deputation from the 1922 Committee ambushed Duff Cooper on the following Wednesday with their grievances. Even Churchill flew into a fury and rounded on the embattled Minister of Information for not only approving Priestley's return to the microphone, but for allowing him to advance 'an argument utterly contrary to my known views'. Priestley 'is far from friendly to the government' he continued, 'and I should not be too sure about him on larger issues.'[20]

The content of the remaining broadcasts appear to reflect that Priestley knew he had enraged Churchill, and agreed to make them less controversial. His talk for 2 February focused on food and the merits of 'communal feeding'. A fortnight later, having given way to the prime minister's 'Give us the tools and we'll finish the job' speech on the previous Sunday, he returned with another 'tame talk' about the monotony of train travel. Priestley had stood by his word to make his *Postscripts* less contentious, but because the critics remained on his case, by the time of his fourth broadcast he was back on familiar territory – the insistence that we were fighting for something more than our existence, followed by another attack on class. Although the talks were significantly toned down, the decision had been made by Duff Cooper to have him removed on the basis that people were objecting to him broadcasting at peak time – paying little regard to the fact that it was Priestley who had made it the 'peak time'! Unknown to the minister, the BBC had arranged for Priestley to do two further talks, meaning there were still three left in total. Cooper (who would finish up doing one of the *Postscripts* himself) wrote to Priestley on 24 March, at first denying the accusation that he had insisted on stopping the broadcasts after the first six and declaring he had no objection to the additional engagements. He then went on to state that 'it is better that you should not monopolise the microphone', and wrote about 'the impossibility of keeping up a high standard when a man is compelled to produce something new regularly every week'.[21]*

Priestley finished the three broadcasts, including a request to speak in tribute to the Merchant Navy in his penultimate broadcast, which he insisted on doing in his own indefatigable style and sticking resolutely to his usual themes: 'If we cannot promise them better living conditions, then to praise them now in wartime would be so much cynical claptrap!'[22] The final script re-emerged from the censor's office in a somewhat mutilated, softened up version before it finally reached the microphone. Priestley remained bitter about the way he was treated, especially so as the BBC and the MOI continually passed the buck of responsibility to and fro. He believed that the order to silence him had come from higher up, and in a preface to his published edition of *Postscripts* he criticised the War Cabinet for failing to realise 'the staggering power of broadcasting', and its under-valuing of the medium as having been a serious weakness in the war effort. While some listeners aired their displeasure at his

---

* Director of Talks Richard Maconachie, who had responsibility over the BBC's home propaganda, also questioned whether a single person should be given the opportunity to acquire such influence. (Letter to Patrick Ryan, 6 September 1940)

removal, others ridiculed the corporation for 'putting Tory MPs on the microphone a week later to talk about the folly of people who talk about peace aims before the war has been won'. Home Service Controller Patrick Ryan assured the embittered Yorkshireman that his *Postscripts* had been among 'the high spots of wartime broadcasting'.[23]

Priestley continued with his overseas broadcasts for the remainder of the war, for which he continued to receive glowing praise. Reviewing a collection of published scripts from *Britain Speaks* for the *New York Times*, Ferdinand Kuhn described Priestley as 'the most popular and effective speaker in wartime England who delivered robust honesty, cheerful defiance and simple straight-from-the-shoulder language that the British people craved in their moment of greatest danger'. Even though people argued that some of his talks were avowed propaganda, Kuhn felt he was '100 times more convincing than the old-style cabinet minister'.[24] In his introduction to the American publication *All England Listened*, Priestley complained, 'I was not prevented from broadcasting to anybody and everybody, only to my fellow countrymen. I was not only allowed, but encouraged to talk on air to the rest of the world.' This was more than a slight exaggeration; within six months of his final *Postscripts*, Priestley was back on the Home Service presenting *Listen to My Notebook* – billed as a programme to 'exploit the entertaining opportunities of the microphone medium' – and also presented *Radio Post* in 1943–44. In fact, so familiar was he around Broadcasting House, that staff remembered him sleeping on the floor during the raids, joking with those around him that 'people often commented that his clothes looked like he had slept in them', so he might as well do so.[25]

In view of his popularity, Priestley's name will always be touted as the man who lit the fuse for the peaceful revolution that led to Churchill being ousted as prime minister at his moment of triumph. Under Churchill, the Tory Party had failed to read the mood of the nation, especially in the latter half of the war, tending to focus on attacking socialism rather than forwarding any constructive suggestions for post-war Britain. Following VE Day, while Churchill focused on events in the Far East, the people at home were more preoccupied with issues of housing, food availability, employment and Social Security – all the things championed by Priestley in the course of his *Postscripts*. While Tory grandees licked their wounds and mouthed accusations of ingratitude – wrongly blaming others for the defeat – the public rejection of Churchill's methods was plainly obvious. Priestley reflected in later years that Churchill deserved to lose the election of 1945, believing him to have been completely out of touch with what the British people were thinking and feeling.

The scripts of Priestley's *Postscripts* broadcasts have become classic writings. Introducing an American publication of the scripts, former 'Murrow boy' Eric Sevareid paid Priestley a glowing tribute:

> It is a great weapon, the voice of a man of courage and compassion and, above all, communion with his countrymen's highest and deepest instincts.

Another man who could also have been adjudged 'the voice of Britain' was the former director of the BBC's European Service, Noel Newsome, who between 1941 and 1944 had broadcast *The Man in the Street*, a programme that reflected his own personal view of the war situation, rather than that of the Foreign Office or the War Cabinet. Newsome very soon had a similar left-wing bias attributed to him by the then Minister of Information Brendan Bracken, who was quick to make his irritation known. It was Bracken who would eventually come to the rescue of the BBC, as difficulties and frustrations blighted early attempts at delivering effective propaganda to Europe on its Overseas Service. It is towards the BBC's wartime programme for broadcasting to Nazi-occupied Europe that we now focus.

8

TALKING TO EUROPE

In October 1935, when a quorum attached to the Committee of Imperial Defence was charged with planning the establishment of the new Ministry of Information, the principal focus had been to create a ministry to oversee home-front publicity. The following year, when the Ullswater Committee recommended that 'in the interests of British prestige and influence in world affairs the appropriate use of languages on the BBC other than English should be encouraged', there was still a measure of aversion within both the government and the BBC towards the idea of engaging in foreign-language propaganda activities. This meant that, as the political problems inside Europe escalated, the range of the BBC's foreign-language broadcasts remained surprisingly small, and not until the annexation of Austria in March 1938 did the government finally began to consider the question of directing propaganda towards belligerent nations.

An analysis of German public opinion carried out through the spring and summer of 1938 discovered that Germans were starved of uncensored news by the Nazi regime, and could prove susceptible to propaganda when presented with hard facts.[1] The government responded in the heat of the Munich Crisis by asking the BBC to broadcast German, French and Italian translations of Chamberlain's key speech. Thereafter the Foreign Office requested that the BBC continue the broadcasts indefinitely to keep listeners in Continental Europe up to date with the British point of view during a time of deepening political crisis. It was then that the BBC finally agreed to start a foreign-language programme separate from the Empire Service to be financed by the government. The corporation would retain responsibility for the broadcasts, but was encouraged to seek Foreign Office guidance on all sensitive issues, while the editorial policy of the new service remained firmly wedded to the non-negotiable principle of truth. Thereafter the service flourished, as bulletins continued to be broadcast in these languages on a daily basis, until the outbreak of war necessitated an increase in foreign broadcasts and an expanded European network generally. Poland and Czechoslovakia were added to the list of services, while further languages were added according to who would become the next victim of Nazi aggression.

Shortly after the European broadcasts had begun, Chamberlain asked the newspaper magnate Sir Campbell Stuart to form a propaganda department, which the latter subsequently established at Electra House in Moorgate – hence it became known as Department EH. The department would later extend its operation to Woburn Abbey in Bedfordshire on the outbreak of war, working alongside the Political Intelligence Department (PID), before coming under the control of SOE in July 1940. In November of that year, when the Empire Service was renamed the Overseas Service, the various BBC European services operated as independent language divisions. Campbell Stuart's team at Department EH typically supplied the propaganda for the German Service, while news and other programme directives were distributed by the European news editor at the central news desk. This was generally a casual arrangement, as relations between the BBC, Department EH and even the Secret Intelligence Service had yet to be defined before the outbreak of war. Department EH exercised its primary responsibility for propaganda based largely on the principles of the 1918 campaigns, with far more emphasis applied to leaflet propaganda to be dropped over Germany than to issuing policy directives for radio broadcasts. In a secret service report delivered to Lord Halifax, the Secretary of State for Foreign Affairs, it was stated that 'the Gestapo hates leaflets mainly because they could not prosecute citizens for reading them; whereas listening to BBC broadcasts was a very hazardous business that only politically active anti-Nazi groups would risk'. The Germans, it tells us, 'were tired of the spoken word, as they were forced to listen to endless streams of Nazi propaganda bombarding them with fascist doctrines in workshops, offices and restaurants'. It was further stated that the German 'is more inclined to listen to music than politics', and that he was 'a born bookworm with a natural penchant for reading'.[2] Little wonder that the need for a BBC German Programme Unit was not formally recognised until November 1940.

When Noel Newsome first entered Broadcasting House on 1 September 1939, he was immediately put in charge of editing European news under the direction of the Overseas News Editor Arthur Barker and Service Controller Stephen Tallents. Having worked as a journalist with the *Daily Telegraph* before being 'requisitioned' for radio, Newsome immediately teamed up with Douglas Ritchie, his one-time sub-editor at the same newspaper. Persons experienced in directing radio propaganda barely existed in Britain in 1939, and it was felt that top-line journalists would be best suited to the role. Newsome's political leanings had not been in tune with the *Daily Telegraph,* an important fact that seemed to go over the heads of the BBC when he was recruited. His new employers would only have had to read his press reports following the Munich Crisis to know that their lead man would eventually set himself on a collision path with both the Foreign Office and the MOI. Newsome had been scathing towards 'Chamberlain and his umbrella man' at Munich, accusing the prime minister of cowardice and betrayal towards an ally, and of 'putting his shameful signature to a document delivering the proud, brave, and free little nation of Czechoslovakia into the mercy of the most odious tyranny'. This had been 'Britain's shabbiest hour – honour had been lost and so had all hope of peace without further dishonour'.[3]

Regardless of his tirades against 'the guilty men', Newsome was thrust into the hot seat of European Service broadcasting, where he would remain until summer 1944. He took note that the number of staff at the service, which including editors, sub-editors, translators and talks assistants, amounted to around thirty men. In its first few months the European Service would be hampered by lack of transmitters, paucity of funding and scarcity of experienced personnel. It was difficult to imagine that the headcount would rise within a few months to a couple of hundred, and then within two years to around 500 men and women.[4] It was Newsome who would set out the BBC's strategy for news as a weapon of war, and go on to direct a huge broadcasting operation mounted in twenty-five different languages for a total of over twenty-three hours a day.

Prior to Newsome's arrival at Broadcasting House, European news bulletins had been the cause of much friction as they ate into home broadcasting time on the regional services late at night. Thereafter an additional wavelength was provided, allowing the different languages to follow each other in a continuous stream, although for reasons unclear the Norwegian bulletins continued to be aired on the Home Service until 1943! In July 1940 additional transmitters were made available, enabling the service to run two separate programmes; however, by the autumn the service was required to compress to a single programme again temporarily to satisfy the broadcasting demands of Department EH and the exiled governments. When the European Service broke away from the Overseas Service in 1941, the service was upgraded to three simultaneous programmes – each devised of languages that would make the most of directional transmitting power. For convenience, each overseas station was given a colour code:

Programme One (Blue) – broadcast to France, Belgium, the Netherlands, Germany, Poland and Czechoslovakia.
Programme 2 (Yellow) – Italy, Austria, Hungary, Yugoslavia, Albania, Greece, Bulgaria and Romania.
Programme 3 (Grey) – Finland, Sweden, Norway, Denmark and Iceland, and at other times to Spain and Portugal.

The broadcasts were arranged cyclically, with the main languages being broadcast at the same time each hour – German on the hour, French and Italian on the half-hour. Transmitters could be switched between programmes as desired to attain the maximum coverage. European programmes were typically in fifteen-minute units, allowing twenty seconds for switching from one programme sequence to another. Further 'colours' were added as more transmitters became available. News bulletins on the European services typically began with the announcement 'this is London calling in the European Service of the BBC', before announcing the various wavelengths on which the bulletins were being broadcast. The European Service worked closely with the BBC's Monitoring Service, which enabled it to transmit 'comparison programmes' such as *Listening Post* and *Flashback* in which the inconsistencies and distortions within enemy propaganda broadcasts were exposed. There were profound difficulties in broadcasting to Europe, where jamming had an obvious nuisance value and could only be overcome by using a larger number of transmitters for a small number of programmes.

The new service had started out with three basic aims – firstly to undermine the will of the enemy to fight, secondly to maintain and stimulate morale in the occupied countries and thirdly to wean the neutrals away from compliance with German interests. Initially, Newsome received no detailed guidance from government about what should be broadcast on the service at this critical time. In the murkiness of the failed appeasement policy, nobody had formulated any formal propaganda directive, meaning evolving situations were dealt with according to more or less spontaneous instincts.* Added to this, the physical separation of the MOI at Senate House, the Enemy Propaganda unit at Woburn and the BBC at Portland Place rendered effective control of its broadcasts impossible. Newsome compiled his early propaganda directives relatively free from government interference up until May 1940, when he received instructions that all Churchill's speeches were to be transmitted in full in every language on the service without fail. This was not something Newsome needed to be told; in a directive of 20 August, he described a recent speech by Churchill as 'one of the most profitable pieces of propaganda we have had in a long time'. Prior to the prime minister's Commons speech of 5 September, he directed his staff to 'clear the decks for our best propagandist, Churchill!' It was important to keep on repeating the speeches, as they were habitually edited on German radio to sound defeatist. Newsome's earlier directives, which do not appear to have survived, were typically couched using tough language towards Germany, immediately followed by attempts to 'stiffen the French into facing up to their obligations' – an approach that met with little success. Thereafter, as nation upon nation began to fall under Nazi control, any thoughts of using the service as a means of stimulating insurgency among people living under occupation was likely to put them in severe danger. It was more vitally important than

* A lengthy unsigned and undated report, likely to have been drafted at the beginning of the war, resides in The National Archives at Kew detailing the benefits of setting up a government body responsible for overseas propaganda.

ever to build trust between the corporation and its listeners throughout the conquered nations of Europe.

Newsome operated under a belief that the war needed to be won in the minds of men who would make the peace as well as on the battlefield, and his opinionated approach often caused friction – 'I was permanently at war with the Foreign Office during my time at the BBC.'[5] In July 1940 he began issuing general directives to key staff, containing an insistence that the subject of war aims and peace aims should be high on the agenda in broadcasts to both occupied and unoccupied countries. There had to be a 'clear-cut comparison' to what a British victory would mean (no return to pre-war conditions) and a victory for Hitler (hell without end!).[6] The freedom that Newsome allowed himself when directing his propaganda ultimately put him on the establishment's radar in the summer of 1940, and gradually the MOI took on more of a presence inside Broadcasting House. On 19 July, J.S.A. Salt was added to the European staff as its first service director to add an additional layer of control and accountability. From this point, Newsome appears to have been more at war with the censors than with the common enemy; frustrations often boiled over – on one occasion he accused MOI 'emissaries' of treating him like 'some type of office boy'.[7] His frustration is summed up in a directive of 8 September 1940, beginning, 'since mention of anything anywhere has come under a ban there is not very much I can say today'.[8] The ministry's constant filtering of information, compounded by what he saw as their ignorance and incompetence, made for an 'impossible situation'. It was a case of 'amateurs dictating to professionals', and he showed little deference towards men in high places, a tendency that won him the respect of junior staff. He had a view of his department as 'backroom boys – anonymous, unhonoured and unsung', which he felt gave him licence to be forthright in his own views: 'We never courted popularity – we got our reward in whatever we were able to achieve.'[9]

Newsome rammed home to his staff that 'it was a cardinal function of the BBC's European Service to tell the truth – good or bad'. He instructed his team that the essence of successful propaganda to Europe was to tell bad news fully, but in a confident tone, and report good news in a sober tone. Good news, he insisted, 'needed little embroidery, and to tell bad news honestly and boldly is a sure sign of strength'.[10] In practice, this sometimes proved to be a difficult path to tread. When the Burma

Road was closed in July 1940, effectively cutting off the supply route to China, his directive to staff of 18 July described the setback as 'knocking the bottom out of all our propaganda'. Broadcasts could not report that Britain had yielded to Japanese diplomatic pressure – effectively 'selling an ally down the river' – and in such situations Newsome typically offset the effects by elaborating on more encouraging events. Often he would broadcast an alternative and more favourable version of events if it would work to Britain's advantage. When the Burma Road reopened three months later in October, Newsome directed his propagandists to bend the truth; the remarks in parenthesis are his:

> The road was not closed in a vain effort to appease Japan (Liar!), but because it was hoped that this proof of impartiality (Save the word) would enable us to act as an honest broker in producing a just settlement of the China war.[11]

Newsome took other more significant liberties with his position, such as allowing the German announcers to broadcast a rejection of Hitler's peace offer after the fall of France without reference to higher authority – a fact noted by Churchill. Later in the war, he welcomed the Soviets as 'our new allies' when announcing the German invasion of the Soviet Union and reported on the Japanese attack on Pearl Harbor long before any announcement from the official broadcasting services. There was never any question of holding news back until the government decided what it was going to do about it. When Hitler threatened to bomb Britain into submission, Newsome, with typical bravado, went ahead and broadcast his own derisive reply; very soon Lord Halifax at the Foreign Office was on the phone berating him for having acted 'in an irresponsible manner'. It was a measure of his effectiveness that Newsome's name very soon appeared on Lord Haw-Haw's list of men who would be brought to trial when the Nazis occupied Britain. 'I asked my father to obtain lethal tablets, he told me not to be stupid.'[12]

The change of prime minister did not invigorate the overseas propaganda effort beyond the powerful effect of Churchill's speeches. All of Chamberlain's appeasers were sidelined – including Director of Propaganda Sir Campbell Stuart – before Churchill decided to place all responsibility for 'black' propaganda and espionage on the shoulders of

Hugh Dalton at SOE, with its remit to 'set Europe ablaze'. Without realising it, Churchill would set in motion a protracted period of internal warfare, first between Dalton and Duff Cooper at the MOI, and thereafter between Dalton and Cooper's replacement, Brendan Bracken, that would endure until the autumn of 1941. In the meantime, the European Service could at least congratulate itself that it had constructed a credible propaganda operation by the end of 1940, both in Axis countries and throughout the occupied territories. A German soldier describing occupied Paris in 1941 reported that the streets were almost deserted at BBC London time, while it was reported in Chambery that 'all Cafe's might as well close at 8 o'clock'.[13] Newsome believed that 'the supreme experience for devotees of the BBC was of course to hear acknowledgement of their own existence', and he and Ritchie tried as best they could to operate a comprehensive operation. German listeners were warned to expect day and night bombing indefinitely, as well as a life of overwork and underfeeding 'so that Göring dressed in white can parade through Paris'. The Italians were told they would prove 'too weak to last the pace' and service editors were directed to emphasise 'their puniness alongside the might of the British Empire, America or Russia'. Newsome took great pains to demonstrate how the language of the broadcasts had to be right. In one directive he noted how in the 'laudable endeavour to achieve liveliness, we sometimes become woolly', with the example:

> In Order to hearten his discouraged airmen, Mussolini has sent a wire to the Italian Air-Force congratulating them on their imaginary successes.

Far less effective than an item that reads:

> Signor Mussolini today wired congratulations to his air-force on their successes. [Meanwhile] It is announced in Cairo that twenty more Italian planes have been shot down with only one British loss.

Newsome also noticed a tendency of sub-editors to comment on news items, 'a practice that must be stopped'. 'Embellishment,' he felt, 'should come from a third party – real or imaginary.' If anyone wished to express a view 'it should come from a source – if necessary invent one!' He favoured the more 'chiselled effect' that could be gained by an economy of words and liked news to be presented in a lively manner – 'we want the weight and authority of The Times with the circulation of the [Daily] Express.'[14]

The early successes of the European Service had been achieved under very difficult circumstances; by the end of 1940 it could not possibly endure for much longer. The service had been conducting its broadcasts from the basement of Broadcasting House, until a landmine exploded on 8 December 1940 and took out the side of the building, causing fatalities. Fires raged for several hours and water from burst pipes and firemen's hoses completely flooded the basement, meaning the whole European Department had to transfer to a less-spacious facility at Maida Vale. Newsome was horrified by the sight of several hundred men and women trying to direct propaganda while herded together like cattle in a pen, beneath a glass roof, at the height of the Blitz. His protestations were at first overlooked following an inspection by Director General Frederick Ogilvie and Service Controller Stephen Tallents, and he subsequently appealed to Harold Nicolson at the MOI, voicing a long-held opinion that the European Service should be split from the General Overseas Service.* On top of this, he argued for greater integration with the Political Intelligence Department in an effort to effect a more formal propaganda policy. The result of this meeting was that Patrick Ryan was transferred from within the corporation to the position of home advisor, while the role of foreign policy advisor went to (Sir) Ivone Kirkpatrick, a man regarded by former colleagues at the MOI as being 'a real terrier' – someone who would 'tear the pants off the BBC people'.[15] Soon afterwards, the European Service was transferred to a much more spacious facility at Bush House, where it would later be joined by the Political Warfare Executive and the PID. The BBC was not pleased about the appointment of Kirkpatrick, a veteran of Gallipoli, in February 1941, for it was feared that he would interfere in its normal editorial processes and channels of control, despite being afforded the right to appeal to the MOI against any advice with which it disagreed.** Both Tallents and Salt had good reason to worry, for the appointment of

* It rests as a shocking revelation in Newsome's memoirs that he 'scarcely saw' Service Controller Stephen Tallents up until this point, p.201.

** Bush House was reckoned to be the most expensive building in the world, costing upwards of £2 million to build. Amazingly, the BBC's entire European operation transferred there in 1941 for a rent of less than £30 a week.

Kirkpatrick marked the beginning of the end of their involvement with the European Service.

Ivone Kirkpatrick turned out to be the ideal man to get at the root of the Overseas Service's problems, and to 'drain the swamp' of inter-departmental aggravations. His years as First Secretary at the British Embassy in Berlin had furnished him with authority and a keen appreciation of what Britain was up against. A seat at the table during the Munich negotiations had led him to the conclusion that Hitler was no ordinary man and could see his contempt towards Britain and the British prime minister. On one occasion, following Chamberlain's departure, Kirkpatrick discovered that Hitler had flown into a thundering rage: 'If that silly old man comes interfering here again with his umbrella, I'll kick him downstairs and jump on his stomach in front of photographers.'[16]

Previously, in February 1940, Kirkpatrick had been seconded to the MOI under Duff Cooper, and picked up immediately that his new minister had one essential ingredient missing: 'an interest in the art of Propaganda'. Even worse, Cooper had appointed the CEO of the London Passenger Transport Board, Frank Pick, as director general of the MOI: 'a disastrous appointment full of calamitous ideas'.[17] Walter Monckton at the Censorship Bureau thought Pick was 'more concerned with expenditure than propaganda', and Kirkpatrick didn't hang around for long at the MOI when he realised how badly the ministry was being run. He knew only too well that propaganda had to be the handmaid of policy, and that the propagandists 'can have no independent policy, and the policy-makers must make proper use of the propagandists'. He also recognised that it had been the total lack of mutual confidence and understanding between the government and the ministry that had led to the disastrous errors of Norway in May 1940, when the truth had been either distorted or withheld.* Within the first few months of his new advisory role, Kirkpatrick made it known that he believed there should be greater co-operation between the MOI and the BBC, as it was imperative that the corporation should be given greater access to secret information if it was to avoid further mishaps. He felt there were too many voices, both at the MOI and in Whitehall, offering guidance

---

* Newsome was haunted by the Norway episode and informed staff that reports of naval battles needed 'very strong confirmation' before being accepted.

that was often contradictory and served to fuel friction, resentment and overall dissatisfaction among the staff.

The organisational changes that Newsome would set in motion became more pressing following the Nazi invasion of the Soviet Union, which changed the climate and gave radio propaganda a new impulse as communists throughout Europe joined in the crusade against fascism. On the day following the invasion, Newsome 'began the day with a light heart', informing his staff that he would be in his office all day to collect payment from those who had 'rashly waged against him' that the invasion wouldn't happen. The war had finally 'straightened itself out', with the forces of fascism in a 'logical and tidy array' against the forces that opposed it all in the same camp.[18] As Newsome saw it, there was little need for constructing propaganda – 'just fill the airwaves with previous German quotes in praise of Russia'. All unconnected features and talks would be scrapped for the day. Thereafter, the Führer's actions were sent up as being the result of a series of setbacks, including his failure to smash Britain, the disastrous performances of his Italian allies and his failure to secure strategic and material resources in the Middle East. Invading the Soviet Union simply to carry on the war was further proof of a policy of aggression at any cost, and it was made known to the German people that their leader had just added another 200 million people to their list of enemies. In a rare intervention, Churchill insisted that all British military actions in the west should be linked to the Soviet–German campaign to reinforce the 'new ally' theme. In a directive of 24 June, Newsome rammed home the line followed by both the prime minister and the Foreign Secretary that Hitler needed to dispose of the Soviet Union quickly to invade Britain and fulfil his commitment to the German people that victory would be achieved in 1941. 'Pin Hitler down to an invasion attempt this autumn' was the propaganda line of the day, with the aim of further depressing the German people when winter came with no end in sight.

With Kirkpatrick's powerful influence at their disposal, things gradually began to improve at Bush House; even more so in July 1941 when Duff Cooper, who was seldom happy in his role as Minister of Information, was replaced by Brendan Bracken, a protégé of Churchill. Since taking over the role in May 1940, Cooper had forever been at loggerheads with Hugh Dalton at SOE over control of propaganda and access to the services of the BBC. Such was the extent of their quarrels, Cooper became depressed and his health began to fail. A memo of June 1941, in which Churchill had informed Cooper he was to take full day-to-day editorial control of the BBC and be responsible for both initiative and censorship, had been the last straw for Cooper. Bracken would run up against the same problems, but for now his remit was to shake up the ministry, which he did so very effectively. He is often cited as the mysterious Irishman who was an effective spin doctor for the War Cabinet, and who also played a key supporting role in the success of Britain's radio propaganda operation. In his memoirs, Ivone Kirkpatrick, whose good opinion was not given lightly, described his former master Bracken as 'a tower of strength'. With Bracken at the helm, a new camaraderie developed between the MOI and the BBC that often faced down interference from other government departments and even the military. Former MP Earl Winterton remembered how Bracken would 'floor critics with an uppercut whenever his actions as Minister of Information were questioned'.[19] Bracken was a man who got things done and certainly impressed Churchill, to the extent that there were times when the two men seemed inseparable. Churchill's wife, Clementine, complained that 'he [Bracken] arrived at Chartwell with the furniture, and never left'.[20]

Following discussions with the chairman of the BBC Board of Governors, Sir Allan Powell, Bracken came around to the idea that it was unsatisfactory that Kirkpatrick did not have a rank at the BBC. Thereafter, the split with the General Overseas Service that Newsome had originally requested was formally actioned, and Kirkpatrick was appointed as controller of the newly independent European Service in October 1941. Newsome was elevated to director of European broadcasts answerable only to Kirkpatrick, who believed in Newsome and allowed him to operate on a long leash. 'I was astonished that I was given so much rope,' he recorded in his memoirs.[21] Kirkpatrick confirmed this in his own memoirs, stating that Newsome and his deputy, Doug Ritchie, had assumed responsibility for every word spoken over the Bush House microphones in the course of the war. As service controller, Kirkpatrick executed his duties efficiently and with the minimum of fuss. Assistant Controller Harman Grisewood remembers him striking out offending passages in service directives with his gold pencil, saying, 'I'm going to biff this out and biff that out,' and recalled: 'He was cleverer than anyone else.'[22]

Meanwhile, Bracken oversaw the creation of a Department for Political Warfare, to be responsible to a Joint Ministerial Committee, and charged with issuing policy guidelines for any government body concerned with political warfare, including the BBC's European services.[*] Officially classified as a secret organisation, the Political Warfare Executive (PWE) was launched in August 1941. Its key directives were the undermining and destruction of enemy morale through sowing fear, doubt and confusion, and fostering a spirit of resistance in enemy-occupied countries. It laid down an insistence that BBC broadcasts should not be incompatible with the impression being made upon the enemy's mind by other methods. This implies that what was said to the enemy, or to occupied countries in Europe, had ceased to be within the discretion of the BBC, and had passed to a new governmental organ. The PWE would ensure unified control of propaganda by regional direction through all media, eliminating competition and overlapping in the process. An insistence that news services should be co-ordinated with other departments proved to be problematical for the PWE, as news was something it found very difficult to control, seeing as it did not typically have instant access to it. Meanwhile, the executive was divided into seven regions (Germany, Italy, France, Low Countries, Scandinavia (Denmark and Norway), Central Europe and the Balkans) each headed by a regional director, and Kirkpatrick was to take charge of interpreting and applying the general directives. The governors at the BBC accepted the new state of affairs, but did not feel the situation excluded them from exercising trusteeship to help maintain the integrity of the service.

The PWE would eventually come under the control of Robert 'Bruce' Lockhart as director general, with Peter 'Ritchie' Calder as director of planning. Before that could happen there would be many more months of interdepartmental 'squabbling', for even on the back of so much reform, the operation remained a complicated entanglement of departments.

---

[*]   The Joint Ministerial Committee consisted of Duff Cooper (Overt), Dalton (Covert) and Anthony Eden (Foreign Policy). By the beginning of 1942, it became clear that the committee was ineffective, and it was disbanded. Thereafter, Eden took overall charge of propaganda policy.

Until February 1942, the PWE was complicated by the shared control of the Minister of Economic Warfare Hugh Dalton at Woburn and Bruce Lockhart at Fitzmaurice Place. Lockhart felt that the propaganda was being hampered by key departments being too widely scattered, causing sectional jealousies to continually intensify. He also expressed frustration that Churchill regarded propaganda as something only of secondary importance: 'teething troubles would have been modified if only the Prime Minister had an interest in political warfare,' he complained.[23]

Dalton, for his part, was furious with the new arrangement, and was especially bitter that much of the responsibility for the 'black' propaganda activities of SOE had been taken away from him. It was he who had originally advocated putting all propaganda to enemy countries under the control of one department, arguing that both 'white' and 'black' propaganda were a single subject because they had the same aim of subverting enemy morale. For that reason, they had to be closely co-ordinated. Dalton's arguments were brushed aside and it was agreed to leave the BBC's propaganda under the guidance of the Minister of Information. As things stood, although the PWE executed propaganda policy, it had no authority over the BBC's open propaganda, and the corporation retained its autonomy over preparation of news items. Dalton's continued frustration meant that he and Bracken seemed to be forever at each other's throats and the squabbles continued relentlessly to an extent that Lockhart believed seriously deterred all progress. Bracken was known to have an aggressive nature: 'a temperament as fiery as his aureole of Celtic hair,' according to Lockhart, yet he always kept it under control. His anger was often feigned and he deliberately baited Dalton, who at one conference called Bracken 'rude, assertive, ignorant, inconsequential, stupid, angular and unreceptive'.[24] The key difference between the warring ministers was that Bracken had influence, in particular the ear of the prime minister. It was Churchill who had agreed to Bracken's plan to move the bulk of the PWE back to London in 1942, in line with the findings of the Browett Committee of November 1941.*

Following accusations of phone tapping the conversations of fellow Labour ministers, Dalton was eventually transferred to the Board of

---

* The Browett Committee was charged with examining the problem of 'overlapping' between the BBC and the PWE.

Trade – a transition further effected by the stinging tongue of Bracken. Despite openly referring to Bracken as a 'Tory Thug', the Labour Party did not lend sufficient support to their man, who went from conducting enemy-directed propaganda to advising women on the home front to 'make do and mend'.[25]

Lockhart was only finally given overall control of PWE in March 1942, having relocated to Bush House along with Rex Leeper, the director of enemy propaganda, and Dallas Brookes, the head of its military wing. Lockhart believed strongly in the power of propaganda to minimise pessimism at home, and to keep alive the hope of ultimate victory. He also believed that nothing annoyed the military more 'than exaggerated accounts of German weakness at a time when the enemy was fighting with undiminished determination'.[26] He pointed to the early offensives in Libya in November 1941 when the first communiqué from Cairo had waxed lyrical in its optimism, which in turn was exploited for broadcasts. When the offensive ended in failure, the Germans had made fantastic capital out of initial over-optimism. The European Service could not make these same mistakes as it was now the largest broadcasting unit in the world, transmitting programmes throughout the Continent for twenty-three hours per day.

Having been co-opted onto the PWE team to represent the BBC's interests, Ivone Kirkpatrick suddenly found himself answerable to three masters – Bracken at the MOI, Lockhart at the PWE, and Ogilvie at the BBC. Kirkpatrick would accept policy guidance from the ministerial committee at the Foreign Office and attend PWE meetings, but it would be for him to decide on how propaganda policy would be executed. Both he and Bracken were of the same mind that the European Service of the BBC should not be a propaganda service in the accepted sense – rather it should be more about countering German propaganda with the truth. This also concurred with Newsome's view, as it would fall on his shoulders to ensure that the European Service broadcasts did not deviate from the prescribed policy.

A further restructuring of the PWE in August 1942 produced a more satisfactory working relationship with the European services of the BBC. Ritchie Calder was appointed to the new post of director of plans and campaigns, a change that led to a marked improvement in the co-ordination of propaganda.[27] Calder had been another journalist making waves over working-class interests in the early stages of the war as a columnist at the *Daily Herald*. He claimed he was virtually press-ganged into taking a desk at the PWE because 'he already knew too much', and came to regard himself as being 'a hostage of secrecy'.[28]

The year 1942 proved to be a testing one for the service, as military disasters came thick and fast. In February, with the disastrous loss of Singapore looming, morale in Bush House was at an all-time low, impelling Newsome to state in his directive of 11 February that 'whatever happens we are fighting like the deuce, and if we go down, we go down fighting'. Frankness could not degenerate into defeatism: 'We want defiance in defeat, not self-flagellation.'[29] Later that year, he began to take a more defeatist tone himself with things going badly in North Africa, although it didn't stop him criticising hysterical newspaper editors who were queuing up to have a go at Churchill. By August the disastrous raid on Dieppe dominated the news, requiring the service announcers to be 'dryer and more laconic than usual, with nothing depreciatory or apologetic about our tone'. Newsome pulled out all the stops to embroider the failed invasion with positivity and had clearly not been deflated by the emerging facts of the disastrous enterprise.[*] 'They have at last had a smack at the Bosch and will go back for some more.'[30]

Away from the internal politics, Director of External Broadcasting Edward Tangye-Lean likened the exceptionally busy floors of Bush House to an 'international barracks where in the underground corridors things look like a civil war on a cosmopolitan scale'.[31] Regional staff varied considerably in size and comparison, with the German service comprising over 100 personnel by the end of 1942. Strict segregation was applied to the various departments, and no doors were allowed to open until the preceding door had been closed to ensure that the German listener could not hear the French announcer. Lean likened it to 'the chambers of a submarine, where you could not enter until the pressure had been adjusted'.[32] Other employees remembered the claustrophobic atmosphere and trying to work against the sound of exploding bombs. This also meant that the studios took on the look

---

[*] Of the 6,086 men that landed, 3,623 had been killed, wounded or taken prisoner within ten hours of the raid. A total of 106 RAF aircraft were lost, along with thirty-three RN landing craft and a destroyer.

of dormitories as nobody wanted to brave the air raids and preferred instead to sleep on the studio floor.

By the beginning of 1943, the European Service was operating an efficient shuttle system, whereby two studios were harnessed to each network – one studio delivering a broadcast, while the programme immediately following was prepared in the adjacent studio. Friction occasionally arose between the services and the PWE, mainly because items of breaking news needed to be broadcast as quickly as possible, and nobody wanted to hang around waiting for an OK from above. By this time, intelligence was being gathered from a multiplicity of sources, including the BBC newsroom, the BBC European Records Unit, the BBC Overseas Research Unit, the PWE Propaganda Research Station, the Press Cuttings and Filing Library at Woburn and the BBC News Information Bureau at Bush House.* It was a complex operation that needed to be up to the moment to be most effective. Kirkpatrick liked news bulletins to be immediately followed by commentaries 'to help citizens living under occupation to interpret events and thereby mitigate for the lack of an independent newspaper'.[33]

Bracken became a staunch defender of the European Service and rose quickly to his feet in Parliament whenever it was criticised: 'It is one of the best and liveliest radio organisations in the world. I wish we could find words adequate to praise the intelligence, energy and resourcefulness of its staff.'[34] He resolutely determined that no outside influence would be allowed to affect the judgement of its news editors. This didn't stop the Tory hierarchy from complaining that Britain's propaganda operation was 'dominated by left-wingers', a charge that Lockhart found difficult to counter as he sat before a Parliamentary committee of Tory grandees.

Lockhart was more than aware that his own PWE had become a hotbed of young and energetic socialists, anxious for Britain to begin laying out a programme of post-war reforms. There was also a strong feeling in the BBC against privilege during a time of war. Service Director Noel Newsome was chief among the 'red dissenters'; the left-leaning bent that had stalled his advancement at the *Daily*

---

* The PWE and the PID also received intelligence from the Foreign Research and Press Service and the Royal Institute of International Affairs.

Telegraph resurfaced again in 1941 when he set up an English-language service, *London Calling Europe*, directly under his control. Newsome began broadcasting his personal version of events as *The Man in the Street*, an initiative that threatened to put him on a collision course with the Foreign Office and the MOI. Much like Priestley's *Postscripts*, Newsome's broadcasts went beyond being simple commentaries on the progress of the war. He had believed from the start that the Soviet Union would eventually be 'won over', and took every opportunity to stir up trouble between the Soviets and her Nazi ally. Later, when the Nazis looked poised for victory in the Soviet Union, and there were rumblings that Britain might conclude a separate peace in the West, Newsome ignored such rumours, and reminded Europeans that 'we were fighting to establish a rule of law and a spirit of freedom and progress, as opposed to a world of Secret Police and the dead hand of tyranny and stagnation'. In a series of broadcasts on the theme 'the projection of Britain', he showcased the way of life being fought for, and even treated listeners to a detailed exposition of the Beveridge Report to highlight Britain's dedication to social justice. It was the broadcast of 17 February 1943, titled *Military and Social Responsibilities*, when Newsome made reference to current debates in Parliament on the issue of social security, that would have angered Bracken the most. 'We all want to know before we enter into a bloody death grapple with this Nazi-Fascist enemy, that the sacrifice will be worthwhile, that the other enemies of humanity, of which the chief is want and insecurity, will also be vanquished.'[35]

Newsome felt that before the country could begin to establish a system of social justice throughout Europe, it had better begin at home. He believed that the sacrifices made 'should not be in vain', and that the plain soldier about to risk his life should be 'inspired by faith in our social and economic plans'. Bracken would scrutinise the scripts for *The Man in the Street* and occasionally return them with written comments such as, 'This red propaganda must cease!'[36] On another occasion he demanded that Newsome be removed from his position for showing him a lack of respect, requiring the diplomatic skills of Lockhart to successfully mediate on his behalf. This kind of outburst from Bracken did not happen often; he was one of the few ministers to recognise the pressure editors were under, and made it known whenever he felt

Newsome had done a good job.[*] He also valued the BBC's independence as a vital factor in winning public trust and preferred a strategy of co-operation, rather than constant censuring of its broadcasts. That said, Bracken was acutely sensitive to political bias, and would always move to avoid the possibility of Churchill giving him a hard time when broadcasts that were leftish in tone were allowed to go unchallenged. For this reason, he seldom authorised the BBC to allow MPs, or those with access to Cabinet ministers, to openly debate or broadcast commentaries of the war situation. Between May 1943 and the beginning of 1944, numerous memos were exchanged between the Foreign Office and the BBC on the subject of satisfying the listeners' interest in foreign affairs by introducing debates between panels of speakers. The head of the Foreign Office news department, William Ridsdale, suggested they broadcast talks by diplomatic correspondents who had enjoyed regular access to Foreign Office Minister Anthony Eden.[37] However, almost every time requests for such broadcasts finished up on Bracken's desk, he poured cold water on the idea in the belief that international affairs could not be placed above party politics: 'To launch the BBC into giving talks about them is certainly to launch home party politics on the air and this is what we are at present trying to avoid.'[38] Bracken's main fear seems to have been that speakers might have appeared impartial, but would not have been regarded in that light by the political parties.

As for Newsome, he might have steered clear of upsetting Bracken for the time being, but continued with his *Man in the Street* broadcasts – effectively making his own propaganda and caring little for the guidance or protocols of the PWE. As the service director, he preferred to set about helping to win the propaganda war in the way he thought most efficient and speedy. Despite being told by his bosses that he was too much of a crusader to have a future in post-war broadcasting, the war had been his personal crusade, and he always enjoyed the support of military chiefs, who also believed he did a good job.[**]

---

[*]   Bracken recommended Newsome for an OBE at the end of the war.

[**] Newsome's wife, the former editor of the BBC's Czechoslovakian Service, Sheila Grant Duff, asserted that there were ministerial attempts to unseat Newsome, and that after the war he was banned by the BBC and his whole war record was shoved aside and forgotten. (Newsome, pp.1, 11)

Throughout the whole of 1943, European transmissions increased by around 40 per cent. Much of that additional time was allocated to the *America Calling Europe* broadcasts prepared by the American Office of War Information (OWI), and relayed directly from New York by the BBC, enabling American views to be heard throughout Europe. The OWI was set up in June 1942 by Roosevelt to meet the demand for news and to counter widespread apathy among Americans. Despite the American public's distaste toward the use of propaganda, it was felt that a slick propaganda operation to control and co-ordinate all war-related information fed to the public was essential. In addition, a Psychological Warfare Branch was created in November 1942 under General Dwight D. Eisenhower that included leaflet propaganda and radio programmes aimed towards demoralising the enemy. It was transformed to a more formal Psychological Warfare Division in 1944, just a few months prior to D-Day.

Getting the US broadcasts up and running presented difficulties due to the commercial structure of America's broadcasting system, and a scarcity of staff with experience of political broadcasting. Initially, the Americans had asked the BBC for time to relay short-wave broadcasts on medium wave throughout Europe and had requested permission to erect three 50kW transmitters. Staff at Bush House remained hostile to the idea of giving up time, and it fell to Kirkpatrick to convince them that it would be an essential demonstration of Anglo-US solidarity in terms of sending the right message to Europe. The Americans were offered six fifteen-minute broadcasts – one in English, two in both German and French, and one in Italian – with a Polish service being added a short while later. A good deal of help and assistance was given to the Americans by Leonard Miall, who was previously in charge of broadcasts in German until 1942, before the PWE sent him to the US to liaise with agencies involved in psychological warfare. Kirkpatrick had a great deal of confidence in Miall as a skilled operator and felt able to cut the Americans some slack in terms of sticking rigidly to any pre-agreed protocol. In his memoirs, Kirkpatrick summed up that 'lack of confidence and suppression of a few American broadcasts was more damaging than the occasional deviation'.

In the months prior to D-Day, the Americans felt they needed to intensify their European broadcasts, as it was clear that their overseas propagandists were struggling to match the effectiveness of their well-polished British counterparts. CBS President William Paley arrived in London in early 1943 with a remit to try to beef things up. Paley, who would become chief of radio at the new Psychological Warfare Division in 1944, took charge of the technical aspects, and saw immediately that the weakness of the transmission system was the biggest problem. He decided that the proposal for the 50kW transmitters was a bad idea, as they would quickly be superseded by the larger British ones. Bracken was insistent that everything possible should be done to satisfy Paley, and with this in mind Kirkpatrick was able to negotiate an increase in US broadcasting time to Europe to twelve hours a day, increasing eventually to fifteen. Kirkpatrick conceded that, although they had been tough negotiations, the key fact that newer, more powerful transmitters were coming into service allowed him to be generous in what he could offer. The Americans were effectively getting a huge increase in transmitting time throughout Europe with a ready-made audience into the bargain – a deal that Kirkpatrick considered to be 'one of the most valuable items of reverse lend-lease'.[39]

This had not been the first time that Ivone Kirkpatrick had been called upon to negotiate on the issue of securing airtime for foreign broadcasters wanting to utilise the facilities of the BBC. In the spring of 1940, Kirkpatrick was called upon to answer demands from the exiled governments of conquered nations who had taken refuge in London and were now requesting airtime to broadcast their own programmes on the BBC's transmitters. As director of the foreign division at the MOI, Kirkpatrick could see the advantages of allowing the displaced governments the opportunity to connect with their people under occupation, as it would afford them the opportunity to counter the tide of enemy propaganda. It was a request that the BBC were at first unwilling to satisfy before Kirkpatrick took hold of the negotiations, and in the case of one occupied country clamouring for airtime, he made an immediate exception.

THE VOICE OF HOPE

One by one, as the countries of Western Europe were knocked out of the war, they either handed over their radio transmitters intact to the Germans, or they were so ineffectively sabotaged that they were able to begin transmitting propaganda within a very short time.[1] When Britain stood alone, Nazi-controlled Europe no longer had the advantage of a free press, and Britain's only contact with those under occupation was through the BBC. By the middle of 1940, the governments of those occupied countries had taken refuge in London, and the BBC was coming under increasing pressure to do whatever it could to facilitate radio contact between the displaced governments and the people inside their conquered territories. By this time, listening to the broadcasts from London was almost universal in the Low Countries and much of Scandinavia, where the majority of the sets used in both regions could receive long-wave broadcasts. The BBC's news bulletins in Danish and Norwegian commenced when the two countries were invaded, while the services in Dutch and Belgian began a month before occupation with the latter being broadcast in French and Flemish on alternate nights. Many people were caught listening and treated harshly; however, the general feeling was that 'a whole people can't be caught', and for millions of listeners throughout much of Europe living under Nazi rule, 'the voice of Britain' effectively became 'the voice of hope'.[2]

Despite widespread disillusionment at the failure of Allied forces to repel the Nazi invasion of Norway, the Norwegians were devoted listeners to the BBC, right up until November 1942 when the death penalty for listening to the broadcasts was established by decree.[3] Early on, the Nazis made vigorous attempts to discredit British news, citing the falsely alleged recapture of Narvik in April 1940 as a prime example. The Nazis had nothing to lose from bending the truth in their news bulletins, whereas the BBC staked everything on re-establishing its reputation for truthfulness. Alongside the BBC's Norwegian broadcasts, Nazi propaganda initiatives were futile – 'nobody in Norway listens to any radio except the BBC', claimed one refugee who had escaped to the US. It was a claim supported by the fact that the Nazis banned the possession of radio sets in Norwegian coastal areas including Oslo, where they had encountered a spirited resistance movement that was difficult to crush. In Denmark, citizens tended to be more easily persuaded towards toeing the Nazi line for their own protection, with the result that no radio ban was ever imposed. It is noticeable that propaganda aims in relation to Denmark typically appeared at the foot of most European Service propaganda directives up until March 1943. At this point a general election had exposed how little support the Germans had in Denmark; the resulting Nazi backlash led to a round of strikes in August that were further inflamed by Danish Service broadcasts, before the *Wehrmacht* seized full control of its former 'protectorate'.

An hour before the Netherlands was invaded on 10 May 1940, Nazi broadcasters denied a rumour about the plans – a typical Nazi manoeuvre calculated to cause disruption and confusion among its intended quarry. On the day of the invasion, the Dutch Royal Family set sail with the intention of landing in Zeeland, where they were unable to make radio contact with the local commander. They proceeded to arrive in London on 14 May in a vessel arranged for them by King George VI. When the Dutch Army finally surrendered on 15 May, Queen Wilhelmina took charge of the Dutch government-in-exile, although relations were often strained by a mutual dislike. Dutch Prime Minister Dirk Jan de Geer did not think the Allies had a hope of winning, and his insistence towards opening peace negotiations with Hitler would result in Queen Wilhelmina removing him from government with the help of Minister for Justice Pieter Gerbrandy. By 16 May, the final Dutch radio station still broadcasting at Hilversum in northern Holland was taken over by German announcers and technicians, and immediately began delivering anti-British propaganda. The Dutch were fortunate that many journalists had managed to get across to England following the invasion. Adrian Pelt, the head of the Information Section at the League of Nations, took the initiative and hastily arranged a meeting between sixteen exiled Dutch journalists and the MOI to discuss the setting up of a new information service for Dutch people, either living under occupation or in exile around the world. It was decided that six of the journalists would form the information service aimed at defending national interests. Another two would work on the BBC's own Dutch programme and the remainder would be split between setting up a weekly newspaper and continuing to work with the press agency.

From the moment of their occupation, listeners in the Netherlands tuning into foreign broadcasts placed themselves at risk of being fined 10,000 guilders and two years' imprisonment.[4] Yet listen they did, and for almost five years of full and partial occupation, transmissions on the airwaves, either directly or specially facilitated by the BBC, were their only link to what was happening beyond the borders of their Nazi-occupied land. Among those who recorded their experiences of listening to BBC news was Anne Frank in her wartime diary, written while in hiding from Nazi persecution in Amsterdam. The BBC's Dutch Service was the lifeblood of all those in hiding, enabling them to keep abreast of current events thanks to the accurate and honest reporting from the BBC. In her diary, Anne reproduced a set of typed rules of the hideout in the secret annex for the next incoming occupant, which included information and rules for radio usage. 'Prospectus and guide to the secret-annexe' boasted among other things:

> Our own Radio Centre, direct communications with London, New York, Tel Aviv and numerous other stations. This appliance is only for residents' use after six-o'clock in the evening. No stations are forbidden, on the understanding that German stations are only listened to in special cases – classical music and the like.[5]

In November 1942, Anne wrote of the occupants of the annex being greatly heartened by Churchill's 'End of the Beginning' speech following the decisive victory for Commonwealth forces at El Alamein. For all Dutch listeners it was always vitally important to ensure the radio was tuned back to German stations after listening, in case it was discovered. It rests as a striking example of the success of the BBC's Dutch Service that in May 1943, the Nazis ordered the surrender of all radio sets owned by the Dutch population, even though it meant sacrificing their own radio propaganda. A great number were not surrendered despite dire penalties, as Dutch citizens everywhere came up with elaborate schemes for hiding radio receivers in unlikely places, including inside books and cigarette cases.[6]

On 9 October 1942, Anne recorded the depression she was experiencing over stories that helper Miep Gies had heard of the rounding up and transportation of Jews, and recorded that 'British radio spoke of the Jews being gassed.' The Netherlands State Institute for War Documentation attributes this knowledge to a broadcast on the BBC Home Service on the 6 p.m. news bulletin of 9 July 1942, during which it was stated that 'Jews are regularly killed by machine gun fire, hand grenades and even poisoned by gas'.[7] This contradicts earlier claims that the BBC deliberately suppressed or ignored news of Nazi atrocities against the Jews, although when press reports were stating that as many as 70,000 Polish Jews had been killed, some by mobile gas chambers, it was a difficult story to ignore. Worries about the possibility of such reports inflaming anti-Jewish tensions in Britain, alongside doubts about whether such stories would be believed, are cited as reasons for the BBC's reluctance to tackle the subject of Nazi atrocities against Jews.[8] It is similarly likely that the Franks' awareness of the mass killings originated from an earlier broadcast on the BBC's European Service on 26 June 1942, in which Newsome spoke of 'Men, women and children being gassed to death in mobile lethal chambers' during his popular *The Man in the Street* programme.[9]

The Home Service, and the Dutch bulletins on the BBC's European Service, was not the only channel of communication from which the occupants of the secret annex received information. In the evenings, when Miep or her husband Henk had finished rendering assistance to those in hiding, they would sneak across the road to hear the news from a neighbour's illegal radio set. Instead of hearing news direct from the BBC, they would hear a familiar voice saying, 'Good evening. Here is Radio Orange from London.* But first, a few messages':

---

* Carel Bendel states in *De Oranjes in de Tweede Wereldoorlog* that the broadcasts began with the words 'Radio Orange Here, the voice of a combatant Netherlands', p.80.

Then it would deliver such statements as 'The bird is walking on the roof'. 'The bicycle has a flat tyre' or 'The car is driving down the wrong side of the road'. Everyone listening knew these were important messages for underground fighters. There was much to lift the hearts of Dutch people under occupation as *Radio Oranje* relayed news of the 250 Dutchmen flying with the RAF and there was temporary hope when it delivered news of the attempt on Hitler's life.[10]

For Miep, and no doubt millions of others living under occupation in the Netherlands, the news broadcasts from *Radio Oranje* pertaining to Allied success was 'strong medicine', and she would regularly lie in bed listening to bombers passing overhead, before anxiously awaiting news from the station of where the bombers had struck.

Radio Oranje broadcasts utilised the facilities of the BBC but remained independent from its own European services. It was the mouthpiece for the Dutch government-in-exile in London; its aim was to counter the tide of German propaganda and provide the link between the Dutch Government and the people of the Netherlands. The MOI considered its role to have been vitally important, and yet historians have afforded very little attention to the service. On 29 March 1944, after hearing Gerrit Bolkstein, the Dutch Minister for Education, Art and Science, announce on *Radio Oranje* that 'after the war, a collection would be made of diaries and letters dealing with the war', Anne Frank began to consider writing a *Romance of the Secret Annex*.[11] She thereafter continued to rewrite the diary for a project titled *Het Achterhuis* (*The Secret Annex*) on loose pages with a view to its eventual publication.

How *Radio Oranje* came into being is a tale not without a significant measure of mystery and controversy. Demands from foreign governments in exile for airtime on the BBC transmitters was a complex problem that at first, neither the BBC, nor the MOI felt able to satisfy. Time was limited, and every minute allocated to governments of occupied countries would chew into the time available for the BBC's own valuable service. Ivone Kirkpatrick – then at the MOI – recalled that these countries had neither the personnel nor the resources to organise efficient broadcasts, and was initially unwilling to sacrifice essential news bulletins 'for the amiable exhortations and generalisations concocted in Allied government offices'. Those Allied governments, who were essentially groups of portfolio-holding ministers with no department or state to administer, would at the very least have to be amenable to British policy directives for their requests to be seriously considered. Both Poland and France had been pushing for airtime, followed by the Netherlands and Belgium; there would prove to be some tough negotiating ahead before any of these proposals could get airborne. In the case of France, General de Gaulle had been allotted five minutes' broadcasting time 'free from BBC interference' for his spokesman Maurice Schumann every night, a concession thought to have been made following the British attack on the French fleet at Mers-el-Kébir.* The Czechoslovakians and Norwegians had no such ambitions of going it alone, preferring a system of collaboration with the BBC whereby programmes were inserted into regular BBC schedules.**

By May 1940, the Dutch Information Service under Adrian Pelt was determined to find more effective ways of strengthening the morale of fellow countrymen in occupied Netherlands and abroad. Pelt wanted the Dutch Government to formally ask the BBC if it would allow time for the service to present its own Dutch programme in an effort to restore contact between the exiled government in London and the population of the Netherlands.*** Since 11 April 1940, contact had only been possible through daily fifteen-minute news broadcasts in Dutch on the BBC's own European Service, with the Dutch having no formal control over the content. Despite Pelt occasionally being allowed to offer advice, the service remained an English instrument of propaganda delivering the English viewpoint; its chief editor was an Englishman and the department was bound by the guidelines of the BBC. Whenever the Dutch Government wanted to address its subjects, it had to ask the BBC to be allotted airtime. Pelt sought to convince ministers that the Dutch Government should have its own broadcasting service in which it had full political control, aside from censorship on military matters.

* In his memoirs, Kirkpatrick asserted that he never had much difficulty with de Gaulle and was indebted to the general for his kindness to him on many occasions.

** The Norwegians were initially offered free time following an intervention from Churchill. The offer was declined. The Czechoslovakians were offered free time in 1943, but continued to follow PWE directives. (Briggs, 1970, pp.247, 426)

*** Pelt had formerly been offered free time by a Paris radio station prior to the French collapse.

The head of the Information Section was supported in his plan by the Dutch Minister of Justice Pieter Gerbrandy, who felt that the exiled government should use all means available, including radio, towards fighting for the restoration of 'free and independent Holland'. In the 1930s, Gerbrandy had chaired numerous radio committees where he had become acquainted with the potential in the new medium, although his enthusiasm for the plan was not shared by Dutch Prime Minister Dirk Jan de Geer, who continued pushing for peace negotiations between Britain and Germany. Since this would affect the Dutch position after the war, he believed that no radio broadcasts could be allowed that might either offend the Germans, or risk inciting the population against their occupiers and endanger the possibility of peace. On 20 May, de Geer had given a speech on the BBC's Dutch Service in which he defended the Dutch policy of neutrality, and urged his compatriots under occupation to behave calmly and with dignity in order to gain the respect of the Germans. Despite de Geer's objections, the Council of Ministers agreed with the proposal to ask the BBC for broadcasting time; Gerbrandy and Pelt secured an appointment with the BBC Director General Frederick Ogilvie on 6 June, and asked for fifteen minutes a day. The core of their argument was that German propaganda encouraging defeatism had to be fought against, and could best be done by a Dutchman, with the Dutch character of the programme being emphasised by using a popular song to announce the service.

Ogilvie was reluctant to give the plan the go ahead, and informed the Dutch that allocation of airtime was not primarily a matter for the BBC. His lack of enthusiasm was prompted by the deficiency of available airtime on the medium wave, and fears that conceding airtime to the Dutch Government would set a precedent for other Allied governments in exile who had also requested airtime. The application seemed to have been definitively cancelled following the fall of France on 22 June, when the MOI received orders from Churchill that as much airtime as possible should be reserved for France. Requests for airtime from other Allied governments were considered low priority until 26 June, when the MOI suddenly changed its mind after Kirkpatrick voiced his approval towards allocating airtime to the Dutch. Kirkpatrick believed there was no need to set a precedent for other exiled governments, as it was considered as essential to counter German propaganda being broadcast from the Netherlands. If the broadcasts were associated with the Dutch Government, and as little as possible with the English, this could take the wind out of the German propaganda that suggested Allied governments were merely puppets of the British.

The following day, the BBC and MOI submitted the request to the Home Defence Security Executive, which was responsible for all security operations, including the use of codes in radio broadcasting.[*] Initially the request was rejected on the basis that allowing foreign governments to communicate with the enemy in their own language could endanger British national security. They did not want to risk the possibility that among Dutch refugees in London there could be any number of German agents at a time when there was a deep suspicion over the level of fifth columnists operating in Britain, a number of which were identified by MI5 interrogators later in the war.[12] The MOI were not dissuaded by arguments that the Dutch could not be trusted and asked the committee to make an exception. Objections could be overcome by incorporating several safeguards, which included allowing the Secret Intelligence Service to vet everyone involved in the broadcasts before they could go on air. Additionally, any other employees involved with the service were not allowed access to the premises of the station until at least forty-eight hours after reporting to the MOI.

The reason for the sudden turnaround in the case of the Netherlands at that point in the negotiations was not immediately clear. Previously, Newsome and Kirkpatrick had been united in the belief that the whole European Service should speak with one voice – the voice of Britain, with news and commentaries following the same line and having the same British imprint. The issue of Dutch airtime had become a more compelling issue on 4 July, when it was announced that all broadcasts from the Netherlands were now under full German control, and they would begin broadcasting to the Dutch East Indies using trusted Dutch broadcasters. At the time, the Indies was a valuable source of raw materials for the

[*] Churchill established the HD(S)E on 27 May 1940, consisting of representatives from the Home Office, the Home Forces, the Security Service and the Secret Intelligence Service. The executive was empowered to consider all questions relating to defence against the fifth column, and to initiate action through the appropriate departments. Its title was changed to the Security Executive (SE) in October 1941.

Allied war effort, including oil, bauxite, rubber and tin among others. It is also possible that the Dutch Government was being favoured because it had openly rejected National Socialism before the war, and indirectly ranged itself against Nazi Germany despite a general policy of neutrality. London also housed the Belgian, Polish, Norwegian, Greek, Yugoslav and Czechoslovakian governments, as well as the Free French representative government. Fierce discussions also took place in Whitehall over allowing the facilities of the BBC to be accessed by a government in exile who had previously wanted a policy of reconciliation with Hitler. The original Dutch policy of neutrality had been aimed at preventing conflict with Nazi Germany, with all radio broadcasts being censored from transmitting anything anti-German. In the summer of 1940, some Dutch ministers were even prepared to accept permanent German domination of Europe, and to consider the possibility of peace talks.[13]

Despite the protests inside Whitehall and accusations of favouritism from other exiled governments, the MOI got its way and on 8 July 1940 the committee agreed to allocate fifteen minutes of daily airtime to the Dutch Government. The MOI insisted that there were compelling reasons for allowing the Dutch Government to combat German propaganda broadcasts to the Netherlands directly, especially as they could now be received in the Dutch East Indies. From 9 December, the BBC allowed the Dutch broadcasts to be relayed continuously in the mornings due to the heavy jamming techniques of the Germans, and broadcasting time was again extended following the American entry into the war in December 1941. By this time the programmes on *Radio Oranje* were also being transmitted regularly to the Indies as far as Curaçao and Dutch Guyana.* Another station called de Brandaris (after the famous lighthouse), intended for broadcasts to Dutch seamen, would eventually be taken over by *Radio Oranje*.

Radio Oranje became a channel for the national cause and the British afforded the Dutch a large degree of freedom to determine the content for the broadcasts themselves. The task of editing the content was given to former VARA board member Jan Lebon and journalist Louis de Jong, who had previously compiled propaganda for the Social

---

* The original time suggested for the *Oranje* broadcasts was useless in countering the effects of German propaganda directed to the Indies.

Democrat Students Movement.[*] De Jong had initially set up a radio facility in Paris that had been forced to close in mid-June shortly before the French surrender.[14] They were the only permanent employees of the service and began work on the fifth floor of Stratton House in the heart of London. This was also the headquarters of the Dutch Government ministries, which occupied three floors, while the Polish government-in-exile operated from the second floor above a French restaurant. They had no experience of making radio programmes and had to focus on the task in hand at a time when a Nazi invasion of Britain was a very real possibility. Their broadcasts would also be carefully monitored by the Dutch Government and particularly the British authorities, who could still exercise influence over what should be broadcast. Gerbrandy had emphasised at a meeting of the Council of Ministers on 14 June that broadcasting counter-propaganda would be an integral part of the struggle for Dutch independence. Another former VARA official, Meyer Sluyser, proposed the name *Radio Oranje* on the premise that only the House of Orange could lead the resistance against the Nazis. Sluyser played a key role in the initial phase by providing guidance on the manner in which the broadcasts should be structured. German influence in the Netherlands was to be countered by keeping alive the realisation that the country was continuing the struggle through the navy, the army, the merchant fleet and the colonies, and that the government in London was continuing to represent their interests.

Early on, the lack of available information about what was happening in the Netherlands made it difficult for the staff at *Radio Oranje* to assess the impact of their broadcasts. News about the course of the war was typically no longer current and was often fragmented, regardless of whether it was favourable or unfavourable. Another problem was the difficulty in overcoming the persistent jamming and constant humming sound present on the allocated wavelengths. The search began for an announcer with a much more powerful voice, and after a fruitless attempt to recruit from among the remaining Dutch soldiers encamped in Wolverhampton, two officials from the Netherlands Department of Foreign Affairs were co-opted to deliver the broadcasts.

---

[*] VARA stands for *Vereeniging van Arbeiders Radio Amateurs* (the Association of Amateur Radio Workers).

Many government ministers were very reluctant to come to the microphone for fear of being identified and exposing their families at home to possible reprisals. Gerbrandy, van Kleffens and the Minister of the Interior, Hendrik van Boeyen, made up the Supervisory Committee that guided *Radio Oranje*. Every script had to be submitted for the scrutiny of the committee, with the exception of Queen Wilhelmina and Marcus van Blankenstein, the chief editor of the London weekly newspaper *Vrij Nederland*. Queen Wilhelmina had effectively launched *Radio Oranje* with a broadcast on 28 July 1940, after consultation with ministers. It would be the first of forty-eight such broadcasts by the monarch. She began on a note of gratitude for the opportunity that the corporation had afforded her and her government:

> I am delighted that thanks to the benevolent co-operation of the English authorities, this Dutch quarter-hour has been incorporated into the broadcasts of British radio, and I express the hope that many fellow countrymen, wherever they may be, will now be faithful listeners of the patriotic thoughts that reach them along this way. And now I am delighted to be the first to speak to you in these fifteen minutes.

Queen Wilhelmina's image would become a symbol of resistance against the Nazis; her late-night broadcasts were eagerly awaited by those living under occupation. Following on from the monarch's opening broadcast, *Radio Oranje* struggled to get its propaganda messages across, despite the freedom from BBC and government interference it was afforded. In the month it took Queen Wilhelmina to remove the 'defeatist' Prime Minister Dirk Jan de Geer from office, he effectively had control of the scripts and was a source of persistent annoyance to the staff. De Geer wanted the broadcasts to be focused on ending the war as soon as possible, a fixation that was reflected in the corrections he habitually made to the scripts. He constantly made defeatist interventions and informed the staff that he expected them to take an objective attitude towards the Germans, including a demand that the word 'enemy' be replaced with 'opposing party', and any reference to the Germans as 'Krauts' was deemed to be 'completely out of the question'.[15] Other accounts of de Geer's negative interference are available from the memoirs of the station staff. Lead journalist Louis de Jong was censured for scripting a broadcast implying that the Netherlands would have her freedom after the war; his script, he was told, 'was pure rhetoric' after the Dutch Ministry of Defence had already stated that there was no hint that Germany would lose the war. On another occasion he was berated for speculating on what punishment should be meted out to the Germans, and was warned to leave the trials of the invaders to the Dutch Government.

Whether or not it was intended at the outset, a primary function of *Radio Oranje* was as a useful medium for refugees to send word home of their safe arrival. Even in this instance, none of the independent services, including *Radio Oranje*, could evade British security regulations laid down for the 'Personal Message Services', and the rules were very strict. All messages sent were subject to a time lag of fourteen days to eliminate the possibility of messages of immediate importance being sent to the enemy, and neither could the same applicant send more than one message every three months. Alternatively, agents of SOE, SIS or PWE in enemy-occupied Europe received and returned messages via the Official Intelligence Message Service, designed exclusively for British or Allied intelligence and propaganda organisation, and was not subject to external censorship. This had its dangers as these bodies were typically unwilling to reject any request made by an ally, meaning a message refused by one censorship system could be passed by another and thus effectively circumvent security procedures.[16]

At the receiving end of the *Radio Oranje* broadcasts were members of the Dutch resistance group, who felt that people in England were poorly informed regarding conditions in the Netherlands. In an effort to improve the situation, physics students Henk Deinum and Marinus Vader successfully built a radio transmitter in the school laboratory, then went on to build another thirteen that were able to transmit vital military information and weather reports to Allied intelligence. Broadcasts were further improved when the Sonotron Company in Amsterdam began selling devices that allowed medium-wave radios to be adapted for short-wave reception, meaning the programmes received would be free from interference. This was crucial as editors of illegal newspapers relied heavily on *Radio Oranje*. Jan Verhagen recorded the station's broadcasts on a gramophone and typed out the reports from the bulletin to be distributed to various illegal magazines, while on the streets leaflets and instructions were discreetly handed to citizens, imploring them to take their orders and instructions from the station. Special coded messages were also broadcast that required the use of a special coding bar to decipher them.[17]

In July 1981, the former chief broadcaster of *Radio Oranje*, Louis 'Loe' de Jong, shared his recollections of three years spent delivering political commentaries for the Dutch people living under occupation. Speaking on Radio Netherlands Worldwide for the benefit of English-speaking listeners, he remembered:

> everyone had to broadcast under a pseudonym. The programmes typically lasted fourteen minutes and forty seconds and because the music generally took up twenty seconds at the beginning and at the end, you only actually got fourteen minutes' broadcasting time.

The music selected for the broadcasts was a 300-year-old tune called 'Orange Open the Gate', which was dropped in 1943 when cases began to emerge of listeners being arrested by authorities loyal to the Nazis after hearing the familiar tune through the thin walls of inner-city dwellings. De Jong remembered that all the programmes were recorded live, 'with the exception of the *Political Cabaret* programme on Saturday evenings for around six months'. One favourite song he remembered from the cabaret shows (that can still be heard in its original recording) was titled 'You're Much Better Off With the British'. All broadcasts were subject to military censorship, even though de Jong could not recall any instance of difficulties arising between the station and the censors. He remembered early attempts to overcome enemy jamming using simple gadgets referred to as 'Nazi Sieves', which were basically two sticks bound together with wire on both sides with a variable condenser or capacitor attached to filter out sound. On a grander scale, such problems could be overcome by situating short-wave transmitters inland, causing the signal to propagate in a different manner. It was generally a serious business; so complex was the information network that *Radio Oranje* frequently managed to stay one step ahead of the Germans by monitoring German transmissions. If an order was given to arrest someone, agents connected to the radio station often managed to warn the target to go into hiding. There were also many coded messages relating to weapons drops for use by the resistance, and de Jong was satisfied that the broadcasts were reaching their target:

> Since we started, around 2,000 Dutch people succeeded in escaping to England. All were interviewed and gave a positive response to the broadcasts. It was also clear from the surge in domestic power during the broadcasts that we had a wide audience.

De Jong also recollected that when the Germans began confiscating all Dutch-owned radios at the beginning of 1943, they gradually lost around three-quarters of their regular listeners. Things got tougher still following the failed Arnhem operation, when, during the famine of the winter of 1944, many houses were without electricity for long periods. It was just prior to the Arnhem episode that *Radio Oranje* contributed towards creating panic and confusion in an event that came to be known as 'Mad Tuesday'. The incident began on 4 September when the BBC's Dutch Service mistakenly announced that intelligence sources in Breda were in touch with British troops. On that Monday evening, Gerbrandy went on air to announce that Allied troops had crossed the Dutch border, and that Breda was being liberated. This announcement, coming around nine months too early, created a huge upsurge of optimism that included people taking to the streets in celebration – a mistaken assumption that fortunately invited no huge reprisal from the Germans. When the Netherlands was finally liberated on 6 May 1945, a special composition titled 'Liberation Poem' was read out on *Radio Oranje*, which delivered its final broadcast on 2 June 1945. A short while later, a bronze plaque was presented to the BBC in gratitude for services rendered to the Dutch that praised 'the fortitude and consolation given to the Netherlands in years of oppression'. Another glowing tribute to the BBC and *Radio Oranje* came from the editor of a Dutch underground newspaper:

> We would have been completely isolated from the outside world, and would have missed the trusted, warm voices which during those long years buoyed and comforted us. A close bond was formed between the voices and us listeners – hidden in a cupboard, or under a bed, or wherever wireless receivers were concealed. It was as if they – the people of Radio Orange and the BBC – were a part of us.[18]

Other governments in exile were eventually afforded 'free time' to deliver their own programmes using the facilities of the BBC. After Belgium had been invaded, King Leopold decided to remain in occupied Brussels, making it difficult for Belgian ministers to secure free time in the short term. BBC Radio Belgique did not transmit programmes specifically for Belgians until 28 September 1940, typically broadcast in both French and Flemish on alternate days, and the Belgians did not secure 'free time' until January 1943.[19] Listeners in Belgium typically resented the political speakers on the service for having escaped the rigours of occupation and avoided joining up with the Free Belgium forces. In early 1941, the BBC's Belgian Service began one of the most effective propaganda initiatives aimed towards the subversion of German rule. Former Belgian politician Victor de Lavelaye worked as an announcer on the service and reported that Belgians everywhere were chalking up 'RAF' and 'V for *Victoire*' on walls throughout various cities. In a broadcast to his compatriots in occupied Belgium on 14 January 1941, de Lavelaye began urging his countrymen to continue doing this, as it annoyed the Germans and undermined their morale.

A few months passed by before Newsome as European Service editor recognised the potential and sought to extend it to other languages; in Britain it was V for Victory, in the Netherlands V for *Vrijheid*, and so on. Newsome's deputy editor, Douglas Ritchie, eventually took charge of the campaign, and broadcast regularly under the pseudonym of Colonel Britton, while his real identity remained a mystery until after the war. Britton transmitted broadcasts in French, German, Dutch, Polish, Czech and Norwegian, and made all manner of suggestions as to how citizens in occupied Europe could further the campaign. This included telling Europeans to sit in cafes with their legs stretched out in a V-shape, and to wave at one another with the fingers spread V-wise. His broadcasts were typically underscored with the slogan, 'The night is your friend; the V is your sign', and very soon the RAF began flying across Europe in a V-formation. Such was the enthusiasm, a 'V Committee' was formed to co-ordinate its adaptation for as many countries as possible. The letter V in Morse Code (three dots and a dash) mimicked the opening notes of Beethoven's *Fifth Symphony*, which was played on the timpani to provide the station identification for all the European services. Churchill referred to the V sign as 'the symbol of the unconquerable will of the people', and it was through the Overseas Service that his famous two-fingered V for Victory sign began life at the BBC.

Colonel Britton was seldom off the front page, despite nobody knowing who was behind the disguise. Ritchie was effectively building a silent V-army of thousands in occupied Europe, especially in France, where thousands had been arrested for distributing paper Vs. Britton would suggest methods of practical sabotage and other effective ways to create havoc and confusion. There were also near disasters, especially when Britton announced in July 1941 that 'there would be a very special announcement on Sunday'; the broadcast was subsequently rebroadcast by *Radio Oranje*, whereupon thousands of Dutch citizens flocked to the coast in expectation of an Allied invasion. As the numbers of shootings and executions multiplied, Ritchie began to feel the weight of responsibility in the knowledge that many of his weaponless listeners would probably die in vain, and referred to his dilemma as being like 'the brake and the accelerator applied at the same time'.[20] He was not so much bothered by complaints coming from SOE about 'encroaching on their territory', rather he was more concerned that such propaganda broadcasts endangered the lives of listeners without any risk to himself, and the brake was finally applied permanently in May 1942. Bruce Lockhart at the PWE, who had ultimately decided to flex his muscles towards stalling the campaign, warmly congratulated Ritchie on a job well done.

Nazi Propaganda Minister Goebbels believed he could neutralise the effect of the broadcasts by instigating his own V-campaign – the success of which is still contended. Even though the V would no longer be forbidden or suppressed, the head of external broadcasting, Edward Tangye-Lean, believed that Goebbels' operation was an intelligent initiative that created confusion and disrupted the campaign.[21] In his memoirs, European Service Controller Ivone Kirkpatrick reflected that the V-campaign had been the most important propaganda initiative conducted during his time at the corporation. Powerfully symbolic as it was, it had essentially been the first organised attempt to damage German morale, and to unite and give hope to the forces of resistance. Before finally going off air, Colonel Britton hinted that at the proper time, the V-army would be called into action against the invaders – 'when a practical line of action is needed'. The end of the war was not yet in view, and to encourage more concrete forms of resistance at that stage in the war would have been foolish.

The BBC's Belgian Service appears to have been similarly successful to that of the Netherlands; tributes were received from the government ministers when it was discovered that nine-tenths of the population listened in to the broadcasts. Antoine Delfonse, the Minister of Communications, described the influence of the BBC on the morale of the Belgian as being 'immense', with broadcasts that were objective, inspiring and bringing real messages of hope in the extreme.[22]

The Polish government-in-exile initially failed to secure broadcasting time free from BBC control after it had relocated to London from Paris following the French surrender in June 1940. The BBC had begun its own Polish Service on 7 September 1939, offering three fifteen-minute bulletins a day, rising to six by 1944. Poland's own broadcasting station, Polski Radio, had delivered its final broadcast from Warsaw two days after Polish capitulation, and began broadcasting from Paris after the government had fled. The BBC worked closely with the Polski Radio staff, who had garnered their own reputation for efficiency and impartiality. Following a visit to London from the Station Director Krzysztof Eydziatowicz in March 1940, a decision was made to incorporate 'Polski' material in the BBC's Wednesday and Saturday broadcasts. As it was now to become the broadcasting arm of the exiled government, the Polish Minister of Information switched the name from Polskie Radio to Radio Polskie to disassociate the station from its former pre-war *Sanacja* regime.

Before the Polish Government could be allocated free time to air its own programmes, there would be major obstacles to overcome, particularly the change in Britain's propaganda directives following the Nazi invasion of the Soviet Union in May 1941. Despite having previously been attacked by Churchill, Stalin was suddenly Britain's ally, and the prime minister now advocated a strong propaganda campaign in praise of the Soviets – without mention of that awful word 'communism'. Britain also adopted a pro-Soviet censorship policy that did not go down well with Poland, who viewed Britain as her principal ally. Asa Briggs claimed that the Nazi invasion 'transformed the war in propaganda terms' and that anything critical of the Soviet Union was now considered 'taboo', while the corporation began referring to 'Russia' rather than the 'Soviet

Union' in its news broadcasts.[23] Thereafter, the BBC began broadcasting programmes on Russian life and literature, and scheduled programmes in observance of Red Army Day on 23 February each year. Following the German defeat at Stalingrad, it broadcast a huge evening in celebration of the Soviet victory live from the Albert Hall. This new directive of rejecting anything anti-Soviet, and playing down or ignoring such atrocities as the Katyn Massacre and mass arrests suffered by Polish citizens at the hands of their invaders, caused many among the Polish community to question the credibility of the BBC, especially when broadcasts were transmitted with the aim of persuading the Polish listeners to assent to Soviet territorial demands. As far as Britain was concerned, it was Allied unity at all costs, regardless of crimes against Polish citizens, and all broadcasts to Poland were required to adopt a firm anti-German tone. By the end of 1941, diplomatic relations between the Poles and the Soviets had grudgingly been restored, and only then, in January 1942, was Polskie Radio finally allowed to broadcast on the BBC wavelengths.

Despite the death penalty having been introduced in Poland for listening in to the broadcasts, those anxious for news were not deterred. After more than two years of fruitless efforts to stamp out 'black listening', the authorities began providing red printed cards for radio owners to hang upon their sets with a message warning them against listening to foreign broadcasts – 'It is a crime against the safety of our race. By the Führer's orders, you will be severely punished.' Goebbels made his feelings on this clear in December 1941: 'There are still people who will not learn. Two death sentences and a number of sentences of forced labour, passed quite recently, prove this.' There is also evidence to suggest that Goebbels' little red cards actually encouraged more people to listen.[24] In Poland, activists produced countless newspapers relying exclusively on material broadcast by the BBC at the risk of their lives.

In the Balkans, the people were also totally dependent on information received from the BBC and shaped their guerrilla campaigns accordingly. German propaganda in this area was particularly problematic as it typically focused on stirring up tensions between ethnic groups. 'Ghosts of the past were just as active in the Yugoslav minds of the present,' observed Kirkpatrick at Bush House as he struggled to reach any consensus with government representatives, who seemed to

THE VOICE OF HOPE

be continually arguing among themselves. The BBC refused to allow individual ethnic groups to broadcast separately, and deliberately steered clear of internal politics in Yugoslavia – reporting only on the continuing struggle against the common enemy. Towards the end of the war, Churchill's unshakable commitment to monarchical rule in both Yugoslavia and Greece created immense difficulties for the propagandists. His insistence that King Peter be restored to the throne of Yugoslavia meant that the PWE was expected to back the Chetnik leader Draža Mihailović, who it was later discovered had been in direct collaboration with the Germans, while Tito's Partisans waged a vigorous guerrilla war against the Axis enemy. Ritchie Calder complained that the PWE was never allowed to refer to the Partisans: 'We had to speak of the "Yugoslav Resistance" including the Chetniks by inference.' To Tito's great indignation, this meant that the Chetniks were getting the credit for the activities of the Partisans – a situation that was favourable to Mihailović. Calder believed that had Churchill been less obsessed with stopping communism and more accepting of the new forces that were emerging from the resistance movements, an alternative to Soviet communism might have been found that could have saved East European countries from falling into the iron grip of Stalin.[25]

Similarly, the PWE believed King George II of Greece had no following among the Greek resistance groups that were often coerced into action via instructions received through BBC broadcasts. BBC Radio Hellas had a particularly receptive audience in Greece, where family members stood guard at the front door while others listened inside. In May 1941, traditional sheep bells and a shepherd flute had been handed over to the BBC by the Greek minister in London to use as a signal to introduce programmes in Greek. When broadcasts began offering instructions on acts of sabotage on machinery that included tanks, the Germans began the wholesale confiscation of sets, after the owners had been told to register them. The Greek government-in-exile were finally afforded 'free time' in July 1942, by which time Churchill had been in Cairo dining with the Greek Royal Family, and had promised King George II of the Hellenes that 'he shall return to his capital on a white horse'. Again, the PWE found themselves in the impossible situation of backing two horses at once. Calder refused to issue directives denouncing the resistance movements as it contradicted the PWE policy that anyone who fights our enemy is on our side. Calder believed that if they sided with the king, the Greek section of the BBC and possibly all the other sections from occupied countries would walk out, as the French Service had done previously over the issue of Admiral Darlan.

Of all the Overseas Services, it was broadcasting to France that was by far the most delicate operation for the BBC, and it is on the French Service that we now focus. The station personnel were faced with the prospect of a split nation to address and had to reach out to a section of the population who had accepted submission to Nazi rule, and succumbed to the advice of the Nazi Propaganda Ministry and Vichy Radio that all British claims of allied kinship with France should be viewed with distrust.

el Newsome, director
European Broadcasts,
October 1943. Newsome
ived at the BBC two
/s before war was
clared and became
central figure in the
gest broadcasting unit
the world, transmitting
ogrammes across
Continent for
enty-three hours a day.
BBC Photo Library)

Ivone Kirkpatrick arrived at the BBC as
foreign policy advisor in February 1941
with the recommendation of being 'a
real terrier who would tear the pants off
of the BBC people'. He was appointed
European Service controller in October
1941. (© National Portrait Gallery)

Minister of Information Brendan Bracken pictured alongside Churchil in 1941. His temperament might have been 'as fiery as his aureole of Celtic hair', yet, unlike his master, Bracken championed the BBC, describing it as 'one of the greatest of our war assets'. (© Keystone/Hulton Archive/ Getty Images)

Amsterdam 1945. Brothers in hiding, Joop and Jan Kuyt, listen in to *Radio Oranje* on an illegal receiver. (© Charles Breijer, Nederlands Photomuseum)

*terijen Telegrafie
Telefonie
stal Telephone
d Telegraph)
rehouse in
sterdam
ntaining
nfiscated radios
owing the
er of 13 May
3. (© Charles
eijer, Nederlands
otomuseum)

arles de Gaulle
oadcasting an
peal to the French
ople to continue
e fight in June
40. 'De Gaulle
d no doubts as to
s destiny as the
erator of France.'
) Hulton Archive/
tty Images)

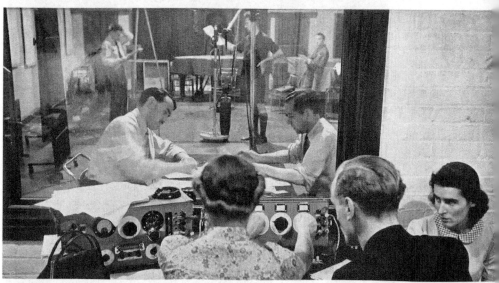

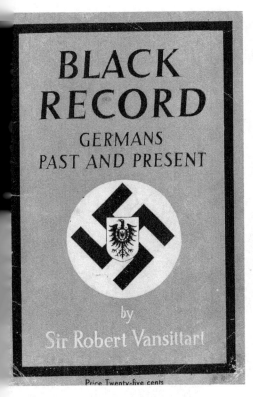

Chief diplomatic advisor to the British Government Sir Robert Vansittart's seven broadcasts on the BBC, made in autumn 1940, were reproduced in book form. His radical ideas made life extremely difficult for the German Service in its attempts to further divide the German people. (Author's Collection)

Heinrich Fraenkel's response challenged Vansittart's theories and produced statistics that gave real hope to the service propagandists in their efforts to appeal to the anti-Nazi element inside Germany. (Author's Collection)

Opposite page: The European Service of the BBC in operation.

Top: Service Director Noel Newsome delivering his propaganda directives for the day. The man with his back to the camera is Assistant Director Douglas Ritchie, who broadcast as Colonel Britton throughout the V-Campaign.

Centre: *London Calling Europe* in production, while in the background actors prepare for a 'feature' programme immediately following. The secretary to the right is worried about timing problems.

Bottom: Editor for the Czechoslovakian Service, Sheila Grant-Duff, advises announcers prior to a transmission going out from London. (All images reproduced by kind permission of Random House)

'One rapidly becomes "propaganda-minded" and develops a cunning one did not previously have.'
George Orwell at the BBC in 1941. (© ullstein bild/Getty Images)

This previously unpublished passport image of Orwell from 1943 was discovered in his secret service file, in which his BBC colleagues reported that he was offering employment to 'friends of his who were connected to the Indian Independence Movement'. He was also described as 'a bit of an anarchist' with 'advanced Communist views'. (Approved for reproduction by the Metropolitan Police IP department)

10

DIVIDED NATION

REACHING OUT TO FRANCE

The prospects for broadcasting effective propaganda on the BBC's French Service rested on a pre-existing reputation for truthfulness that the corporation had steadily built up among French listeners during the run-up to war. Director of External Broadcasting Edward Tangye-Lean observed that the French were not given to psychological thinking, and that 'the intelligentsia were at one with the workers' in their distrust of homespun propaganda. Just as the French listener praised the BBC for 'sticking soberly to the news', so he or she denounced the French radio for the condescending manner in which it kept its citizens in the dark. Cross-Channel correspondence received by the BBC indicated that listeners turned to the station as a more reliable source of information than the official state-run radio *Radiodiffusion Nationale* (RN). The BBC's reputation for delivering honest news, however disheartening, was in contrast to the heavily censored public network at home. Shortly before the French capitulation, when the British and French Ministers of Information forged a collaboration agreement, one worker from Lyons wrote alarmingly that he was afraid that the BBC bulletins 'will lose much of their interest'.[1]

French listeners were targeted from Germany by *The Traitor of Stuttgart*, the antisemitic Paul Ferdonnet, who sought to drive a wedge between Britain and France. Ferdonnet's broadcasts typically argued that Britain would gladly 'let France die on its behalf', and he taunted listeners with the claim that 'Britain provides the machines while France provides the bodies'.[2] Much like the British fascination with Haw-Haw, the French could not get enough of Ferdonnet's compulsive broadcasts on Radio Paris, and winning over the spellbound listener was always going to be a challenging assignment for the European Service, especially as relations had become somewhat strained during the early months of the war. Before a shot was fired, the MOI had been anxious to counteract German statements comparing the cost of living among the German working class to that of Britain and France, and informed the BBC that it was simply not advisable to talk about 'our high standard of living' given our current relations with the French.[3] Additionally, there had been reports from the British ambassador in Paris of 'unfavourable comparisons' made between the size of the BEF (390,000 men from thirteen divisions) and the French forces totalling around 3.5 million. It was incumbent on the Secretary of State for War to remind the French that the BEF was 'an advanced guard only', and the decision was made to quote numbers of men rather than divisions in future bulletins transmitted to France.* When the fighting finally began, the Allies were swiftly routed, and by 25 June 1940 the battle for France was lost after just forty-six days of armed combat; the terms of the armistice saw the country split into two separate occupied and unoccupied zones. Thereafter, the propaganda transmitted to and from France would arguably become the BBC European Service's most complex operation.

The fall of France compounded a level of Anglo-French ill-feeling that the German propagandists wasted no time in exploiting. Encouraged by Ferdonnet's oft-repeated claim that 'Britain would fight to the last Frenchman', the Germans invested more time and effort in Radio Paris than in any other station. Despite this increased effort, the technicians at the BBC Monitoring Service remained unimpressed and regarded the Nazi propaganda operation as a 'sterile and desperate business' offering little to consolidate the victories it had helped towards achieving. Programmes typically featured lead announcer Dr Friedrich Sieburg attempting to sell the ideals of the National Socialist Movement and claiming that Germany had been misunderstood; 'Occupation?

---

* It had previously been reported in France that the BEF comprised fifty-five divisions.

No! Europe has come together in a solid block for its own benefit.'[4] It was important for the BBC's French Service to swiftly eradicate any thought about 'lack of brotherliness', and any talk of the French 'letting us down', or of Britain 'betraying the French', had to cease forthwith. Refugees arriving in Britain, relaying conversations from home about France carrying the whole of the burden, could not be allowed near a microphone.[5] It was bad enough that anti-British radio propaganda repeatedly reinforced French suspicions by raking over past British belligerence towards France, including stoking up fears that Britain still harboured designs on taking over the French Empire.

A short while later, when Churchill ordered the scuttling of the French fleet at Mers-el-Kébir on 3 July, it was immediately seized upon by enemy propagandists as yet another example of British treachery towards France. The head of the new unoccupied Vichy State – the decorated 'war hero' Marshal Pétain – made direct reference to Dunkirk and Mers-el-Kébir in an official broadcast, accusing Britain of both deserting and attacking France.* Doug Ritchie at the BBC easily countered this by resurrecting Admiral Darlan's final order not to surrender the ships to Britain and not to obey any further order – a clear indication that Darlan was acting under German command. For Ritchie, the action was justified by the claim that 'anyone who obeys the enemy's orders is also the enemy', and highlighted the scuttling as 'staggering proof of Britain's desire to preserve Anglo-French friendship'. By spurning the opportunity to have the ships interned in the French West Indies, rather than allow them to be used against Britain, Pétain had effectively condemned the fleet to its fate. Newsome rejoiced that 'Britain had forestalled Hitler' and he instructed his propagandists to exploit the victory over Pétain from every angle.[6]

With France now conquered, Britain was suddenly under imminent threat of invasion. Out in the streets, people openly speculated that 'now France had fallen the date has been set for London', while others commented cynically 'we will be much better off without the French!'[7]

---

* The scuttling of the French fleet had caused unease and anger among the BBC's French section, requiring Newsome to use all his powers of persuasion to convince them it was the right thing to have done. The MOI reported that morale in Britain increased after the scuttling. (Report on Morale, 05-07-40 (NA))

The head of the BBC's French Service, Darsie Gillie, emphasised to his team that they must try to put their own fears aside and focus on the job in hand; there was no official government strategy for propaganda to the occupied countries at the time, leaving Newsome to determine the direction of the broadcasts on his own initiative. The BBC sought to provide an authoritative news service for the people of France, and to reinforce the message further all pro-British propaganda on the French station was spoken almost exclusively by French nationals, each with a special clause in their contract stating they were not compelled to broadcast anything they regarded as being against the French national interest. The success of the service depended largely on building up a strong bond of trust between the BBC and the French listeners, which meant reporting successes and failures truthfully and carefully weighing up their significance to avoid being undermined by enemy propaganda. It was also important to display a degree of sensitivity towards the extreme stressfulness of living under occupation, for even in the summer of 1941, when French morale had recovered slightly, violent hatred between Frenchmen was still the order of the day. One had to accept that there were those willing to resist their oppressors and those who were not, and the BBC's French Service announcers were careful not to offend either.

Newsome initially urged Gillie and his team to focus on revitalising French morale, promoting a strong belief in British resolve, and fostering hatred of not only the Germans, but of the Nazi-created Vichy state. This would involve counteracting Anglophobia, rebuilding confidence in Britain's power to continue the war, and exposing German attempts to create divisions between the two countries. The warm welcome given to French refugees in Britain would also need to be highlighted to counter the backlash against Nazi propaganda that claimed Britain was preventing the return home of French soldiers stranded after Dunkirk. The up-to-the-moment responses to the BBC's propaganda gathered from the BBC's Monitoring Service was vital during this time. In a broadcast on 3 August 1940, the French Service programme director – the well-known theatre director Michel Saint-Denis, operating under the alias of Jacques Duchesne – urged the French people not to be taken in by German efforts to create divisions between Britain and France, and to be mindful of not betraying 'the camp that fights for freedom'.[8] BBC propagandists appeared to have recognised the need to constantly illuminate the opposing alliances; it was Britain and 'Free France' set against Nazi Germany and its Vichy collaborators, who had turned France over as a satellite of the conqueror. French citizens who had accepted the armistice signed by Pétain on 22 June were to be under no illusions about the resolve of the French dissidents who had elected to continue to fight from Britain to liberate France from its chains. In London, Maurice Schumann openly criticised Vichy's puppet leaders for abandoning the defence of France by begging for an armistice on 'the most humiliating terms', including handing over 400 million francs to the Nazis every day.

By the summer of 1940 all parties, including Churchill, agreed that as much airtime as possible should be reserved for directing propaganda in the service of Britain's conquered neighbour. Aware of the popularity of the BBC's French Service, Alexis Luger, the former head of the French Foreign Ministry, had previously informed the prime minister that 'with clever use of the wireless, the BBC might be able to turn public opinion around'. This was also pertinent to French North Africa, where Churchill emphasised the importance that news was 'broadcast to the highest point', and empowered Duff Cooper with 'the full authority to make the BBC obey'.[9] Churchill's typically aggressive tone towards the corporation seems unduly harsh, for it was the BBC that helped to bring General Charles de Gaulle to the forefront of French politics. De Gaulle had only just been appointed Minister of War on 5 June, before flying to London four days later tasked with brokering a deal with Britain by the Reynaud-led government. Believing he had convinced government representatives that the two countries could resume the fight against Hitler as a unified force, he returned to France only to discover that Reynaud had been replaced by Pétain, who was already set to sign an armistice with the new occupiers. Having immediately escaped back to London in the company of Churchill's personal representative in Paris, General Spears, he asked the British Government if he could make an appeal to Frenchmen to continue the fight. Churchill consented, and on the 18 June 1940, de Gaulle informed his compatriots that 'the flames of French resistance must not be extinguished – will not be extinguished'. This first address began a process that would stimulate the legend of a 'Free France', although the general was absolutely furious that the speech had not been recorded. De Gaulle's statement had been broadcast on the same day as Churchill's 'Finest Hour' speech, and the significance of an address by the little-known former tank commander was not appreciated. De Gaulle, who was typically described as 'a difficult man who radiated authority', was persuaded to deliver a second, recorded, broadcast on 24 June calling on 'all Frenchmen who want to remain free to listen to my voice and follow me'.[10] It was initially believed that hardly anyone heard the original broadcast, until French citizens who became key operatives in the resistance organisations testified otherwise.* Paris resident Odile de Vasselot remembered she joined the resistance after hearing de Gaulle's appeal of 18 June:

> I was on my own in my room, listening to a little radio, and I went to tell my family in the living room: do you know what's happened? De Gaulle is in London! My grandfather shouted out: 'The war's not finished yet! There's still hope!'[11]

Others, she remembered, said he was a traitor for disobeying Pétain. She had known the then Colonel de Gaulle as a family friend, of whom her grandfather (a general) used to say 'de Gaulle was the only intelligent soldier because he wanted a motorised army, with tanks':

> We used to rip posters and draw Lorraine crosses [the Free French symbol] on walls with chalk. On posters of the Vichy Propaganda Minister Philippe Henriot we would put speech bubbles saying 'I'm a bastard.'[12]

From 19 June, the day after de Gaulle's appeal, six fifteen-minute bulletins in French were broadcast daily on the service. This was followed by a fifteen-minute entertainment slot called *Ici la France* (*This is France*) a programme for French citizens broadcast by the familiar voices of RN staff who had taken refuge in London. On 30 June the amount of broadcasting time allotted to the French Service was further augmented, and *Ici la France* was increased to half an hour. Jacques Duchesne was appointed to lead what became the first truly national programme broadcast by the BBC to occupied Europe. On the other

---

* After hearing de Gaulle's initial broadcast on 18 June 1940, Henri Guegant also became inspired towards assisting Frenchmen anxious to continue the fight by arranging safe passages to England.

side of the Channel, Radio Paris represented the voice of occupation in the new domestic broadcasting framework, fronted by French presenters under the direct control of the Germans. The Vichy Radio service pumping out its own propaganda from unoccupied France was viewed as 'lacking the glitter' of the Paris station – listeners commented that it 'stank of the Bosch attempting to fill us with shame'.[13] When the RAF had strategically bombed the Renault factory, Vichy Radio described it as 'the criminal aggression of a former ally who allowed our soldiers to go to their deaths alone'.[14] The French painter Jean Oberle was a regular speaker on the BBC French Service, where he focused on fuelling French distrust of the Paris service by constantly referring to it as 'the microphone of the occupier' and its 'Radio Paris lies'. On top of this, service personnel regularly mocked the German propaganda coming from Paris by rewriting the works of popular French songs, often utilising a full orchestra to enhance the broadcasts.[15]

In the weeks following the fall of France, a large number of the BBC's French Service personnel were lured back across the Channel due to family ties, leaving Pierre Bourdan to become the regular announcer on the service. His first broadcast from London on 3 August 1940 proclaimed to the French people: 'We are in England because England remains the enemy of Germany.' On 26 August, his colleagues at the service, Jacques Brunius and Pierre Lefèvre, confirmed the decision to conduct propaganda from London by declaring: 'I prefer to see the English in their country than the Germans in mine.'[16]*

Despite being labelled by Vichy as 'England's Servant', de Gaulle continued to broadcast on the BBC in an effort to raise morale in his homeland, cutting a powerful presence on his visits to Broadcasting House. One member of the service later recalled: 'I do not remember ever hearing him fluff his lines, and he was always courteous and found time to thank the recording engineer after he had finished.'[17] Newsome was also impressed by de Gaulle; in his memoirs he remembered how the tall, angular, haughty and deeply impressive general stalked into the studio, sat down and opened his broadcast with the typically arrogant declaration, *'Français c'est moi, le Général de Gaulle, qui vous parle'*.[18]**

*   Attributed to Jean Oberle.

**   'France this is me, General de Gaulle, speaking to you.'

Newsome frequently spent time in the company of de Gaulle away from the BBC and recognised in him a man who had no doubts as to his destiny as the liberator of France: 'He was not the type to inspire affection, but was a great source of intelligence that I could not always get from the British authorities.'[19] While some of the BBC French section tried to excuse the capitulation and armistice, de Gaulle believed it was 'not only a capitulation, but a submission to slavery that Frenchmen would not accept, either for reasons of honour, common sense and the highest interests of the country'. In the weeks following the French surrender it soon became clear that, although a large number of people had fled to the only country still holding out against Nazi aggression, others had stayed with a view to undermining the occupiers from within. Armed with this knowledge, de Gaulle was determined to assert whatever influence he possessed towards building up an effective resistance operation inside France. This would entail the creation of an active network of committed partisan units that would assist the future liberators at the designated hour. The general was driven by a deep anxiety that the French Army should be seen to play a credible part in the deliverance of France from her occupiers. He was particularly fearful of France becoming a breeding ground for left-wing radicals if the French forces were not in evidence, and with the BBC occasionally at his disposal, de Gaulle promoted a strong anti-collaborationist message through his broadcasts.

Despite an often-strained relationship that would become exacerbated by difficult decisions that lay ahead, Churchill was largely sympathetic to de Gaulle's position and aims. Newsome was also determined to lend whatever assistance he could to the general, and issued a directive to the French Service on 15 July urging announcers to make every attempt to instigate a spirit of resistance in France. In practice, the spirit of resistance and the creation of partisan units that de Gaulle coveted did not happen spontaneously. It took a significant amount of time for such groups, or 'circuits', to rise up from the demoralising effect of defeat. The perceived strength of the German forces alongside the comparative weakness of Britain in retreat offered little real incentive to potential French agents weighing up the risks of being associated with the resistance, and not until the war began to turn in favour of the Allies were sufficient numbers encouraged to join. For many people, their first act of resistance was to listen to BBC broadcasts that provided the inspiration for an underground movement in France to flourish steadily. André Philip, who later became Commissioner of Labour under de Gaulle, was acutely aware of the level of organisation and discipline that had to be internalised, which often proved problematical as potential resistance groups could not always agree politically or tactically among themselves. With the exception of communists who had experienced guerrilla warfare in Spain, very few Frenchmen had the necessary experience required for proactive resistance. Up until the German invasion of the Soviet Union in May 1941, communists had remained aloof to the 'capitalist struggle' and when they did finally become involved, resistance groups across France under the banner of Front Nationale began to flourish.[20]

Before the BBC could effectively begin assisting any resistance movements, awkward logistical problems would need to be overcome. The Allies' hasty abandonment of the struggle in northern France had allowed Hitler to organise his forces free from Allied scrutiny. The speed and scale of the Nazi invasion had caught the Special Intelligence Service under the command of Colonel Stewart Menzies on the back foot, and it was now confined to operating in neutral countries. It would help the BBC's propagandists immensely if Menzies could get intelligence-gathering agents out in the field. British organisation of clandestine operations inside France did not begin until 5 May 1941, when radio operator George Noble was parachuted into the Châteauroux area in central France. Within two days, Noble had formed his link with London and by mid-June had organised the equipment drop, although he had to wait in a field for two days, unaware that bad weather had delayed the operation. It was Noble who suggested using cryptic messaging on the BBC to notify circuits on the ground of impending operations; with the result that the system of *messages personnels* was born – a game changer in enabling the clandestine services to operate more efficiently.* The broadcasts might not have been propaganda per se, but each time the Germans heard these coded messages it meant another act of sabotage or worse was in the pipeline. By the end of 1941,

---

* Georges Begue at SOE has also been credited with proposing the use of the BBC to transmit coded messages.

the joint secret services of Britain and France had established twenty-nine intelligence agents in the field with twelve radios transmitting regular information back to London.[21] These sets proved to be a vital communications facility for intelligence gathering and for special operations planning. Clandestine broadcasting was more difficult in Vichy, where radio detection devices were able to identify foreign service broadcasts very easily and hunting them down was a major priority. Despite listening to BBC programmes being banned in Vichy from October 1940, people did listen and placed much value on the broadcasts, as one correspondent to the *Radio Times* commented:

> Tell the BBC how much they help us to keep our spirit high, and how pleased we all are when we can get them on the radio. Cheer up, and God bless you all. We are sure to win![22]

Difficult days still lay ahead for the French Service, with de Gaulle becoming increasingly frustrated over a perceived lack of support, refusing to believe that his followers amounted to a minority and that so many of his compatriots had chosen to side with Vichy. He also questioned why there was so much concern about the post-war political situation and a return to a democratically elected government, particularly as he viewed the democratically elected socialist regime of Leon Blum as responsible for his country's downfall. De Gaulle also suspected that the BBC was obstructing him, as the Free French were given only partial control of the French-language broadcasts, under the belief that 'they did not speak for everyone'. The Allied forces still viewed Vichy (who had condemned de Gaulle to death in his absence in August 1940) as being more representative of French opinion, believing they would eventually come onside. De Gaulle also had other problems; hardly anyone in France knew what he looked like. He was simply a voice and nothing else, and neither were the Frenchmen involved in the BBC service necessarily 'Gaullists', rather they were independent announcers subsidised by the BBC and unattached to the general. De Gaulle's only regular concession was a five-minute slot under the title of *Honneur et Patrie*, when, typically, a representative of the general Maurice Schumann would speak to the French people on his behalf. All further requests for 'free time' were refused.

If de Gaulle had been provided with all the available knowledge, his prickliness would have been difficult to understand, as reliable reports indicated that around a third of all French people were essentially 'Gaullists' on the basis that he was continuing the fight.[23] He also underestimated the devotion of French people to the BBC – now being referred to as Radio Londres. In a letter to the BBC, one listener wrote that he had surveyed the 150 households in his village to discover that 110 had wireless sets, and out of those 105 listened regularly to the BBC.[24] Before becoming an announcer for the BBC French Service, Franck Bauer was sent on missions in occupied France with the Free French forces, and remembered that the resistance only listened to BBC radio:

> It was in French but scrambled by the Germans and very hard to find just the right place to listen to it. When we'd finished we turned the button to another station, in case the Germans came in and looked. There were funny coded messages – the carrots are cooked; the fruits are not yet ripe ... Sometimes young people had told their families if they got to England they would transmit a message.[25]

Bauer quickly came to realise the importance of his role as an announcer. 'We were listened to by millions of people every night. So I presumed we were doing a pretty good job.' He remembered the slogan that he continually repeated on the BBC service to denounce the German propaganda stations: *'Radio Paris ment, Radio Paris est allemand.'* (Radio Paris is lying, Radio Paris is German). Announcers typically included popular French songs, poems and comedy in their broadcasts, which always began with a selection of personal messages.[26]

Meanwhile, de Gaulle was not alone in his frustration at the perceived lack of progress. He had a powerful ally at the BBC in Newsome, who complained to the MOI in October 1940 that 'the propaganda effort was being undermined by the vacillation and confused thinking of the Foreign Office'.[27] He had earlier been banned from broadcasting anything favourable towards de Gaulle following the failed assault on Dakar, and was then told to delete an announcement that the Vichy Government had gone over to the enemy – essentially the whole reason for de Gaulle's declaration of a newly constituted political authority.[28]

The MOI was of the opinion that the French were ultra-sensitive to any criticisms of the Vichy leader Pétain – affectionately referred to as 'The Lion of Verdun' – and requested that the BBC continue to be polite towards the marshal. Newsome agreed that to continually attack Pétain would widen the divisions between the French people, but any endorsement of Vichy over de Gaulle made broadcasts aimed at the oppressed peoples of Europe seem utterly pointless. Up until September 1940, the British Government had not been over-concerned with the BBC's anti-Vichy propaganda, which typically demeaned its puppet government as a servant of Germany. In a directive of 6 July, Assistant Editor Doug Ritchie had instructed the propagandists to 'treat Vichy as though it were Germany', and outlined the 'clear distinction between the handful of dotards, purblind idiots and traitors posing as the government of France and the French nation – our comrades in arms'.[29] The following day, Newsome also condemned the perpetrators who believed that 'at the stroke of a pen they could convert free and democratic France into a totalitarian slave state', and warned the French that Vichy was 'a prostitute of the Axis who would not even collect her fee'.[30]

In August 1940, multiple broadcasts were transmitted to France commending the heroics of the few during the Battle of Britain, and simultaneously playing up French participation in air raids over Germany. Later broadcasts praised the fortitude of Londoners in the face of repeated bombing raids, setting the city apart as a symbol of defiance. Britain was effectively showcasing herself as unconquered and resilient, and firmly committed to continuing the fight against Nazi Germany alone if need be. Among its most important broadcasts at this time was Churchill's stirring declaration (in his best French) of British solidarity with France, broadcast on 21 October 1940. A critical strategy of winning over the French was to foster the belief that things were being done in line with 'our shared interests' and not solely to execute British policy alone. French Service broadcasts had to be careful not to alienate a defeated ally, rather it sought to appear sympathetic to the position of a valued and respected friend and had no ambitions other than to see her liberated and restored to her former standing. As late as 14 July 1943, British Foreign Secretary Anthony Eden spoke on the French Service, re-advocating 'the restoration of

France to her full sovereignty and to her natural place among the great powers of the world'.[*]

In September 1940, *Ici la France* was rebranded as *Les Français Parlent aux Français* (*The French speak to the French*), to serve as a conduit for the broadcasting of commentaries on the progression of the war. The programme was regularly preceded by a five-minute slot entitled *Honneur et Patrie* (*Honour and Homeland*), intended to promote the political and tactical aims of de Gaulle's 'Fighting France' movement. *Les Français Parlent aux Français* would remain at the heart of the BBC's French Service for the next four years, and very soon extended right across southern Europe with the intention of reaching French prisoners of war. As the popularity of the service excelled, the wave of anti-British propaganda coming from Vichy and via Radio Paris was largely unsuccessful, as people generally desired a British victory largely on account of their hatred of the Germans, rather than any sense of affiliation or admiration towards Britain. As early as May 1941, the Germans had begun to accept the superiority of British propaganda to France and began confiscating radio sets across regions of northern France. Vichy had warned its citizens that 'British propaganda was more deadly than steel', to which the British countered 'deadlier than steel for the axis because truth is stronger than steel'.

The popularity of the BBC's broadcasts was confirmed by the amount of mail it received from occupied France; amazingly over 1,000 letters dating from June 1940 until the end of 1943 are stored in the BBC's Written Archives. There can be little doubt that there were sympathetic readers among the strict Vichy censorship departments who deliberately allowed letters to slip through; thereafter they would be processed by British military intelligence before reaching the microphones of the BBC. The corporation took every opportunity to broadcast positive letters it had received from French listeners, correspondence that the enemy typically dismissed as being faked. Of particular interest were letters reporting on the ambivalent attitude towards Pétain, as it allowed British intelligence to gauge

---

[*] Eden's promise was undermined in November 1943, when Jan Smuts, the South African Premier who had been co-opted to the British War Cabinet, gave a speech in which he predicted the post-war disappearance of France as a great power.

public opinion and the BBC to assess the impact of its propaganda. The level of incoming mail was further intensified in January 1941 with the introduction of the regular programme *Courrier de France* (*Letters from France*), which was broadcast on the French Service on Friday evenings until February 1943. The success of the programme led to German attempts in July 1941 to tighten the control of mail, although after the controls had been introduced some 195 letters still arrived at the European Service headquarters, confirming the failure of the initiative.* The service occasionally undertook more daring methods in its efforts to raise the morale in the occupied region, particularly so on May Day 1941 when the BBC aided a Gaullist attempt to appropriate the bank holiday in the city of Angers. An order was broadcast for people to make their way to the town hall at 6.30 p.m. in silence wearing tricolour ribbons or rosettes if they so wished. It was felt that eye contact alone would carry the message of mutual recognition and hope.[31]

In August 1941, the recently created Political Warfare Executive urged propagandists to emphasise the key fact that the goal of a 'Free France' depended upon Britain coming through victorious. This message was reinforced the following year when a directive of 12 July 1942 stressed that the French could only be expected to take an interest in British actions and affairs 'only in so far as these affect the liberation of France, and France's own future'. It was to be a tough baptism for the new BBC/ PWE alignment, where developments would push the bond of Anglo-French trust to the limit – such as British military action in regions of the French Empire, or the RAF's strategic bombing missions over French territory. The early struggles for influence over public opinion had focused largely on protecting the integrity of the French Empire. In response to Pétain's broadcast on Radio Vichy in October 1940 that collaboration with Germany would ensure 'French unity', the BBC responded that such collaboration would bring demands from Germany that would chip away at the 'intact French Empire'. The argument would surface again in May 1941, when Vichy allowed Germany to use airbases in the French mandate of Syria. This action presented the French Service with a valuable opportunity to refute enemy propaganda that

* Fifty-seven of the letters were from the occupied zone and 136 from Vichy. (Tangye-Lean, p.168)

had accused Britain of having designs on French territory, identifying Germany as the more serious threat to French overseas interests.

The aggressive tone of Vichy propaganda intensified further in May 1942 when Britain captured Vichy-controlled Madagascar to prevent it falling into the hands of the Japanese. Shortly afterwards, the BBC purposefully announced that Madagascar would remain French territory – effectively countering Radio Vichy's proclamation that British promises to restore Madagascar to France could not be relied upon in the light of historical precedents. Then in June 1942, a British-led Allied campaign in Syria introduced the sensitive issue of Britain fighting against French forces – effectively 'spilling French blood'. Vichy propaganda directed towards these issues largely failed owing to the tendency of French listeners to be more concerned with events happening closer to home. Forward information concerning planned bombing raids over France was a much more delicate affair, and BBC announcers had to stress the strategic importance of the action, and to justify its effects in terms of the destruction of the enemy's war machine. Where heavy casualties had occurred, the dead were portrayed as innocent victims of German decrees that compelled French citizens to work for the occupier. Enemy propaganda accusing Britain of bombing indiscriminately without regard for the consequences tended to be rejected by listeners, who viewed such action as the inevitable consequence of Germany's exploitation of French factories. The British Government took to broadcasting warnings through the French Service in an effort to keep casualty numbers as low as possible. French agents abroad reported just prior to D-Day that opinion had begun to turn against the Allies in some regions as the bombing raids intensified.

When the Allies landed in French North Africa in November 1942 at the beginning of Operation Torch, the response from Vichy was similarly scathing as it decried 'the occupation of our Africa by the Anglo-Saxons', and condemned 'the savage amputation of part of our Empire'.[32] Huge controversy between Britain and the Free French followed in Algiers when Vichy's Admiral Darlan, who was present when the Allies had landed – seemingly 'converted' to become head of French North Africa with Allied recognition. The Allies had effectively used the 'traitor' Darlan as an expedient to secure swift French co-operation in North Africa, much to the disgust of de Gaulle. Newsome remembered that the policy of recognising Darlan over de Gaulle 'caused eruptions' among the announcers on the French Service. Not only did it create huge difficulties for Bruce Lockhart at the PWE, it no doubt put a smile on the face of Dr Goebbels as de Gaulle's supporters declared they could no longer broadcast on the BBC as it would suggest acceptance of Darlan's position. Subsequently they staged a mass walkout on 3 December, and only returned following Darlan's assassination on 24 December, by which time German troops had occupied Vichy, effectively declaring Pétain and his puppet government redundant. Meanwhile, Jacques Duchesne, whose overwhelming enthusiasm underscored the success of *Les Français Parlent aux Français*, hung around with those that remained to produce his programme, which was then cut short to hear an assurance from President Roosevelt that relations with Darlan were merely 'a temporary expedient'.

With the service personnel back at the microphone, the BBC was the principal means by which Frenchmen could follow the progress of their fighting forces overseas. Transmitters in Algiers were weak in comparison, and the French had already acquired the habit of listening to the BBC. Other developments following the occupation of Vichy included the curtailment of the popular programme *Courrier de France*, after the enemy had ramped up efforts to prevent correspondence from reaching Britain. It was replaced with *Courrier d'Angleterre* (*Mail from Britain*) from 3 March 1943, featuring letters that reflected daily life in Britain and illuminated the friendship and ties between the two countries. To achieve a greater air of authenticity, the letters were typically written by BBC employees who had lived in France, although they adhered closely to PWE guidance. Another series of broadcasts that ran from March 1943 showcased the hard work being done by both the military and on the home front in the interests of the war effort. *Chronique d'Angleterre* (*News from Britain*), focused on such things as military exercises, the functions of the Home Guard and the Women's Land Army – simple self-promoting propaganda that could not be easily countered. It essentially provided French listeners with a positive illustration of Britain at war and a snapshot of English daily life. Morale in French homes was also further boosted when popular humourist M. Pierre Dac made his way to Britain across the Pyrenees in 1943 and gave great encouragement to French listeners with his broadcasts from London.

It was at this point in the war that the ever-evolving superiority of the Allies began to illuminate difficulties in the area of propaganda directed to those living under occupation. Broadcasts frequently stimulated morale by reporting convincing evidence of Germany's likely defeat, and news editors were told to be cautious and reserved as over-cooking a story could easily encourage over-sanguine hopes, impatience and danger of premature insurrection in certain countries. Newsome did not always agree with this line of constantly warning listeners against over-optimism:

> The high ups tended to want small reverses treated as calamities and to soft-pedal our successes. I always felt radio should be used to undermine the enemy's morale – not shore it up. Also to stimulate friends in occupied countries into active resistance, and not to encourage passive resignation.[33]

Newsome believed that radio propaganda had as much potential in determining the duration of the war as had the armed forces, and felt the government was being over-cautious. In its defence, the government recognised the potential of the BBC to encourage the co-operation of resistance movements with Allied forces of liberation, 'but only at what it believed to be the appropriate moment'. In 1943 the introduction of broadcasts directed towards editors of the clandestine press in Europe played a valuable role in keeping partisan elements informed, providing valuable, up-to-date information. It was reported that some clandestine newspapers reported instructions from the BBC word for word.[34] Jean Moulin, a representative of de Gaulle's Free French movement in London, was charged with unifying the resistance groups in readiness for the day of reckoning, which he succeeded in doing with the creation of the *Conseil National de la Résistance* in April 1943. Within two months, Moulin had been tortured and murdered by the Nazis, and the unified resistance faction he created suspended all immediate plans for guerrilla warfare, and persevered with its pre-invasion functions aided by the BBC under the guidance of the PWE. This included gathering intelligence, aiding escaped prisoners and stranded air crew, facilitating 'black' propaganda and sabotage.

In all its propaganda operations directed to occupied Europe, the BBC had achieved varying degrees of success. Aside from being 'the voice of hope' in countries such as the Netherlands, where the occupation had been exceptionally brutal, in France the corporation had succeeded in helping to bring people onside with the man who would become the figurehead of French liberation in the person of Charles de Gaulle. With regard to the assistance given to aiding and empowering resistance units, post-war tributes echoed the statement made three years earlier by the Interior Minister for the Free French, André Philip, who had spoken to a newspaper correspondent after arriving in Britain from France in 1942:

> If we have resistance in France it is because of the BBC. Its influence has been tremendous, possibly one of the greatest influences in French history.[35]

In December 1944, after their country had been liberated, the people of France wrote around 4,000 letters to the BBC in praise of its wartime service. The corporation also received a visit from the director general of the French radio network Radiodiffusion Français, who also paid a glowing tribute:

> The whole of France was dependent on the transmissions of the BBC. The enormous majority got from them their faith, their hope, and the certainty of victory. The salvation of an entire people is the most sensational of exploits that radio has to its credit.[36]

In its attempts at delivering propaganda to enemy countries, the BBC would require an even stronger measure of support from the highest levels of government if its strategy was to achieve a similar level of success. Regrettably, it was an operation that would be largely stifled by, among other difficulties, a high level of government obstinacy that limited its chances of success considerably.

11

BROADCASTING TO THE ENEMY

Among the German diplomats in London in the late 1930s was Count Albrecht Bernstorff, a former worker of the German Embassy and outspoken critic of the Nazi regime. Bernstorff had resigned his diplomatic post in disgust at the direction his country was heading and taken a banking job in Berlin that enabled him to visit London regularly. He came armed with a mine of information for his old friends in the UK capital, one of whom was the future director general of the Political Warfare Executive, Bruce Lockhart. On one such visit in December 1938, following a long diatribe on the likely course of Hitler's future intentions, Bernstorff afforded Lockhart one sound piece of advice: 'Tell your Government to increase your broadcasts in German!' before making it known that during the Munich Crisis nearly all Germans, including the leading generals, listened in to the BBC's German bulletins. Bernstorff was eventually taken to a concentration camp, where he was later executed, leaving Lockhart full of admiration for his friend's cast-iron courage. Bernstorff's advice no doubt found its way to the BBC, where broadcasts to Germany would become the corporation's biggest propaganda operation on its European Service, with combined broadcasts to Axis countries in Europe amounting to almost eight hours a day.

At the start of the war, the BBC's German section did not exist as a permanent entity, and still had to be properly established in its basic structure. The pre-war fledgling service consisted of a few German announcers, translators and British editors and commentators who were preparing news and talks in shifts in the 'German Room' at Broadcasting House. There was no programme unit as such, and they received most of their information for broadcasts from the enemy propaganda unit at Electra House. Newsome took a particular interest in the service when he arrived, with an insistence that, more than any other station, it was essential that news was always 'precise and accurate, before resorting to amusing exposures of Nazi ineptness'.[1] He also believed that the psychological war should emphasise the themes of German consciousness of guilt and past defeats, and playing up the strength the United Kingdom derived from its own tradition of victory. It was a sound platform to begin upon, for any deviations from the truth would leave the service vulnerable to any number of eavesdroppers, including Dr Goebbels' radio monitors who were known to be cross-listening to the BBC's European broadcasts, always on the lookout for inconsistencies. For this reason, Newsome impressed upon his staff that 'they were fighting just as much as anyone in the armed forces, and that for them the battle was very much on'.[2] On rare occasions when the mantle slipped, and the service broadcast misleading information that was likely to damage the credibility of the service, Newsome did not hold back in apportioning blame directly to the War Office.

The task of directing propaganda into the heart of the enemy was also a challenging one for an abundance of reasons. Not only was enemy-directed radio propaganda still a novel and untried process, there were also difficulties owing to the technical limitations of the receivers and the typical German radio set. Added to this was the fact that the outright banning of opposition to the Nazi regime had fostered a mood of apathy among a large proportion of Germans, and a general distaste towards a medium that already dripped with propaganda.

Early efforts to connect with German listeners were also hindered by constant anti-German rhetoric emanating from the Permanent Under-Secretary for Foreign Affairs, Sir Robert Vansittart, whose mostly inaccurate claims were being repeatedly ridiculed on the Nazi propaganda transmissions. Vansittart promoted a view of Germans as 'a race of bone-headed aggressors', 80 per cent of which were 'the moral and political scum of the earth who had to be hamstrung and broken'.[3] Worse was to follow when Vansittart began a series of broadcasts on the BBC Home Service at the height of the Blitz called *Black Record*, comparing Nazi Germany with the antics of the butcher bird gobbling up his naively unsuspecting neighbours. His favourite themes included

'German envy of Britain's empire', 'the lust for world domination that has been stirring inside them for generations', and condemning its 'formerly penniless leaders as having grown fat on political plunder'. Such wild generalisations created difficulties for the service, particularly when he openly condemned 'the brazen horde' of some 80 million Germans that needed to be 'policed for a minimum of a generation' – effectively using the Nazis' own methods to keep them subdued. In Britain people bought into Vansittart's theories – a published version was made into a talking book for the blind – while George Orwell noted that Vansittart's 'Hate Germany' pamphlet was 'selling like hot cakes'.[4] Fortunately for the German Service, Vansittart's ill-informed judgements were easily disproved by Jewish refugee Heinrich Fraenkel, who published an immediate reply bearing the title *Vansittart's Gift for Goebbels*. Fraenkel's repost was prefaced by Ernest Bevin's May Day speech offering a message of kinship and support to the German workers, and thereafter effectively utilised bare facts to address the controversy caused by the seven broadcasts. At the core of Vansittart's argument was an assumption that, aside from a few well-meaning individuals, Hitler had the entire German people behind him – a theory that was easily disproved with reference to what happened in the elections of November 1932:

> The Nazi Party was rapidly declining. It had been overblown with millions of malcontents – victims of the slump – lured in by desperation, rather than Hitler's glib tongue and splendid showmanship. Yet after the landslide of the November election the party was broke to the wide, and in what looked like a hopeless situation. Hitler moodily threatened suicide – a few weeks later he was in power. How had it happened? Goebbels grandly calls it the 'Socialist Revolution' – it was nothing of the kind. It was just a bargain with big business and the Junkers – strong in money, power and influence.[5]

Fraenkel's key point was that it was big business, rather than the people, who had smoothed Hitler's path to the Chancellorship at the head of a coalition government (in which the Nazis held only three of the twelve seats). Thereafter he squeezed out his opponents and replaced them with his own henchmen prior to enacting a reign of terror – before

Hindenburg's death, combined with a little faking of his 'last will and testament' by Goebbels, confirmed him as Führer.[6] Fraenkel also provided figures that proved Hitler had only commanded 50 per cent of the electorate, an indication that there were millions of potential dissenters inside Germany who might defy him if they could be reached.* This was an encouraging revelation for the propagandists at the BBC's German Service.

Before attempting to reach those potential 'dissenters', the German Service propagandists had to overcome yet another awkward problem often referred to as the dilemma of the two Germanys. Up until the spring of 1941, neither the government, the BBC nor the public could agree on whether a measure of separation existed between the Nazis and a large section of the German people, many of whom might want to free themselves from the yoke of Nazism.** Many people believed that, rather than fighting against the German people, Britain was fighting a new brand of Fascist ideology, and on that basis propaganda to Germany should seek to further split public opinion and to support efforts to challenge and overthrow the regime. Chamberlain still believed right up until the day before war was declared that he could forestall Hitler by broadcasting 'an appeal to the German people' on the German Service on 2 September.[7] Having failed to urge the 'good' German people to 'arise and prevent the Führer from besmirching the good name of the Reich', the Foreign Office continued to dissuade the German Service from parodying or caricaturising Hitler for comedy purposes for fear of driving the less hostile element towards supporting him.

The service complied with the directive until April Fool's Day of 1940, when they aired a spoof parody of Hitler by Martin Miller called *Der Führer Spricht*. Robert Crossman, the head of the German section at Department EH, had seen the four-and-a-half-minute production at the Austrian Exile Theatre and arranged for Miller to reproduce the show for radio. Miller had effectively captured the Führer's vocabulary,

---

*   These were the semi-constitutional elections of 5 March 1933, five weeks after Hitler's appointment as Reich Chancellor.

** In February 1941 George Orwell reported 'there is still a division of opinion over whether we are fighting the Nazis, or the German People'. Davison (2009), pp.291–2

intonations and rhythm very effectively in the production, in which he announces his intention to subjugate the United States to the German Reich. By applying his typical measure of warped logic, the Führer demands that the USA must become a German protectorate, and thereafter his ambitious plans include reinventing the New York skyline, removing the Statue of Liberty to alleviate traffic congestion and renaming the White House 'the Brown House'. *Der Führer Spricht* was viewed as a somewhat defiant venture, for not until June 1940, when Britain faced its gravest moment of crisis, was the distinction between the 'two Germanys' finally abandoned. Thereafter, to ensure that German listeners could not consider themselves among the victims of Hitler's aggression, the BBC was asked to refrain from using the word 'Nazi' in its future German-language output.* Meanwhile, Crossman concluded that the show had been a successful venture, and thereafter commissioned a whole series of Hitler speech parodies from Miller that were broadcast on the BBC German Service between 1940 and 1942.[8]

Ivone Kirkpatrick, who would become controller of the European Service following the major reorganisation in the autumn of 1941, had departed Berlin and relocated to the Foreign Office at the start of the war. Curious to know how Chamberlain's Department of Propaganda into Enemy Countries' operation at Woburn was progressing, he seized an opportunity to pay a visit, and was unimpressed by what he saw. 'The staff were keen and doing their best, but they were hopelessly handicapped by a number of factors.' Kirkpatrick witnessed a unit that was out of touch with its government owing to their physical separation, and also discovered that very few people in the organisation had any first-hand knowledge of Nazi Germany. There was little regard for the potential within radio propaganda, while 'the great bulk of their work was producing leaflets that only reached a small proportion of Germans'.[9]

When Churchill became prime minister in May 1940, his arrival did not make it any easier for the propagandists to win over the citizens inside Axis countries, nor to trigger any form of popular rising against the war.

---

* The Soviets also subscribed to the theory of the two Germanys following Barbarossa, and called on the German people to unite against the common enemy. Their logic indicates a belief that the people ceased to be Germans the moment they put on a uniform.

By the end of 1940 the corporation was still out of favour with Churchill; during a Cabinet meeting in November he had described the BBC as 'the enemy within the gates', and the new prime minister was firmly against their demands for the formulation of a war aims policy. Churchill's insistence that the military position did not justify launching 'ambitious schemes for post-war settlements' made it difficult for the European Service to sketch out any credible alternative to Hitler's rule, nor were they able to emphasise any social or economic reconstruction plans. This was despite an official memorandum of December 1939 stating that 'there can be no useful propaganda without a clear policy, no clear policy without defined purpose'.[10] Churchill believed that to voice an aim for any 'fair deal for our enemies' at this stage would be resented by the British public, and informed the BBC their time would be better spent countering German economic and financial propaganda. He suggested to BBC bosses that the economist John Maynard Keynes be asked to broadcast a rebuttal before Roosevelt could seize the initiative in his inauguration speech due in January 1941.[11]

In October 1940, Hugh Carleton Greene, the future director general, took charge of the BBC's German Service, and despite throwing himself into the role with regular daily meetings of staff, he could offer little to tempt enemy subjects beyond the promise of self-determination as enshrined in the Atlantic Charter. Later in the war when Churchill and Roosevelt agreed on a policy of 'unconditional surrender' at the Casablanca Conference in January 1943, the scope for political warfare against Germany was further disabled, as no encouragement for the overthrow of Nazism could be offered to any alternative political group inside Germany. This meant that during the final two years of war the BBC had no distinctive propaganda policy towards Germany beyond attempts to demoralise enemy forces and subjects alike. The service propagandists could only warn the opponent that war criminals would be punished, but that no collective revenge would be taken against those who withdrew their support for the regime.

When Kirkpatrick formally began his association with the BBC in 1941, his principal role involved getting propaganda policy agreed with various government departments. For the German section he was a useful man to have around given his years in Berlin as First Secretary at the British Embassy, where German colleagues had not been shy of providing him with information on 'Hitler's way of life' at the Berghof. In April 1942 Kirkpatrick was able to incorporate this information into a broadcast for the service, following a claim Hitler had made in the Reichstag about having not had three days' leave since 1933:

> I have paid two visits to Berchtesgaden and I must say I envy Hitler his holidays at the Berghof. Breakfast in bed in a bedroom overlooking Salzburg and the Alps. Later in the morning Hitler appears in a Tyrolese costume or a country suit. If the weather is fine there is a walk on the mountain-side. Dietrich, the Press Chief, is ready at hand with the latest press news, diplomatic telegrams, military reports and so on. But the sun is shining and the Fuhrer has no time for politics. Dietrich is told to go away. Lunch is in the dining-room on the first floor, in a little bow window overlooking the valley. Alpine flowers are on the table. Three waiters in SS uniform are in attendance. After lunch chocolate and cakes in the large sitting room downstairs. In the afternoon, tea on the terrace under a gay umbrella.[12]

And so on; Kirkpatrick continues his recollections of Hitler's serene and idyllic existence that sometimes lasted for weeks. It was blinding propaganda that would have stuck deep in the throat of every German workman, who would 'gladly give up his leave for a few days' rest in the enchanting atmosphere of Berchtesgaden'.

The rising popularity of the BBC's German Service became a growing source of agitation for Goebbels and his Propaganda Ministry; special wardens were employed to go from house to house to detect BBC broadcasts. In one report a small town of 25,000 inhabitants was mentioned in which there had been no fewer than 200 denunciations of persons for listening in; eight who had dared to listen publicly in a restaurant were also prosecuted. Offenders were shamed in the local press as having subjected themselves to 'spiritual self-mutilation' and classified as 'traitors, saboteurs and fornicators'.[13] Press extracts of men condemned to penal servitude or even death for listening to the BBC were gathered as evidence of how widely the BBC's broadcasts were being heard. Goebbels' ministry estimated that around a million people were listening, although such estimates were treated with scepticism as most people were too reluctant to talk about it.

Even children had been taught by the party that it was their duty to inform on listeners.

Goebbels was also worried about the *Forces Programme* on the German Service that began in January 1941, and was later discovered to have been listened to prolifically among the German Army. It was the 'Letters Home' section that concerned him the most, mindful of the demoralising effect that these could have on soldiers after the events of the last war. Following a heavy air raid he was known to have cut the post from an entire district to prevent this scenario from being repeated. Alongside the *Forces Programme*, the service began broadcasting the *Navy Programme* from November, intended to promote the overwhelming strength of British sea power for the ears of the German Admiralty.

Shortly after being appointed European Service controller in August 1941, Kirkpatrick set about dividing the now independent service into regional organisations. German News Editor Hugh Carleton Greene became German regional editor and took charge of the whole of the German output, including news. In compiling the programmes, the BBC frequently made use of German exiles, provided they spoke English well and proved able to translate quickly and accurately. It was an unlikely alliance, although leading scriptwriter Robert Lucas suspected that he and his fellow exiles were forever being regarded with suspicion.[14] The corporation was careful not to give the impression that it was running a service for refugees with their own agenda, and so the aim was to leave German listeners with the clear understanding they were listening to what was described as 'the sincere expression of an English point of view'. Service staff were also explicitly warned from the beginning that the broadcasts had to sound 'as English as Yorkshire Pudding'.[15]

Because of the dangers posed to listeners, announcers were trained to be brief, and to say only the most important things, and programmes seldom lasted more than seven or eight minutes for the same purpose. Above all, it was important to address the target as though he or she was just a fellow human being, rather than a Nazi, as in the dark confines of the listening place, he or she was free from the hypnotic Nazi propaganda and as such a human being again. Carl Brinitzer, one of the translator/announcers in the BBC German Service, invented a new broadcasting technique that aimed to increase comprehension by paring down sentences to bare essentials, mainly because listeners in Germany often had to decrease the volume of radios to barely audible levels. Brinitzer believed that content delivery was the critical ingredient, even if it meant that information was packaged into prose that defied syntactic conventions.[16]

The German Service began at five o'clock in the morning with the twice-weekly *Workers' Programme* presented by Patrick Gordon Walker, aided by two German socialists. Timed to coincide with the shift changeover, it regularly championed the devotion of Britain's labour organisations towards victory, presenting a faithful picture of English workers and the Labour Movement. Frequent reference was made to the new social order for Britain outlined in the Beveridge Plan of December 1942. There was much criticism of National Socialism and its claim to have brought greater prosperity and better working conditions to the workers. In *Voices in the Darkness*, Edward Tangye-Lean provides a reproduction of a broadcast delivered in January 1941, less than a fortnight after Hitler had promised to deliver a quick victory:

> Goebbels and Hitler tell you that a British victory would mean the destruction of the German People. If that were true you would go on fighting to the last man. But is it? Remember you are not fighting a small clique of international financiers but free people. It is not the City of London but the millions of members of the British Trade Unions and the Labour Movement who are the deadly enemies of Nazi Germany, and our Labour leaders are collaborating with the Churchill government. When we win, peace terms will be made only with our consent. We want not the destruction of Germany but a world in which the German and British peoples work together as friends.

The overriding message of the remainder of the broadcast was that the longer the war lasted, the more difficult it would become to achieve a just peace. The service aimed to persuade the German workers to take an active line in the face of inevitable defeat. The choice was peace now or justice later.

The most important programme on the German Service was the news bulletins. From 1941 the hourly reports were followed by analysis given by the German section commentators Lindley Fraser, Hugh

Carleton Greene, Richard Crossman and Sefton Delmer. There was a strict separation between the news, which had to be scrupulously objective, and the commentaries that allowed the government view to be aired via the commentator. The propaganda element that typically mirrored the government line was invested in the latter, which meant the commentators were required to confer regularly with the relevant government departments. Lindley Fraser, who by the spring of 1941 was talking to Germany two or three times a week, focused on the meaning and consequences of even the most minor of Allied successes. The announcers knew the Germans were listening because their own broadcasts were filled with counter-answers to the BBC broadcasts. It wasn't only about convincing the German listeners that they were being 'systematically misled by their Nazi overlords', it was as much about telling them what the British were really like and what they stood for.

The news bulletins were particularly well received in POW camps, where Captain Harry Roberts of the REME Corps remembered news being 'given out on a room-by-room basis by a member of the wireless team under very strict security arrangements'. Roberts remembers the Germans continually holding snap searches to try to discover the illicit radio, and, having failed, took to severing the electricity supply during news broadcasts.[17]

German listeners occasionally enquired about the absence of commentary broadcasts by the great German intellectuals from among the exiles. Despite such requests, well-known critics of the Nazi regime, whether on political or racial grounds, were typically prevented from addressing Germans on the BBC service, a policy that was deemed essential for upholding the corporation's commitment to objective truth. External artists were able to script and translate news and features, but were only occasionally allowed to broadcast in features or as newsreaders. It was deemed essential that all commentaries had to be spoken by British voices, although the BBC did sometimes make exceptions.[18] Among the intellectuals who were given a voice over the airwaves was the celebrated novelist Thomas Mann, who emigrated to the United States following the Nazi invasion of Czechoslovakia in March 1939. Mann began broadcasting an anti-Nazi feature called *Deutsche Hörer* (*Listen Germany*) on the service from October 1940. The programmes were between five and eight minutes long, and his message was simple: 'With Hitler there will never be peace – he is incapable of peace.' Two main themes dominated Mann's broadcasts – responsibility for prolonging the war, and the fate of Germans afterwards: 'Only if you free yourselves, can you have the right to share in the approaching freedom of a new world order.' Early on, it was difficult for Mann to get his message across when news of victories 'rain down on you as the fire-bombs of your monstrous rulers rain on London'. As the war turned in favour of the Allies, Mann was able to give extracts, interspersed with the chronology of what actually happened, giving extra credence to his prophetic realism. Works of the great German poets – Matthias, Holderlin, Schiller and Goethe – who had been discredited by the Nazis and would have aligned themselves with Mann, were read out to give an authority to cultural programmes that would otherwise have been difficult to attain.[*]

Mann's eldest daughter, Erica, was also involved with foreign-language broadcasting initiatives on both sides of the Atlantic. As a well-known actress, writer, and political activist who opposed Hitler, she delivered broadcasts directed to potential audiences in both enemy-occupied territories and Nazi Germany. In 1942, she assisted the Roosevelt administration in setting up its own German-language broadcasts, after it had been discovered that soldiers were being targeted by two American women recruited by enemy propagandists to demoralise GIs in all manner of ways. This included casting doubts on the likely success of their missions and implicating their wives and girlfriends 'running about with men unfit for military service'. Mildred Gillars from Ohio and Rita Zukka from New York broadcast regularly between 1942 and 1945 from Berlin and Rome respectively; unfortunately for Goebbels and his treacherous recruits, most GIs found humour in these desperate women and invented nicknames for them including 'Berlin Bitch', 'Berlin Babe' and finally 'Axis Sally' – the name that stuck for all eternity. Meanwhile, between autumn 1940 and early 1943, Erica Mann addressed listeners in Germany and Austria on seventeen occasions, highlighting 'the bad, evil and hopeless cause for which they were fighting that the rest of humanity would never permit to prevail'. Listeners were warned

---

[*] German Radio denied this and claimed that Goethe would have been piloting a Stuka. (Tangye-Lean, p.75)

not to underestimate the Allies' determination to fight it out to the end, regardless of whatever sacrifices it would take, and that it was in their hands to shorten the disaster by making an end to it themselves. The Nazis deemed that Mann's broadcasts were important enough to warrant a rebuttal in *Der Völkische Beobachter*.* Even Lord Haw-Haw did her the honour of responding to her broadcasts after she had described the German people as 'behaving like comatose rabbits'.[19]

Another heavily contested debate arose within the German Service over the question of whether the German viewpoint could be converted through the medium of satire. Cracking war-related jokes at home had been a very successful strategy for raising home-front morale, leading scriptwriters to wonder whether German citizens could be won over to English humour in the same way and, importantly, would they risk life and limb hidden under a blanket with a primitive radio set to listen to satire? Austrian exile Robert Lucas, who joined the BBC as a scriptwriter in 1940, certainly thought so, and set about writing his first comedy contribution titled *Die Brief des Gefreiten Adolf Hirnschal* (*Letters from Private Adolf Hirnschal*). The programme featured fictitious letters written by a soldier on the front line to his wife that he reads to a comrade prior to mailing. Hirnschal is depicted as the obedient Nazi who admires his Führer, and yet his rhetoric somehow exposes and ridicules the theories and proclamations of the Nazi hierarchy. During the course of his writings, he comes to recognise his own shallowness and naivety at 'jumping for joy' at the news he was being sent to the Eastern Front to fight against a nation whose previous alliance with Germany had been described by his Führer as 'irrevocable and irreversible'. Lucas's scripts were very effective at exposing the unashamed hypocrisy within National Socialism.

Another contributor who believed in the power of satirical propaganda to influence opinion among Germans was the German-Jewish writer and art historian Bruno Adler. Having fled from Nazi persecution in 1936, Adler scripted programmes of just a few minutes' duration aimed at the plain citizens of Germany struggling to overcome the rigours of war. One Adler creation incorporated into the German Service broadcasts was written specifically for the *Frauen-Sendung* (*Women's Programme*).

---

* *The Nationalist Observer.*

For German women, explanations for the severe shortages of just about everything were difficult to attain when there was a complete news blackout on the British blockade. Aware of this, Adler came up with a character in the shape of a Berlin housewife called Frau Wernicke (played by Annemarie Haase) who inadvertently uses straightforward common sense to expose the contradictions in National Socialist arguments to the point of absurdity, and rarely uses a phrase that does not incorporate a tone of subversive cynicism. Her monologue typically referred to wartime problems such as food shortages and the endless bombing raids that blighted her everyday life. Whatever enthusiasm she derived from life under Nazi rule is dampened by her answers to her own questions – her tradesman husband was forced to close his business and her daughter's ambitions were stifled through being forced into another year of state labour. Evidence later emerged that suggested *Frau Wernicke* evolved into one of the most popular programmes among Germans tuning into the service. Another programme that went out in a similar vein was *Aus der Freien Welt* (*From the Free World*), which exposed further difficulties of life under National Socialism and its effect on German culture, in particular the arts. Banned jazz records were played in addition to works by German composers who had fled the country.

Bruce Adler later teamed up with Norman Cameron to compose another satirical series called *Kurt and Willi*. This consisted of a dialogue between two friends who would meet up in a Berlin café regularly to discuss current events and everyday life in Berlin. Kurt Kruger is a somewhat naive schoolmaster, while Willi Schimanski works in the German Ministry of Propaganda. Willi cynically exhorts the dishonest rhetoric of the highly skilled propagandist; however, in response to Kurt's stolid belief in the proclamations of Nazi propaganda, he subtly exposes the hidden absurdities, to the immense disappointment of his friend. The fact that the satire was based on secret intelligence material gave a level of credibility to Willi that even impressed Goebbels.

European Service Director Noel Newsome was not a fan of employing satire for enemy propaganda purposes. Aside from a fear that the humour might not translate very well, he was doubtful about whether it was a worthwhile exercise when programme time was limited. 'If *Kurt and Willi* was genuinely funny it could only have served the lamentable purpose of easing the tension in Germany, just as, for instance, wisecracks about doodle bugs reduce tension here about robot bombs.' On the other hand, if it was not funny Newsome believed it to be a complete waste of precious broadcasting time. Lucas remained adamant that the programmes had been worthwhile and a clutch of thank-you letters received after the war appear to support his view. In other letters, former listeners stated that the satirical content on the BBC's German Service had 'saved me from suicide' or 'given me the moral strength not to become compliant'.[20] It seems that, as in the case of BBC Variety's own subtly 'propagandistic' comedies such as *ITMA*, humour directed towards the German people had similarly made the unbearable bearable.

Another source of conflict between the BBC and the PWE arose out of a scheme hatched in 1941 to transmit propaganda on enemy-controlled wavelengths. The plan, which had the backing of the prime minister, involved the purchase of a huge 500kW transmitter called Aspidistra from RCA in the United States. Under the current laws, the transmitter could not be used legally in the United States, and so it was purchased by the British Government at a cost of £111,801 4s 10d. The transmitter survived the journey through U-boat-infested waters, and a hole 50ft deep was excavated in the Ashdown Forest, near Crowborough in Sussex, to install the device. The mast wasn't so lucky and had to be rebuilt after the ship carrying the original had been torpedoed. Originally intended to be commissioned under the control of Department EH, rather than the BBC, Aspidistra was one of the most powerful broadcasting instruments in the world. By the time it was installed, Department EH had merged with other units prior to the formation of the PWE, who had no immediate use for the transmitter, and the BBC was therefore given temporary access to it.

The great advantage of Aspidistra was its dual ability to reach into the heart of Germany and to change frequencies almost instantaneously. This enabled it to cut in on enemy broadcasts that had been silenced during Allied bombing raids, allowing it to transmit demoralising news into the original programme. The clarity of broadcast in these 'intrusion operations' confused the Germans, who were convinced it was coming from a local source. Aspidistra also enabled announcers to impersonate ground control to sow disruption and confusion with the aim of steering fighter aircraft away from bombing raids. Originally there had been no concrete plan to utilise the facility for 'black' transmissions, until Sefton Delmer at the PWE finally acquired it for his purposes. Delmer, who had previously created the station *Deutscher Kurzwellensender Atlantik* transmitting 'black' propaganda into Germany with limited success, utilised the transmitter to set up a fake station for German soldiers called *Soldatensender Calais*, which began broadcasting in October 1943. The programme mainly consisted of banned jazz music interspersed with commentaries attacking the Nazi hierarchy and morale-sapping news items compiled to unsettle the listener.

While the various departments were haggling over the use of Aspidistra, MPs in Parliament were becoming concerned about the secrecy of the BBC's enemy-directed propaganda operation, and in February 1942 they accused the MOI of having lost control of what was being said across the airwaves. Their chief complaint was that they had scarce input and very little knowledge about what was being broadcast:

> We have the ludicrous situation at present that we are not given proper facilities for knowing what is being said in our name and in the name of our country on the wireless to our deadly enemies in a moment of deadly peril.
>
> The real truth is that this is being made a sort of little secret business for a lot of little secret experts, who are not experts at all, and it is high time that the winds of criticism blew roughly through the whole thing.[21]

Other criticisms accused the service propagandists of having a tremendous belief in starting a revolution in Germany, without any fixed idea about what the nature of the revolution would be. Others complained about the propaganda talks as being 'leftish in character', under an assumption that it was a war of 'the Working Class against Fascism', or a war 'for or against Socialism'.[22] These complaints would not have gone down well with regional editors who were responsible for enemy propaganda, and the MOI poured cold water on the rebuke, insisting that the BBC's policy of total honesty in reporting, in particular its openness in admitting defeats and not crowing over victories, stood the service in good stead for all of its enemy-directed propaganda. As the war began to turn in favour of the Allies, this strategy paid off as more Germans began tuning in to the BBC service to hear accurate news, despite the severity of the penalties and constant jamming of the frequencies. Previously, German propaganda had thrived on the basis of military might and invincibility, before deadlock and the ultimate defeat at Stalingrad triggered a change in the tone of the broadcasts. Reports that previously focused on the offensive were now centring on the defensive – issuing denials and rebuttals – as not only had the Nazis lost the battle at Stalingrad, they had also lost the propaganda initiative. Of the 91,000 German prisoners taken, few would be heard of again for some considerable time. German prisoners in Britain fared better thanks to the BBC's German Service, where programmes would feature the names of German POWs; and from 1943, a quarter of an hour each night was spent relaying messages recorded by them to their families. On one occasion a family in Germany arranged a Requiem Mass for a soldier who was believed to have been killed. When they heard over the BBC that he was still alive, their first thought was to cancel it, until they realised this would let the authorities know they had been listening to illegal broadcasts. The family went ahead with the service, only to discover there were no mourners present at the church, they having heard the original broadcast themselves.

Gradually, as the prospects for an Allied victory became more certain, the BBC was easily able to exploit exaggerations and deficiencies in German propaganda. A weekly programme, *Sefton Delmer antwortet Hans Fritzsche*, was aired shortly after German propagandist Fritzsche had spoken on the German home service, and Delmer was able to refute his claims with irony and sarcasm. Another regular series, *Hitler versus Hitler*, exposed the failure of the Nazi regime better than most. The BBC possessed an impressive catalogue of speeches by Nazi leaders, and was easily able to illuminate contradictions and broken promises by using extracts from Hitler's own speeches.

By the spring of 1943, broadcasts to both the German and the French services were relegated down the ladder of importance when the main thrust of the European propaganda broadcasts was directed against the Italians in a determined effort to accelerate their elimination from the war. Disaster in Tunisia, and the likelihood of Nazi invasion, made ordinary Italians want to get out of the war as soon as possible, and it was here that Newsome saw an opportunity to make a significant difference.

However, broadcasting to Italians presented other difficulties, for although they had accepted the Nazi brand of fascism, they were also tied down by the Gestapo, and little progress would be made by ridiculing them as the press had done. Radio had gained in popularity in Italy more than in any other country, with 2 million additional sets registered between December 1939 and May 1940. Over 70 per cent of them were able to receive short-wave transmissions.[23]

There was little co-ordination between Italian and German radio, as each typically broadcast conflicting accounts of the same incident. Penalties for listening to the BBC were less severe, except among the younger element, who were expected to become 'good fascists'. Others were ordered to hand in their radio sets, only to get them back rendered incapable of receiving anything other than a local transmission. Colonel Harold Stevens, widely referred to in Italy as *Il Colonello Buonasera* (Colonel Good-Evening), was the lead propagandist on the Italian Service Radio Londra. Born of an Italian mother, Stevens spoke fluent Italian, and became a very popular figure throughout Italy through an ability to speak persuasively, as he openly deplored the disastrous situation in which his country had placed itself. Many of his broadcasts were news commentaries relayed in a casual and friendly manner, and never moved away from the assertion that the Italians themselves were responsible for their plight on account of their tolerance of the Nazi regime. Now they were being 'badly used' and it was emphasised that nothing would save them from the wrath of the Royal Navy if they continued the struggle. Italy had been 'severed by her rulers from her true friends and made to fight against the civilisation of which she belongs'.[24] Stevens implored them to understand that the occupation, their economic hardships and acute shortages were the fault of one man only, Benito Mussolini. For Edward Tangye-Lean at the BBC, the essence of Colonel Stevens' success was that 'he challenged the Italian tendency to tolerate the war with fatalistic jokes'.

By 1943, things had changed in the shape of promises of support from British and American armies staring out towards southern Italy from the north coast of Africa. The Italians were particularly receptive to BBC broadcasts by that time, as a large number were already convinced that Germany would ultimately be defeated. The Italian Service not only built on such defeatist talk, but did all in its power to convince the Italians that 'Italy had already lost the war'. Listeners were told that Germany would not make an all-out stand in defence of its Axis partner, but merely use her as a battlefield for a fighting retreat to the inner fortress of Europe. Additionally, there was much discussion at the War Office over how best to handle the strength of propaganda directed towards Italians prior to the invasion of Sicily.[*] A memorandum from Secretary of State for Foreign Affairs Anthony Eden in May 1943 suggested that a change from hard to soft propaganda be made at once, rather than immediately prior to the assault. This was rejected by the War Cabinet on the grounds that the object of the propaganda should be 'to weaken the resistance of the Garrison in Sicily, and the best way being through the families of the soldiers' – an opinion shared by SOE.[25][**] Propaganda to Italy was something that both Churchill and President Roosevelt also felt strongly about; a telegram issued from Washington to the Joint Chiefs of Staff on 24 May outlined the position:

> We cannot tell the Italians that if they cease hostilities, they can have 'peace with honour'. We cannot get away from unconditional surrender. Tell them they will be treated by Britain and the United States of America with humanity, and that the Italian people will be constituted into a nation in accordance with the principles of self-determination. The latter would not include any form of Fascism or Dictatorship.[26]

The success of the radio campaign became apparent when the Allies landed in Sicily on 9 July, where troops were received as liberators (rather than invaders) with flowers and demonstrations of enthusiasm. In one Sicilian town, Allied troops were surprised to discover the words 'Viva Stevens' scrawled on the walls. Another notable success for the Italian Service was revelations of strikes in Fiat factories just prior to Mussolini being overthrown on 23 July 1943. Following his fall and the capitulation of Italy, the BBC rejoiced in the success of its contribution, and thereafter the service exploited it to the full against Germany as a sign of the incipient break-up of the entire Nazi-Fascist system.

---

[*] Operation Husky.

[**] Minister for Labour Ernest Bevin spoke of the advantage of having a ready supply of radio sets for issuing to civil populations 'as we drive out the enemy'.

Allied armies supported by the propagandists at home had split the Axis – meaning the BBC's Italian Service was the first to see its target knocked out of the war. It was estimated that before the fall of Mussolini there were more 'black' propaganda listeners in Italy in relation to radio owners than in any other country.[27] When Germany took control of north and central Italy, radio had been suspended, meaning the only way Italians could find out what was going on was through the BBC.

Following the armistice, the main objective of the Italian Service was to rekindle the fighting spirit of Italians now that they were a co-belligerent against Germany. Encouragement was given to those who had taken to the mountains to fight a guerrilla campaign, with instruction given to factory workers about how to obstruct the German war machine. By the end of 1944 the main information programme, *London Calling Italy*, was increasingly gaining in popularity among the reinvigorated Italians. It is said that the Germans shrank from imposing the death penalty on the Italians for listening to the BBC, as it would have meant shooting an entire nation.[28]

The success of the Italian venture effectively illustrates how enemy-directed propaganda typically accelerates processes already in operation, rather than achieving any practical objective on its own. While the European Service might have been celebrating a notable measure of success in helping to turn Italian opinion around, there were other BBC employees who had decamped to a disused department store in Oxford Street with the aim of delivering a different kind of propaganda. Among a maze of partitions and shelving units, they laboured away in a determined effort to direct the right kind of message to the farther regions of the world. Among the most difficult targets was India, the jewel in Britain's imperial crown, where tensions had already been simmering between ruler and ruled long before the name of Adolf Hitler became known.

12

HEARTS AND MINDS

THE EASTERN SERVICE

In December 1932, the BBC extended its reach significantly when it began short-wave transmissions aimed towards English-speaking people throughout the British Empire. The new Empire Service was commissioned just in time for the first Christmas Day address by a reigning monarch – a tradition that continues to this day. King George V was able to reach out to men and women 'so cut off by the snow, the desert, or the sea, that only voices out of the air can reach them'. By the mid-1930s the programmes were receiving high praise by those in the service of empire; serving soldiers at Fort Sandeman in British Baluchistan had known nothing of the devastating earthquake in the province's capital Quetta in May 1935 until they heard about it on the BBC. A year later the corporation broadcast the sad news of the death of George V to the four corners of empire, and thereafter kept the dominions in the information loop as the subsequent abdication crisis unfolded.

The service had been set up to enable greater ties between the mother country and the empire through the means of radio broadcasts. The first director general, John Reith, first broached the idea to the India Office in 1924 as a means for disseminating British views and values to an even wider public scattered around the dominions. The first radio station in India had been opened in Mumbai (then Bombay) in July 1927 by the Viceroy Lord Irwin, although it was not until 1932 that the BBC's Empire Service addressed listeners in India, with a broadcast lasting no more than ten minutes. Following the Italian invasion of Abyssinia in 1935, the BBC was encouraged to extend the reach of its Empire Service to counter Italian propaganda being directed towards the Middle East with the aim of undermining British interests in the area, including Palestine. By 1937, the service was broadcasting for twenty-one hours a day in English to primary audiences in all parts of the empire, at convenient listening hours according to local time. The four main services – Pacific, Eastern, African and North African – each broadcast to secondary audiences in other parts of the world. The service went out on the short wave for primary listeners and was rebroadcast on medium wave by local stations, thereby increasing the size of the audiences.

The government had been anxious to get a BBC Arabic Service started and it finally went on air on 3 January 1938; its first foreign-language broadcast attracted a large and enthusiastic audience, having been targeted by official government pamphlets encouraging them to listen. This was followed in March by broadcasts in both Spanish and Portuguese directed to parts of Latin America, purely for the dissemination of news. Britain at this time was still very much focused on a policy of appeasement with the fascist dictatorships and continued to reject the use of any direct political propaganda. Only with the entry of Japan into the war in December 1941 did the corporation resume ramping up facilities for the service at the request of government, anxious to improve links with British subjects in the subcontinent and the Far East. In February 1942, the BBC spent over £400,000 on improvements to services, enabling it to consolidate and extend its overseas services in accordance with Parliament's wishes.[*] The growth in the number of foreign languages in which broadcasts could be transmitted on the Overseas Service since the beginning of the war was remarkable. In September 1939, the BBC was broadcasting bulletins and programmes in ten languages, including English, rising to forty-one by the end of December 1941. So far as news bulletins were concerned, the rate of expansion was similar, rising to

---

[*] At the start of the war the BBC had only one short-wave transmitting station for the Empire Service located at Daventry. New sites had to be built, including Rampisham in Dorset, Start Point in Devon, Clevedon in Somerset, Skelton in Cumbria and Wooferton in Shropshire.

ninety-seven a day – fifteen in English, of which three were for European and twelve for empire services. Naturally this great expansion entailed a significant increase in staffing levels, amounting to just under 600 new appointments in 1941 alone.[1]

In November 1942, an Overseas Forces' Service began with the aim of providing troops further afield with a valuable morale-boosting link with Britain. With regard to enemy propaganda, overseas staff, including Kirkpatrick, saw very little value in broadcasting anything to Japan beyond straight news, while Chinese Radio was controlled by the Chinese Ministry for Propaganda, which effectively limited the scope for any political co-operation.[2] Added to this, the reception from Britain was poor, and the service was continually hampered by power outages.

Following the declaration of war, the British Government did not have to wait too long to discover where India stood in terms of supporting the national effort. A statement on 15 September 1939 on behalf of the Indian National Congress Independence Party was presented to the War Cabinet by the Secretary of State for India on 27 September. It indicated that 'India was in full sympathy with the allies, but any co-operation would be withheld until a full statement from Her Majesty's Government of their war aims in their application to India was forthcoming'. The Cabinet unanimously agreed that it would be undesirable to enter into any formal commitments at this early stage, and responded that without Britain's help India was virtually defenceless against external aggression.[3] The British Government was more worried that the BBC was unconcerned with transmitting news bulletins to India, and criticised the corporation's indifference towards the listening public in Britain's most treasured imperial possession. There was a critical need to keep subject peoples informed through regular news broadcasts and commentaries, and the BBC needed to up its game considerably if it was to avoid stinging criticism from members of both houses, such as this from Viscount Astor in October 1939:

As I understand it, when war started, the B.B.C. ceased to relay news to India, and Germany had a free run. One has only to read the papers to see that there is considerable difference of opinion – a potential trouble in India in connection with our war aims, and it would be a great pity if we did not take full, immediate, and adequate steps to deal with the accusations which are coming from Berlin accusing us of Imperialism and all that sort of thing.[4]

Such criticism was inevitable; Berlin was speaking to India in half a dozen languages, including Hindustani, and immediate action was required to put the BBC on at least an equal footing with Germany. In November 1939, the Empire Service was renamed the Overseas Service, and thereafter it continued to expand as the number of staff required to keep the various channels ticking over rose significantly. The India Service began broadcasting in May 1940, typically countering the Nazi broadcasts by focusing on British culture and music, along with occasional news bulletins. The reception to the service was lukewarm. In July 1941, the journalist Kingsley Martin launched a bitter attack on the MOI and the corporation in an editorial for the *New Statesman*, citing the solemnity of the service, and of failing to appreciate that Indians despised European dance music; 'plenty of Indians would welcome serious talks on literature and other topics which recognise their equality of interests'.[5] German propagandists had studied Indian tastes and susceptibilities, and war news from Berlin had proved to be a great attraction for Indian listeners. Programmes typically featured classical music selections, coupled with the aim of promoting German culture as being more highbrow than the British. The BBC countered this by emphasising the cultural links that already existed between the two countries, and later by allotting time at the microphone to broadcasters sympathetic to the aims of the National Congress. The war of words raging over the question of 'on which side India's interest might be better served' could not be won without a considerable programme of expansion. This resulted in the Eastern Service swiftly outgrowing its allocation of space, and in June 1942 it was transferred to a disused department store in Oxford Street. By that time the service had increased the number of languages for its broadcasts to India to include Marathi, Gujarati, Tamil and Sinhala. With over 250 million Indians being fluent in Hindustani, the BBC had originally prioritised that language, with Bengali having been introduced a year later in 1941.

The business of formulating propaganda directed towards the people of the dominions presented a different and very challenging undertaking for the BBC when compared with other forms of political warfare. Unlike in the enemy and enemy-occupied territories where the intention was to spread disaffection and to motivate and provide guidance for resistance groups, the aim of the propagandist working for the India Service was to appeal to subjugated peoples to side with their oppressors over the 'common enemy'. This was a difficult task given the delicacy of wartime relations between Britain and India, particularly at a time when the independence movement was in the ascendency. The corporation had to reflect the views of the pro-independence National Congress Party, even though many of its staunchly anti-British leaders, including those of the Quit India Movement, had been slung in jail. Reflecting on the task that faced them, one former employee remembered that 'nobody pretended that broadcasts from London could dissipate the fog of India's political troubles, but it can project a beam of light into the gloom and consolidate common misunderstandings'.[6]

The chances of successfully disseminating radio propaganda to India was also hampered by the fact that just over one in every 4,000 Indians possessed a radio, and the department laboured away, unsure of whether they were having any real effect on the hearts and minds of the Indian intelligentsia.* The Germans certainly believed it to be worthwhile; Axis propaganda to the subcontinent was ramped up significantly in 1941 when the former president of the Indian National Congress Subhas Chandra Bose arrived in Berlin, having escaped from house arrest in British India. Bose was received warmly by the Nazis, who took an opportunistic line of sympathy to the independence cause, and furnished him with funds to set up the Free India Radio Service that enabled him to direct propaganda against the British Raj. Recognising the danger posed by Bose and the serious threat to India from Japan, Newsome at the European Service responded by attacking the National Congress leaders being led on by Bose in his popular *Man in the Street* broadcasts. The Indian Congress Party had begun a movement of resistance against the British 'for fighting a war with the Japanese that was likely to plunge the strategically vital subcontinent of India into political turmoil'. Newsome went on to attack Gandhi and Nehru, 'who had professed themselves to be bitter enemies of Hitler, and now demanded the abolition of the one authority capable of defending India's

---

* In India in 1940 there was one radio for every 3,875 people. (Davison, 1996, p.119)

freedom against the Japanese'. India's pacifists, he argued, would not be allowed to interfere with Britain's attempts to smash Hitlerism. Much sympathy for their cause had arguably been lost by such a stand, leading Newsome to conclude that 'India will achieve her freedom *in spite of*, rather than *because of*, her self-appointed leaders'.[7]

Much about the day-to-day running of the BBC's India Service can be learned from the experiences of the esteemed political writer Eric Blair, known by his pen name George Orwell, who joined the staff of the BBC in August 1941. Born in 1903 in India, where his father worked as a civil servant, Blair had failed to distinguish himself as a King's Scholar at Eton College. Instead of going up to Oxford with his Eton pals, he had joined the Imperial Police, where he served his time in Burma – an experience that he famously described as 'five wasted years within the sound of bugles'. His selection for a job organising propaganda for the BBC was a strange one; his deep anti-imperialism having been the hallmark of his first published novel as George Orwell, *Burmese Days*. It was a work that initially could not be published in Britain for fear of libel action, rather than for Orwell's rages against imperialism where 'every white man is a cog in the machinery of despotism', which are arguably among the novel's chief merits.

Orwell's experiences in Burma, where his every opinion on every subject was dictated to him by 'the Pukka Sahib's code', underpinned the social conscience that shaped his early literary development. He knew where he stood and was no longer averse to going against the establishment on sensitive issues. A good example is the case of the novelist P.G. Wodehouse, who was under investigation in the summer of 1941 after being publicly maligned for broadcasting five talks from Berlin to America. Before Wodehouse was eventually cleared, Orwell published an essay titled *In Defence of P.G. Wodehouse* that effectively defended a potential traitor banned by the BBC, and whose books had also been withdrawn from public libraries. A file detailing Orwell's political sympathies, formerly held by the Security Service, makes for interesting and amusing reading: 'Blair (Orwell) came under notice of the Wigan Borough Police in February 1936 in connection with his Communist activities in Wigan,' and previously 'seems to have eked out a precarious living as a freelance journalist in France'. Another report notes that he worked at a bookshop for a man called Westrope, who 'holds Socialist views' and considers himself an 'intellectual'. Regardless of Orwell's allegedly 'dodgy past', his security check came back 'nothing recorded against' and he was accepted onto the staff of the corporation. A Special Branch report from much later in the file describes him as being 'practically penniless when he found work with the BBC'. Although his salary of £640 a year was the best he had earned since leaving Burma, to describe him as penniless is not strictly true. Orwell's workload was quite prolific throughout 1941 and included four broadcasts on literary criticism for the BBC's Eastern Service programme, We Speak to India, that he scripted and took part in between 29 May and 19 June 1941. In his Complete Works, Professor Peter Davison remarks that the irony 'that he was only paid well when working directly or indirectly for the Raj' would not have been lost on Orwell.[8]

Orwell had not only impressed the BBC with his earlier broadcasts, he also captivated them with his particular interest in the Far East, and his experience of being amongst the Burmese people. Taken alongside his proven literary abilities and impressive connections, he was considered to be the perfect fit to head up a highbrow staff aiming to reach Indians of superior educational grounding. This would include editing over 200 newsletters for broadcast to India, Malaysia and Indonesia in English; and translated for broadcast in Gujarati, Marathi, Bengali and Tamil. Orwell had only recently expressed an opinion about the BBC to the editors of the American quarterly Partisan Review before agreeing to work for the corporation:

I believe that the BBC, in spite of the stupidity of its foreign propaganda and the unbearable voices of its announcers, is very truthful. It is generally regarded here as more reliable than the press.

A little over five months after writing that letter, Orwell had signed up to become a contributor to the BBC's 'stupid foreign propaganda' he had previously derided. Throughout a period of well over two years, Orwell worked firstly as talks assistant, then later as talks producer, for the India section of the Eastern Service. An enormous body of work that he did for the station, running to over 2,000 pages, has survived and has since been published in the aforementioned Complete Works. At a time when Indians were already the target of German propaganda questioning whether enslaved people should willingly die for their masters, Orwell, who was a committed anti-imperialist and a voice for pro-independence, was now under contract to direct radio propaganda in line with the government's plan. This would involve promoting the British view of situations rather than his own, and without compromising the corporation's reputation for objectivity and honesty.

Orwell spent his first two weeks as an employee on a BBC induction course at Regents' Park, which he contemptuously nicknamed 'the Liar's School', before starting work in the Indian section under Zulfaqar Ali Bokhari, who went on to become director general of Radio Pakistan. Bokhari was answerable to Eastern Service Director L.F. Rushbrook Williams, who was responsible for making sure the broadcasts concurred with the British Government line. Aside from the newsletters on the war situation, Orwell's responsibilities also included organising a number of cultural, educational and political programmes on general issues including propaganda. In his introduction to the vast collection of Orwell's BBC papers, Peter Davison regards the Indian Service's attempt at distance teaching as the most remarkable aspect of Orwell's propaganda work. Orwell inherited this body of work almost as soon as he arrived at the BBC and immediately set about expanding the range of courses to incorporate an additional thirteen on a wide diversity of subjects. The courses were supplemented by talks involving many distinguished speakers from the worlds of literature and science. Orwell also wrote a good many propaganda talks of the 'government advice' type on subjects such as 'paper rationing' before he noticeably moved away from all that to a much more sophisticated kind of propaganda embedded within his cultural and educational programmes.

Edward Stourton, in *Auntie's War*, believes that Orwell's propaganda work placed him in difficult territory – leading him into 'a betrayal of everything he stood for'.[9] At the time, it was an accusation that Orwell was not unaware of; after all, much of the Axis propaganda *and* the BBC's counter-propaganda involved ignoring passages in Nehru's speeches. In his *War Diary* in April 1942 he refers to the betrayals and contradictions that working for the BBC had forced upon him, and concluded that 'sooner or later we all write our own epitaphs'. Having said that, a committed anti-imperialist he may have been, but Orwell was at pains to inform the subject peoples not to believe the assurances of liberty for the conquered peoples being churned out by the Nazi propaganda machine, including high-sounding promises of freedom being directed towards the 'coloured peoples' now under British rule. Orwell emphasised this point in an essay published in November 1941 titled *All Propaganda is Lies*:

> This comes, it should be noticed, from men who only yesterday were openly describing the coloured races as the natural slaves of the white, and who described negroes, for example, in Hitler's own words as 'Semi-apes.' And even while the German wireless woos its Indian listeners with promises of independence, it woos the British public by declaring that Germany has no wish to break up the British Empire, and praises the British for the civilising work they have done in India.[10]

This was typical of the tone Orwell adopted in his efforts to keep Indian subjects onside in his radio broadcasts; he acknowledged that he was rapidly becoming 'propaganda-minded' and developing a cunning he did not previously have. He was also quick to counter criticism coming his way, particularly from the literary critic George Woodcock, who accused him of using radio propaganda to 'fox the Indian masses'. 'Does Mr Woodcock really know what kind of stuff I put out in the Indian broadcasts?' Orwell began. He pointed out that most of his broadcasts were aimed at Indian left-wing intellectuals, some of them bitterly anti-British. The intention was not to 'fox the Indian masses'; rather it was to present an awareness of what a fascist victory would mean to the chances of India's independence. 'Propaganda cannot fight against the facts,' he wrote in 1943, and he kept his corner clean by refraining from the added colour and distortion of the type of propaganda he despised. He also believed that radio had the effect of making war a more truthful business, and felt that critics should actually find out what he was doing at the BBC before attacking his good faith.[11]

In 1943, Orwell edited a book titled *Talking to India*, which contained transcripts of a selection of broadcasts, alongside examples of the Axis propaganda being broadcast by Chandra Bose reproduced for comparison. In his introduction he asserts that most Axis propaganda to India was poor; however, he regarded Chandra Bose to be 'the high water mark', and noted that for propaganda purposes 'Bose is reduced to pretending that the Axis powers have no imperialist aims' and that 'the enemy consists solely of Britain and the USA'.[12] After an illuminating comment reflecting how Bose had been obliged by his position to change tack on his view of the Sino-Japanese War (despite having been prominent on various 'aid' China committees), he then focuses on aspects of the war deliberately omitted by Bose. This included any admission that Germany was at war with the Soviet Union, the fact that both Italy and Japan possessed subject empires, or that the Germans were forcibly holding down some 150 million people in Europe, 'none of which fitted in with his general propaganda line'.[13] It was clear to Orwell that Bose was forcibly obliged by his Berlin masters to avoid mention of certain major issues of the war affecting a vast percentage of the human race. To suggest that Orwell's propaganda was in some major way a betrayal of his ideals is to ignore the distinction between honest and dishonest propaganda. Little wonder Orwell was more than happy to allow samples of his own BBC broadcasts to stand alongside those of the Axis!

Even though he worked diligently in what he regarded as 'a small and remote outpost in the radio war', Orwell found the work both tedious and frustrating, and could never escape the feeling that his efforts were a waste of time. Earlier in his *War Diary*, when he had been at the BBC for six months, he described its atmosphere as 'something halfway between a girls' school and a lunatic asylum', and concluded the entry by stating that 'all propaganda is lies, even when one is telling the truth – I don't think this matters so long as one knows what one is doing, and why'. He may have been right about the limited impact of what he was doing, but as his comment suggests, he had become very good at it. When the corporation suggested to him that it would like him to broadcast as George Orwell, rather than Eric Blair – effectively putting his literary reputation on the line – he was able to extract considerable licence from the BBC to conduct the programmes on his own terms. Not only did this give him a much greater freedom of speech, it also afforded him greater political licence when he insisted that his commentaries always followed 'what is by implication a left line'. How could he not at a time when he was also under contract to supply regular contributions to the American, communist-backed quarterly *Partisan Review*.

In the course of his mammoth undertaking to compile *The Complete Works*, Peter Davison uncovered a plethora of interesting information on Orwell's time at the BBC that suggests he tended to follow his own propagandist agenda, rather than one that might have been forced upon him by the BBC. A good example is his penchant towards organising broadcasts on the subject of prison literature, at a time when India's future leaders including Gandhi and Nehru were in prison. Orwell had informed the presenter Reg Reynolds that it was something he particularly wanted to put across in India so far as it is possible. Additionally, he commissioned the writer K.S. Shelvankar, whose 'Penguin Special' *The Problem of India* had recently been banned in the country, to deliver a number of talks, and despite protests from Bokhari, these all went ahead. Orwell also arranged talks on what Indian culture had given to the west, citing E.M. Forster's *My Debt to India* and two talks on philosophy by C.E.M. Joad – a household name in Britain courtesy of the BBC programme *The Brains Trust*. As Davison points out, none of these could be classed as 'lying propaganda'. Talks arranged on the subject of great books such as *The Social Contract*, *The Koran* and *Das Kapital*, as well as discussions on major social problems such as *Moslem Minorities in Europe* and *The Status of Women in Europe* can be seen as an enlightened form of propaganda that went right over the heads of the 'higher-ups'. There were other talks by Indian intellectuals in various Indian languages that could be construed as having been a much more innocuous form of propaganda – tackling such subjects as *The Beverage Report*, *The History of Fascism* and *The Japanese Threat to Asia*. Other talks looked to India's future and covered such subjects as minorities and cultural expression – broadcasts that often involved distinguished experts in their field.

It was the people Orwell was mixing with, rather than the content of his broadcasts, that brought him back onto the radar of the Security Service when he applied for clearance to Allied HQ in 1943.* His recently released security file contains tales that gossiping BBC informants had reported about him to Special Branch: 'He has a good many Indian

---

* Orwell was in line to be sent to West Africa as a war correspondent for *The Observer*. The appointment failed to materialise.

friends and has offered employment to K.S. Shelvankar' (whose books were banned by the Indian authorities). Another informant responded that 'he is telling some of his friends that his department was trying to get Mulk Raj Anand on the staff'. Anand was a socialist writer and propagandist who had been active in the Indian Independence Movement. The India Office was strongly opposed to his appointment, but Orwell somehow managed to get his friend on board. Orwell was also described by colleagues as being 'a bit of an Anarchist', 'a man of advanced Communist views' and 'a man in touch with extremist elements' who had 'thrown in his lot with Victor Gollancz', the left-wing publisher. He was also described as 'dressing in a Bohemian fashion', both at his office and during his leisure hours.

Orwell's stint with the BBC had not been a happy one. His resignation letter was clearly filled with frustration, as this abridged section indicates:

> I am tendering my resignation because, for some time past, I have been conscious that I was wasting my own time and the public money on doing work that produced no result. I believe that in the present political situation, the broadcasting of British propaganda to India is an almost hopeless task.

It is difficult to assess Orwell's belief that it was all a waste of time, as there is little evidence to counter his assumption. The service certainly continued to expand during his time, with twelve Asiatic languages being incorporated within the forty-seven being broadcast by the BBC shortly before his resignation.[14] Orwell had always been acutely aware that it was the English speakers who were most likely to have access to short-wave radio sets, and that the most important broadcasts were the three-quarter-hour transmissions aimed at the English-speaking Indian population, rather than the European population or the British troops in India. In terms of the literacy figures, Orwell records in *Talking to India* that there were 5 million Indians literate in English and several millions more could speak it – a figure that added up to only 3 per cent of the population.[15] He could only console himself with the fact that no attempt was ever made to boycott listening to the BBC in India.

On another level, Orwell's time with the corporation was not completely wasted either, in terms of his own literary ends. The amount of 'stupid propaganda' from Europe that appeared on his desk, along with the difficulties he encountered in being able to broadcast exactly what he wanted, helped him to form his vision of the Ministry of Truth in his famous novel *Nineteen Eighty-Four*. His description of the ministry's canteen is said to be based on the facility at Bush House, and Room 101, where he attended policy meetings for the Eastern Service at 55 Portland Place, also entered the novel's lexicon.

Finally, on the question of whether India with her aspirations of freedom had anything to fear from a Nazi victory, it is worth consulting the memoirs of Ivone Kirkpatrick, the former controller of the BBC's European Service, who recalled an incident that occurred during his time at the Foreign Office. As First Secretary at the British Embassy in Berlin, Kirkpatrick effectively had a ringside seat throughout the critical discussions prior to the Munich Crisis in September 1938, and accompanied Foreign Secretary Lord Halifax and British Ambassador Neville Henderson during their respective interviews with the volatile and unpredictable Führer. At the very mention of India, Hitler had been quick to air his views on British policy:

> He could not understand, he said, why we tolerated disorder, or wasted time in parley with Congress. The remedy was quite simple; 'Shoot Gandhi' he said in his sharp staccato accent. 'And if that does not suffice to reduce them to submission, shoot a dozen members of congress, and if that does not suffice, shoot 200 and so on until order is established. You will see how quickly they will collapse as soon as you make it clear that you mean business.

As Hitler continued his tirade – a clear indication that he intended to massacre countless hundreds of India's National Congress until they cowered to his will – Kirkpatrick looked across at the Foreign Secretary and studied his expression: 'Halifax gazed at Hitler with a mixture of astonishment, repugnance and compassion.' The feeling that it would have been a complete waste of time to argue had long taken hold.[16]

EPILOGUE

THE INVASION OF EUROPE

In May 1943, the Allies formally decided to undertake a cross-Channel invasion of Europe, code-named Operation Overlord, under the direction of the Supreme Headquarters of the Allied Expeditionary Force (SHAEF), with Dwight D. Eisenhower appointed as Supreme Commander. Thereafter, SHAEF created its own Psychological Warfare Division in the interests of integrating all propaganda directives within the specific requirements of the central command. A new international broadcasting service for troops serving under SHAEF would be launched with operational control residing with the BBC, although Eisenhower would retain the power to amend or censure the content of 'invasion news' bulletins, which began on 7 June 1944.

On 20 May, Eisenhower had delivered a special broadcast on the European Service to the people under occupation in Western Europe. With the exception of de Gaulle, the leaders of exiled governments thereafter followed suit to inform their people that they would be instructed through the medium of radio in relation to what was expected of them when the time came to act. They were to observe the enemy closely, collect all possible information about troop movements and to take certain precautions for their own safety during the fighting. Eisenhower had been anxious for de Gaulle to declare himself fully behind the invasion, believing it would be critical towards achieving controlled co-operation with resistance movements inside France.

The general already considered himself to be the chosen leader of France, and regarded Eisenhower's speech as an insult to both him and his countrymen on the grounds that the Supreme Commander had spoken of 'affording the French people the right to choose the representatives and government under which they wished to live'. He flat-out refused to endorse the speech, unaware that 47 million copies had already been printed. Meanwhile, in the Netherlands hand bills were being distributed in towns and cities appealing to citizens ready to help the liberators *not* to act arbitrarily, rather to observe instructions to be broadcast on *Radio Oranje*.[1] Care had to be taken by both the station and the editors of clandestine magazines to ensure that news broadcasts being transmitted from London were not unduly optimistic, and reproduced as accurately as possible. A near disastrous situation had occurred on 5 September 1944 when *Radio Oranje* reported that 'liberation was near', an announcement that sparked excitement and panic throughout Rotterdam. Following the failed Allied military operation at Arnhem later that month, when it was clear that the war was going to last considerably longer, a new magazine, *Special Bulletin of Free Netherlands*, was published by the central leadership in an effort to keep over-optimistic civilians better informed.

At 10 p.m. on 5 June 1944, all the European Service regional directors were gathered together to be briefed for the first time that the invasion was in progress. Further meetings took place in which General de Gaulle was left furious after being told that the D-Day speech he finally intended to make on the BBC would have to be vetted. Eden was adamant that the general was not to be trusted and informed the PWE at 4 a.m. on the morning of D-Day that his broadcast must be scrutinised by censors at the Foreign Office. Ritchie Calder remembered that 'when the General arrived at around lunchtime to broadcast, that idea withered as we met him, killed by the frost of his look'; thereafter he entered the studio and delivered a magnificent broadcast, moving those present to tears. 'De Gaulle typically had pulled a fast one,' remembered Calder, 'he was recognised only as the president of the Provisional French Government. In the broadcast he had deliberately left out the *Provisional*. Like Napoleon Bonaparte, he had crowned himself.'[2]

Other D-Day broadcasts were directed towards the Poles who had been forced to serve in the German Army, and to the resistance movements in occupied nations who were told to disorganise the enemy in any way possible and to protect all industrial installations. On 5 June the French Service had broadcast the first verse of Paul Verlaine's poem *Chanson d'automne* to let resistance fighters know that the invasion would begin within twenty-four hours. Later that evening the announcer broadcast a further signal as an order to the resistance to begin cutting wires and telegraph cables. These were tense moments for the French Service as it was later discovered that a 'personal message' delivered shortly afterwards had aroused suspicion, triggering a stage II alert among the German Fifth Army at the Pas-de-Calais.[3] Shortly after midnight on 6 June the first airborne landings began, and years of trust built up between the BBC and the overseas listener would finally bear fruit for the good of the military. On the morning of 6 June, the BBC's French Service took twenty minutes to broadcast its *messages personnels* instead of the usual five to ten.[4] Thereafter, some 200 coded messages (some real, some fake) would be transmitted every day.

In Bush House, Newsome instructed European regional editors that they had a 'tremendously responsible job to do', for 'the great day to which all our efforts in the last four years have been leading up has arrived'.[5] Thereafter he led them through a PWE-OWI directive that they were to adhere to rigidly, as there was to be no variation whatsoever in the presentation of news in the different languages. As events unfolded, the European Service would transform into a rapid, comprehensive news service, supported only by authorised comment. Every editor was told to convey the impression of complete confidence in ultimate success. Newsome would thereafter transfer to SHAEF's own Psychological Warfare Division, leaving Ritchie to succeed him as European Service director for the remainder of the war. Controller Ivone Kirkpatrick also departed the European Service for the Political Intelligence Department in the autumn, to be replaced by Overseas Controller Beresford Clark.

The day 6 June 1944 witnessed not only the greatest military operation in modern warfare, but also the greatest ever media operation ever organised. Alongside 300,000 men from a dozen nations going into battle were 500 accredited war correspondents – most of them assigned a rank and in uniform.[6] Throughout preparations for D-Day, the BBC was kept in the information loop to enable its war correspondents to become suitably prepared for what lay ahead. In 1943, the corporation had set up a specialist war reporting unit to train and organise its reporters for the coming battle. This would involve special instruction in military skills as correspondents went on assault courses, reported on mock battles and learned how to live rough, and also how to use their broadcasting equipment in case their engineers were killed or wounded. Reporting on both the Allied invasion and the accompanying air support carried a considerable element of risk that would inevitably cost some reporters their lives.* As early as 8 May, the BBC's News Division Controller Patrick Ryan had briefed his team of correspondents that they had been chosen to undertake the most important assignment in broadcasting to date, and thereafter wished them good luck.

The British Government and armed forces fully supported the presence of the BBC, but the US-led command of the invasion force opposed giving its reporters special treatment. Field Marshal Montgomery had to convince SHAEF that the BBC was a special case because its broadcasts were heard throughout the English-speaking world, and just as importantly, were heard in the countries that were being invaded. 'Monty' fully believed morale to be 'the greatest single factor in battle' – believing that he too could make good use of the microphone to keep in touch with his armies. 'If they could feel they actually knew their commander-in-chief that would be half the battle.'[7] Eisenhower eventually consented and informed the news media that 'our countries fight best when our people are best informed. You will be allowed to report everything possible, consistent, of course, with Military Security.' War correspondents were typically given the honorary rank of captain, although the more senior correspondents such as Wynford Vaughan Thomas and Richard Dimbleby were assigned the rank of major.

The onus on correspondents to deliver the news efficiently, accurately and responsibly was huge. Reporting on the progression of ground operations as the Allies advanced into Europe would be as instantaneous as wartime news reporting had ever been. There would be no time to polish material, while most commentaries would be

---

* The BBC's Kent Stevenson died while reporting on a raid over north-west Germany two weeks after D-Day, and Guy Byam was killed in a US Air Force raid over Berlin on 3 February 1945. (IWM)

delivered unscripted and impromptu. The BBC team would have its own censorship unit attached to it that would receive instructions direct from army intelligence. Frank Gillard remembered that it was a tense time – 'nobody wanted to utter a word that would put a single fighting man in peril'.[8] Everyone who used the microphone was aware that the enemy would be monitoring every word that was said, meaning that reporters had to be careful not to raise enemy morale in the process. Reporting would essentially be a right-first-time process in which there would be no opportunity to rectify mistakes, as yesterday's news would pass swiftly into history in the shadow of unfolding events. The bar had been set high by previous correspondents at home in their effectiveness in enlightening listeners to the reality of aerial bombardment. Now it was the turn of the overseas correspondents; it was no longer about simple propaganda as people wanted to know what war looked, sounded and smelt like from looking over the shoulders of the men in battle.

For the BBC Home Service, the commencement of Operation Overlord began with a vague broadcast at 8 a.m. on 6 June warning people in enemy-occupied countries living near the coast that 'a new phase of the allied air offensive had begun'. News of the actual landings was not broadcast until 9.32 a.m., when John Snagge began reading out the prepared communiqué in a special bulletin.* The corporation had stolen a march on the earliest editions of the popular press by an hour, an early indication that the press would for evermore be headlining events of which listeners to the BBC were already aware. The supremacy of radio in reporting the invasion was reinforced by Montgomery, who preferred to release news over the BBC, rather than respect the age-old prerogative of the traditional press, leading to a considerable degree of ill-feeling between BBC correspondents and press reporters.[9] The supremacy of the BBC was further emphasised by a 9 p.m. broadcast on D-Day by the king, for which 80 per cent of the population listened in. From that day forward, the corporation would continue to be the voice of SHAEF throughout Europe for the remainder of the war, allowing the fighting men to maintain a valuable morale-boosting link with home as the operation progressed.

---

* The BBC Monitoring Service heard news of the D-Day landings on German radio hours before the official Allied announcement.

Within two days of the invasion, Bomber Command had delivered over 9 million leaflets in 'drops' throughout Nazi-occupied Europe. Leafleting would become the main thrust of the propaganda effort following the D-Day landings and would be critical towards warning citizens to take cover, as it was believed that the softening-up process through strategic bombing could cost over 80,000 French lives. Churchill was anxious that the French must remain 'among our friends' in the new post-war Europe. At home, the fireside public generally got its information about the progress of the invasion from a specially devised half-hour commentary programme on the BBC called *War Report* that first aired after the nine o'clock news on D-Day and every day thereafter until final victory was achieved. In the following months, these regular dispatches were listened to by 10–15 million people every night, both in Britain and by unknown thousands in Nazi-occupied Europe under the shadow of the Gestapo. It was a window on the war that took the listener to the heart of the action wherever things were happening, carrying with it the hopes of the nation, and of those living under Nazi tyranny. For millions of people, *London Calling* was the voice of freedom and it was for this reason that the Secretary of State for War had insisted that the BBC must have the full co-operation of the army. At this time the Minister of Information, Brendan Bracken, felt it was about time the BBC started trusting the general public with war news, whether it was good or bad. Bracken was constantly reminding the government that it was 'the responsibility of the BBC to report news, and if it adopted too restrictive a view of its functions, it would lose all credit for impartiality'.[10] There was a distinct form of morale-boosting home propaganda to be defended; if the public did not get news from the BBC they would get it from the US news media – reports that would more likely emphasise American rather than British efforts.

With so many regular bulletins and such an intensity of unfolding events, problems were bound to arise from time to time over the content and how on-the-spot reports were coming across. People began to ask if it was right to expose the public to the appalling realities of war, as descriptions of live events were typically followed by the sound of German machine-gun fire. Newspaper reporters readily took the opportunity to criticise the corporation's war correspondents' reporting of events by asking if it was 'necessary to hear the gliders crash, the machine guns rattle, and to make the people of this island realise that their men were giving blood only a few miles away?' The feeling at the BBC was 'yes it was', and the corporation defended its position with the revelation that on D-Day alone over fifty official despatches had been received at Broadcasting House.[11] American listeners were kept informed of events in northern France and beyond in a special programme called *Combat Diary*. These invasion reports were rebroadcast on at least 725 radio stations in the US, where the BBC's excellent coverage received handsome praise in the *New York Times*. The American Station Broadcasting in Europe (ASBIE) also began broadcasting prior to D-Day in collaboration with the BBC. By the eve of the invasion broadcasting was effectively a joint Allied operation as over 200 periods a week were being devoted to the *America Calling Europe* programme.

The BBC's European Service continued to play an important role in support of the invasion forces. Ever since the disastrous defeats in North Africa and at Stalingrad, it was noticeable that more and more Germans began to listen to the broadcasts, including the 'black' stations. These numbers increased further following the Allied invasion of France, to the extent that by the autumn of 1944 it was estimated that between 10 and 15 million Germans were tuning in regularly.[12] With the invasion in progress, the BBC's European Service editors continued to countenance information on the proposed shape of post-war Europe beyond 'unconditional surrender'. Exiled governments typically looked to London for information on 'currents of thought' on the free world as potential stimulants.*

Additionally, the sheer scale of the aerial bombing campaign also hindered any chance of success the PWE might have had in their efforts to divide the German people. With the odds of any success stacked against them, the German Service focused on maintaining the right balance between the discouragement of Germans and not nourishing premature hopes of imminent victory. Hitler helped in this respect by proclaiming that Germany would 'fight to the end with the

---

* Churchill protested that he had never heard the term 'unconditional surrender' until the Casablanca Conference, a claim that the PWE knew to be completely untrue. Being bound by the Official Secrets Act, Calder could not divulge the fact that 'unconditional surrender' had been dropped on his desk in the week before Casablanca.

utmost ferocity'. In the weeks before D-Day, the main objective had been to concentrate the attention of the German soldier on the enemy within (i.e. the Party) rather than on the enemy outside. After D-Day the themes were switched to the hopelessness of continuing the war, the folly of useless sacrifice, and the incompetence of Germany's leaders.

As the Allied forces gained the upper hand, so the intensity of the propaganda war gradually moderated. The Belgian Service officially ended on 5 September, and in October when the Allies formally recognised the establishment of de Gaulle's Provisional Government following the liberation of Paris in August 1944, the importance of the BBC's French Service diminished rapidly, with the final broadcast of *Les Français Parlent aux Français* being aired on 22 October.[13] When the Radio Luxembourg transmitter was captured by US forces that summer a valuable asset was acquired, enabling Newsome and others to provide valuable broadcasting assistance to the German section. Direct control of propaganda by the Political Warfare Executive ceased when a country was liberated, but the government's connection to the services broadcast to the liberated country were maintained indirectly through the MOI. Broadcasts to Norway and Denmark and to countries still actively at war remained within the orbit of the PWE. Churchill felt that since such statements broadcast by the BBC carried such great authority, he thought it was essential that the government should retain full control of all broadcasts to countries with which Britain was still at war, and where the lives of British soldiers were at risk.[14] As the Allies began making inroads into Germany and bringing areas of the country under their military control, the BBC assisted in the process of denazification by providing programmes that exposed the dominant myths in National Socialism, including its theory of racial science.

During the final days, it was a testament to the power of truthfulness that the Germans were listening in to the BBC in an effort to discover what was happening in their own country. This tendency extended right down into Hitler's bunker in Berlin, where in the final stages of the war, the Führer had become increasingly concerned about critical military information being leaked to the enemy, snarling to his generals, 'I wonder if we can get this order to the troops before we hear about it over the BBC.'[15] Communications were often restricted at vital times, especially when the antenna positioned above the bunker was twice knocked out by artillery fire. In his book *The Berlin Bunker*, J.P. O'Donnell considered it 'a delightful irony that Adolf Hitler, in the last days of his life, received his world news round-up from the BBC broadcasts'. Heinz Lorenz, of the Nazi Propaganda Ministry, edited the broadcasts and in the last days was assisted by Hans Baur. It was by this means that Hitler was to learn of the defection of Himmler.[16]

Finally, on Wednesday, 2 May 1945, immediately following the final broadcast of *Kurt and Willi*, the BBC broadcast news of Hitler's death to the German people in a German-language broadcast direct from London.[17] This included an account by Admiral Dönitz of the Führer 'fighting valiantly in front of his troops' and a description of the red Soviet flag flying above the Reichstag.

After Germany had surrendered there were significant cuts in broadcasting hours to Europe, though no BBC language service was actually scrapped. The cuts came mainly because governments in exile and foreign broadcasters alike returned to their liberated nations, although the French Service survived the worst of the cuts and broadcasts to Germany actually increased. The new pattern for overseas broadcasting was set out by the British Government in July 1946, which foreshadowed the Cold War. In the near certain knowledge that other powers would continue to employ the medium of radio to state their position to international audiences, the British viewpoint would never again be allowed to go unheard across the airwaves.

Meanwhile, high praise in recognition of the BBC's wartime operation at the end of the war was generous and plentiful, although one of the most notable tributes had long been voiced by an unlikely source. When Brendan Bracken had been appointed Minister of Information by Churchill in 1941, Churchill expected his protégé to throw his weight around where the BBC was concerned; however, unlike his mentor, Bracken gradually became a staunch defender and great admirer of the corporation. During the closing stages of the war he lauded its achievements:

Let us recognise that the BBC is one of the greatest of our war assets. We have taken the BBC too much for granted. We have never considered the ability and the sheer hard work which have enabled it to rise to the heights it has attained in this war. The BBC has lightened the darkness of occupied Europe; it has strengthened the will of the populations there to resist. It has been a faithful servant to the British public and to the British Empire. It has earned our gratitude and the hatred of the totalitarian powers.[18]

NOTES

1. WHEN RADIO CAME OF AGE

1   A. White, *BBC at War*, p.17.
2   BBC Yearbook, 1940.
3   S. Baldwin to J. Reith, 16 July 1926, quoted in A. Briggs, *The History of Broadcasting in the United Kingdom, Vol. 1: The Birth of Broadcasting*, p.384.
4   Locker-Lampson/Henderson, Hansard, HC deb, 3 December 1930, Vol. 245 cc.2195–6.
5   BBC Yearbook, 1941.
6   D. Welch and J. Fox, *Justifying War: Propaganda, Politics and the Modern Age*, p.81.
7   A. Briggs, *The History of Broadcasting in the United Kingdom, Vol. 3: War of Words*, p.18.
8   J. Seaton, *The Media in British Politics*, p.135.
9   J. Reith, Memorandum, 26 January 1940 (NA CAB 67-4-20).
10 Grant-Ferris, Hansard HC deb, 15 February 1939, Vol. 343 cc.1808–13.
11 Briggs, *The History of Broadcasting in the United Kingdom, Vol. 3*, p.163.

2. RADIO PREPARES FOR WAR

1   J.B. Priestley, BBC *Postscript* – broadcast on 22 September 1940.
2   A. Marwick, C. Emsley and W. Simpson, *Total War and Historical Change 1914–1955*, p.25.
3   P. Knightley, *The First Casualty: The War Correspondent as Hero and Myth-Maker from the Crimea to Iraq*, p.84.
4   R. Greenslade, 'First World War: How State and Press Kept Truth Off the Front Page', *The Guardian*, 27 July 2014.
5   Cabinet Meeting, 1 November 1933 (NA CAB 24/244).
6   T. Aldgate and A. Marwick, *Between Two Wars*, p.165.

7   Knightley, *The First Casualty*, p.86.
8   E. Tangye-Lean, *Voices in the Darkness: The Story of the European Radio War*, p.57.
9   *The Listener*, February 1935 (Dr Goebbels never actually appeared on the balcony).
10   C. Stuart, *The Reith Diaries*, p.219.
11   *Radio Times*, 21 March 1941.
12   J. Seaton and J. Curren, *Power Without Responsibility*, p.118.
13   *The Week We Went to War*, BBC, 7 September 2009.
14   J.A. Thomas, *A History of the BBC Features Department 1924–1964*, pp.68, 110.
15   E. Wilkinson and E. Conze, *Why War? A Handbook for Those Who Will Take Part in the Second World War*, p.31.
16   Ibid.
17   J. Gardiner, *The Children's War: The Second World War through the Eyes of the Children of Britain*, p.59.
18   MOI, *Reports on Morale*, 4 June 1940 & 17 July 1940 (NA INF 1/264).
19   MOI, *Reports on Morale*, 1 July 1940 & 11 July 1940 (NA INF 1/264).
20   White, *BBC at War*, p.21.
21   Ibid., p.22.

3. NOT THE WAR WE EXPECTED

1   S. Garfield, *We Are at War: The Diaries of Five Ordinary People in Extraordinary Times*, p.20.
2   BBC Yearbook, 1944.
3   Garfield, *We Are at War*, p.24.
4   Noted by John Colville, soon to become Winston Churchill's private secretary.
5   M. Yass, *This is Your War: Home Front Propaganda in the Second World War*, p.6.
6   Briggs, *The History of Broadcasting in the United Kingdom, Vol. 3*, p.191.
7   T. Bouverie, *Appeasing Hitler: Chamberlain, Churchill and the Road to War*, p.302.
8   Garfield, *We Are at War*, p.233.
9   MOI, *Public Opinion on the Present Crisis*, 15 June 1940 (NA INF 1/264).
10   Greenwood, Hansard, HC deb, 11 October 1939, Vol. 352 c.383.
11   P. Martland, *Lord Haw-Haw – The English Voice of Nazi Germany*, p.38.
12   War Cabinet meeting, 16 September 1939 (NA CAB 65/1).
13   Briggs, *The History of Broadcasting in the United Kingdom, Vol. 3*, pp.110, 151.
14   Memorandum (NA CAB 67-4-20).
15   War Cabinet minutes of 30 January 1940 (NA CAB 65-5-27).
16   Briggs, *The History of Broadcasting in the United Kingdom, Vol. 3*, p.36.
17   V. Gielgud, *Years of the Locust*, p.181.

18   A. Goody, 'BBC Features, Radio Voices and the Propaganda of War 1939–1941'.
19   *The Listener*, 566, 16 November 1939.
20   *The Listener*, 602, 25 July 1940.
21   Stuart, *The Reith Diaries*, p.253.
22   South, Hansard, HC deb, 11 June 1940, Vol. 361 cc.1231–40.
23   Both letters were quoted in the above debate.
24   Cooper, Hansard, HC deb, 11 June 1940, Vol. 361 cc.1231–40.
25   Memorandum by Home Intelligence Dept of MOI, 17 June 1940 (NA INF 1/257).
26   MOI, *Daily Reports on Morale*, July/August 1940 (NA INF 1/264).
27   MOI, *Public Opinion on the Present Crisis*, 14 June 1940 (NA INF 1/264).
28   MOI, *Daily Reports on Morale*, June/July 1940 (NA INF 1/264).
29   'Stories of the Battle of Britain 1940', *The Spitfire Site*, 5 June 2010, spitfiresite.com/2010/06/this-week-in-the-battle-of-britain-1940-dunkirk-over-triumph-or-defeat.html.
30   *Radio Times*, 14 June 1940.
31   *Radio Times*, 21 June 1940.
32   Davison, *George Orwell: Diaries*, pp.245, 304.
33   Ibid., p.249.
34   H. Irving, 'If the Invader Comes', *Talking Humanities*, University of London, 18 June 2015, talkinghumanities.blogs.sas.ac.uk/2015/06/18/if-the-invader-comes/.
35   P. Addison and J. Crang, 'In Search of the Dunkirk Spirit', *BBC History Magazine*.
36   Garfield, *We Are at War*, pp.263, 267, 272.

4. STRIKING THE RIGHT CHORD – WARTIME NEWS

1   Fletcher, Hansard, HC deb, 15 February 1939, Vol. 343 c.1837.
2   B. Bracken, Note to War Cabinet: *The Work of the BBC*, 2 March 1943 (NA CAB 66-34-40).
3   Ibid.
4   I. McLaine, *Ministry of Morale: Home Front Morale and the MOI in World War II*, p.28.
5   Memorandum (NA CAB 67-3-44).
6   War Council Meeting, 16 December 1939 (NA CAB 65/2).
7   War Council Meeting, 18 December 1939 (NA CAB 65/2).
8   Supreme War Council minutes (NA CAB 65-56-147).
9   E. Stourton, *Auntie's War: The BBC during the Second World War*, pp.93–6.
10   N. Newsome, *Giant at Bush House: At the Heart of the Radio War*, p.207.
11   MOI, *A Summary of Public Opinion on the Present Crisis*, 18 May 1940 (NA INF 1/264).
12   N. Harman, *Dunkirk: The Necessary Myth*, p.235.

13   Ibid., p.236.
14   Ibid., p.243.
15   MOI, *Public Opinion on the Present Crisis*, 27 May 1940 to 29 May *1940* (NA INF 1/264).
16   *London Review of Books*, Vol. 40 No. 18, 27 September 2018.
17   BBC WAC, Radio News Bulletin, 31/05/1940, Bernard Stubbs.
18   Spitfiresite.com (uploaded 16 August 2020).
19   Ibid.
20   D. Welch, *Propaganda, Power and Persuasion: From World War I to Wikileaks*, p.34.
21   J. Gardiner, *Wartime Britain 1939-45*, p.202.
22   MOI, *Public Opinion on the Present Crisis*, 1 June 1940 (NA INF 1/264).
23   Ibid.
24   BBC *Postscripts*, 8 June 1940.
25   *The Pride of Britain*, broadcast 29 May 1942.
26   MOI, *Public Opinion on the Present Crisis*, 3 June 1940 (NA INF 1/264).
27   Ibid., p.12.
28   MOI, *Report on Morale*, 7 August 1940 (NA INF 1/264).
29   Davison, *George Orwell: Diaries*, p.251.
30   MOI, *Report on Morale*, 17 September 1940 (NA INF 1/264).
31   Davison, *George Orwell: Diaries*, p.266.
32   MOI, *Report on Morale*, 29 July 1940 (NA INF 1/264).
33   J. Fenby, *The Sinking of the Lancastria*, p.247.
34   Newsome Directive, 23 September 1940 (CAC NERI 1/3/1).
35   BBC WAC, Radio News Bulletin, 14/07/1940, Mark Gardner.
36   MOI, *Report on Morale*, 15 July 1940 (NA INF 1/264).
37   W. Churchill to D. Cooper, 26 June 1940, in W. Churchill, *Their Finest Hour*, p.151.
38   MOI, *Reports on Morale*, 17 August 1940-19 September 1940 (NA INF 1/264).
39   Woolfersten, 'A Day at the BBC Newsroom at the MOI', *Radio Times*, 24 April 1941.
40   Briggs, *The History of Broadcasting in the United Kingdom, Vol. 3*, p.591.
41   War Cabinet minutes, 28 June 1940 (NA CAB 65/7).

5. COURTING AMERICA WITH 'THE MURROW BOYS'

1   BBC Yearbook, 1941, pp.58-9.
2   Ibid., p.59.
3   Winterton, Hansard, HC deb, 23 October 40, Vol. 1365 cc.1095-7.
4   J. Porter, *Lost Sound: The Forgotten Art of Radio Storytelling*, p.91.
5   BBC Yearbook, 1943, p.83.
6   Stourton, *Auntie's War*, pp.223-4.
7   Newsome Directive, 6 November 1940 (CAC NERI 1/3/1).
8   W.H. McNeill, *America, Britain and Russia*, p.778.

9   N. Lemann, 'The Murrow Doctrine: Why the Life and Times of the Broadcast Pioneer Still Matter', *The New Yorker*, 23 January 2006, www.newyorker.com/magazine/2006/01/23/the-murrow-doctrine.
10 J.B. Priestley, *All England Listened: The Wartime Postscripts of J.B. Priestley*, p.v.
11 Newsome, *Giant at Bush House*, p.293.
12 W. Churchill, *The Grand Alliance*, pp.539–40.
13 Newsome Directive, 9 December 1941 (CAC NERI 1/3/4).

6. MAKE THE PEOPLE SMILE AGAIN

1   A. Calder, *The People's War: Britain 1939–45*, p.18.
2   Briggs, *The History of Broadcasting in the United Kingdom, Vol. 3*, pp.87–8.
3   War Cabinet minutes, 15 April 1942 (NA CAB 65/26).
4   BBC Yearbook, 1941.
5   White, *BBC at War*, p.5.
6   D. Shellard and S. Nicholson, *The Lord Chamberlain Regrets: A History of British Theatre Censorship*, p.117.
7   Ibid., p.120.
8   BBC Yearbook, 1944, p.30.
9   Briggs, *The History of Broadcasting in the United Kingdom, Vol. 3*, p.101.
10 White, *BBC at War*, p.24.
11 Ibid., p.25.
12 *Radio Times*, 13 February 1940.
13 *Radio Times*, 5 March 1940.
14 T. Kavanagh, *Tommy Handley*, p.9.
15 F. Worsley, *ITMA 1939–1948*, p.3.
16 Ibid., p.4.
17 *Radio Times*, 18 August 1939.
18 Garfield, *We Are at War*, pp.86–7.
19 Ibid., pp.132–3.
20 BBC WAC, script, ITMA 19/09/39, Tommy Handley.
21 Ibid., p.32.
22 *Radio Times*, 16 January 1942.
23 Worsley, *ITMA 1939–1948*, p.11.
24 H. Strauss, Hansard, HC deb, 17 February 1942, Vol. 377 cc.1729–30.
25 Kavanagh, *Tommy Handley*, p.10.
26 Ibid., pp.13–14.
27 Briggs, *The History of Broadcasting in the United Kingdom, Vol. 3*, p.537.
28 Hickman, *What Did You Do in the War, Auntie?*, p.50.
29 Kavanagh, *Tommy Handley*, pp.12–13.
30 *Radio Times*, 1 May 1942.
31 Foreign Office memo (NA FO 800-309-1).

32 Kavanagh, *Tommy Handley*, p.255.

33 White, *BBC at War*, p.8.

34 V. Lynn, *Vocal Refrain: An Autobiography by Vera Lynn*, p.92.

35 Ibid., p.97.

36 M. Deniert, *Lale Andersen: Verfolgung und Auftrittsverbot*, web.archive.org/web/20050117114217/http://www.lale-andersen.de/html/w_1943.htm.

37 Hickman, *What Did You Do in the War, Auntie?*, p.117.

38 Listener Research Weekly Report No. 62, 29 November 1941.

39 BBC Board of Governors minutes, 4 December 1941; Briggs, *The History of Broadcasting in the United Kingdom, Vol. 3*, p.523.

40 S. Nicholas, *Millions Like Us: British Culture in the Second World War*, pp.81–2.

41 Gardiner, *Wartime Britain 1939–45*, p.136.

42 H. Thomas, BBC internal memorandum to Assistant Director of Variety, Bangor, 24 March 1942.

43 C. Baade, *Victory Through Harmony: The BBC and Popular Music in World War II*.

44 *Radio Times*, 21 January 1944.

45 Earl Winterton, Hansard, HC deb, 7 March 1944, Vol. 397.

7. CROSSING THE PROPAGANDA LINE

1   Earl of Radnor, Hansard, HL deb, 19 March 1930, Vol. 80.

2   *Morning Post*, 27 February 1931.

3   Lord Gainford, Hansard, HL deb, 19 March 1930, Vol. 80.

4   T. Mills, *The BBC: Myth of Public Service*, p.36.

5   Lord Halifax Foreign Office correspondence (NA FO 800-309-1).

6   War Cabinet minutes, 18 December 1939 (NA CAB 65/2).

7   Davison, *George Orwell: Diaries*, p.261.

8   Buittenhuis, 'J.B. Priestley: Britain's Star Propagandist in World War II', *English Studies in Canada*, p.445.

9   Priestley, *All England Listened*, p.xvi.

10 Briggs, *The History of Broadcasting in the United Kingdom, Vol. 3*, p.193.

11 *Radio Times*, 21 July 1940.

12 *Radio Times*, 26 July 1940.

13 J.B. Priestley broadcast, 21 July 1940.

14 MOI, *Reports on Morale*, 20 July 1940 & 6 August 1940 (NA INF 1/264).

15 D. Cooper to War Cabinet (NA INF 1/869).

16 Baxter, Hansard, HC deb, 13 March 1941, Vol. 369 c.1406.

17 Foreign Office minutes, 29 July 1940 (NA CAB 65/57).

18 *Time* magazine, 4 November 1940 (PAB).

19 N. Hanson, *Priestley's Wars: Soldier, Broadcaster, Campaigner*, p.284.

20 Memo for W. Churchill to D. Cooper (January 1941), quoted in N. Hawkes, *The Story of J.B. Priestley's Postscripts*, pp.14, 24.

21   D. Cooper to J.B. Priestley, 21 March 1941 (PAB).
22   Priestley, *All England Listened*, p.xix.
23   Letter from Patrick Ryan to J.B Priestley, 27 March 1941 (PAB).
24   Copy in Priestley Archive, University of Bradford.
25   *Radio Times*, 9 May 1941.

8. TALKING TO EUROPE

1   Seul, *British Radio Propaganda against Nazi German during the Second World War*, p.25.
2   Secret report to the Secretary of State for Foreign Affairs, 29 January 1940 (NA CAB 65/11).
3   Newsome, *Giant at Bush House*, p.191.
4   Ibid., p.201.
5   Ibid., p.235.
6   Newsome Directive, 1 July 1940 (CAC NERI 1/3/1).
7   G. Johnston and E. Robertson, *BBC World Service: Overseas Broadcasting, 1932–2018*, p.116.
8   Newsome Directive, 8 September 1940 (CAC NERI 1/3/1).
9   Newsome, *Giant at Bush House*, p.203.
10   Newsome Directive, 9 December 1941 (CAC NERI 1/3/4).
11   Newsome Directive, 8 October 1940 (CAC NERI 1/3/1).
12   Newsome, *Giant at Bush House*, p.230.
13   Tangye-Lean, *Voices in the Darkness*, p.152.
14   Newsome Directive, 9 December 1941 (CAC NERI 1/3/4).
15   Newsome, *Giant at Bush House*, p.278.
16   I. Kirkpatrick, *The Inner Circle*, p.135.
17   Ibid., pp.149–50.
18   Newsome Directive, 22 May 1941 (CAC NERI 1/3/3).
19   Earl Winterton, *Orders of the Day*, p.303.
20   M. Bloch, *Closet Queens: Some 20th Century Politicians*.
21   Newsome, *Giant at Bush House*, p.235.
22   Quoted in Hickman, *What Did You Do in the War, Auntie?*, pp.113–114.
23   B. Lockhart, *Comes the Reckoning*, p.143.
24   Balfour Conference papers, cited in P. Ellis, *The Political Warfare Executive – A Re-Evaluation Based Upon Intelligence Work of the German Section*.
25   Bruce Lockhart to Anthony Eden, 6 March 1942 (NA FO 898/10).
26   Lockhart, *Comes the Reckoning*, p.143.
27   Briggs, *The History of Broadcasting in the United Kingdom, Vol. 3*, p.381.
28   J.R. Calder, 'Technology and Human Rights' (speech), Assembly for Human Rights, 22–27 March 1968.
29   Newsome, *Giant at Bush House*, p.218.
30   Newsome Directive, 20 August 1942 (CAC NERI 1/3/5).
31   Tangye-Lean, *Voices in the Darkness*, p.37.

32 Ibid.
33 BBC Yearbook, 1943, p.104.
34 Bracken, Hansard, HC deb, 8 April 1943, Vol. 388.
35 S. Grant-Duff, *The Man in the Street (of the BBC) Talks to Europe*, p.91.
36 Newsome, *Giant at Bush House*, p.299.
37 Ridsdale to Eden, 7 May 1943 (NA FO 954-23A-196).
38 Sendall (Bracken's Private Secretary) to Ridsdale, 20 May 1943 (NA FO 954-23A-200).
39 Kirkpatrick, *The Inner Circle*, p.167.

9. THE VOICE OF HOPE

1   Tangye-Lean, *Voices in the Darkness*, p.108.
2   Ibid., p.205.
3   Ibid., p.204.
4   D. Van Der Heide, *My Sister and I*, p.92.
5   A. Frank, *The Diary of Anne Frank*, p.53.
6   Verzetzmuseum, Amsterdam.
7   BBC Written Archives Centre.
8   S. Ward, 'Why the BBC Ignored the Holocaust', *The Guardian*, 22 August 1993.
9   Grant-Duff, *The Man in the Street (of the BBC) Talks to Europe*, p.63.
10 M. Gies and A.L. Gold, *Anne Frank Remembered*, pp.206–7.
11 N.A. Caplan, *Revisiting the Diary of Anne Frank*, p.84.
12 Internal Foreign Office memo, 31 December 1942 (NA KV/3).
13 O. Sinke, *Verzet Vanuit De Verte: De Behoedzame Koers Van Radio Oranje*, pp.32–3.
14 *A Voice Across the Water*, Radio Netherlands Worldwide, July 1981.
15 Sinke, *Verzet Vanuit De Verte*, p.51.
16 Internal Foreign Office memo, 31 December 1942 (NA KV/3).
17 Verzetzmuseum, Amsterdam, Exhibit 19014.
18 BBC Yearbook, 1945.
19 Briggs, *The History of Broadcasting in the United Kingdom*, Vol. 3, p.429.
20 Tangye-Lean, *Voices in the Darkness*, p.190.
21 Ibid., p.193.
22 BBC Yearbook, 1943, p.105.
23 Briggs, *The History of Broadcasting in the United Kingdom*, Vol. 3, pp.11, 357.
24 Tangye-Lean, *Voices in the Darkness*, p.60.
25 Calder, University of Edinburgh Spring Lecture, 1965.

10. DIVIDED NATION - REACHING OUT TO FRANCE

1   Tangye-Lean, *Voices in the Darkness*, pp.106–7.
2   J. Jackson, *France: The Dark Years 1940–44*, p.117.
3   Meeting of Foreign Office Ministers, 14 December 1939 (NA FO 800).

4   Tangye-Lean, *Voices in the Darkness*, p.146.
5   MOI, *Report on Morale*, 15 June 1940.
6   General Directive, 5 July 1940 (CAC NERI 1/3/1).
7   MOI, *Report on Morale*, 17 August 1940 (NA INF 1/264).
8   BBC French Service broadcast, 2 August 1940.
9   W. Churchill to D. Cooper, 11 August 1940, in Churchill, *Their Finest Hour*, p.580.
10 Hickman, *What Did You Do in the War, Auntie?*, p.116.
11 *The Connexion – French News and Views*, 25 April 2018 (uploaded 6 October 2020).
12 Ibid.
13 Tangye-Lean, *Voices in the Darkness*, pp.146–7.
14 Ibid., p.147.
15 Ibid., p.110.
16 K. Chadwick, 'Our Enemy's Enemy: Selling Britain to Occupied France on the BBC', *Media History*.
17 'Vive le Generale', *BBC World Service*, 8 February 2007, www.bbc.co.uk/worldservice/history/story/2007/02/printable/070122_html_40s.shtml.
18 Newsome, *Giant at Bush House*, p.225.
19 Ibid., p.228.
20 C. Emsley et al., *The Impact of World War II*, p.25.
21 E. Wake-Walker, *A House for Spies: SIS Operations into Occupied France*.
22 *Radio Times*, 8 August 1941.
23 Tangye-Lean, *Voices in the Darkness*, p.153.
24 BBC Yearbook, 1943, p.104.
25 *The Connexion – French News and Views*, 25 April 2018.
26 Ibid.
27 Johnson and Robertson, *BBC World Service: Overseas Broadcasting*, p.116.
28 Ibid., p.117.
29 Doug Ritchie Directive, 6 July 1940 (CAC NERI 1/3/1).
30 Newsome Directive, 7 July 1940 (CAC NERI 1/3/1).
31 R. Gildea, *Marianne in Chains*, p.149.
32 Chadwick, 'Our Enemy's Enemy'.
33 Newsome, *Giant at Bush House*, pp.317–18.
34 BBC Yearbook, 1944, p.78.
35 BBC Yearbook, 1943, p.105.
36 BBC Yearbook, 1945, p.113.

11. BROADCASTING TO THE ENEMY

1   Johnston and Robertson, *BBC World Service: Overseas Broadcasting*, p.112.
2   Ibid.
3   A. Glees, *Exile in Great Britain: Refugees from Hitler's Germany*, p.88.
4   Davison, *George Orwell: Diaries*, p.292.

5   H. Fraenkel, *Vansittart's Gift to Goebbels*, p.5.
6   Ibid., p.6.
7   Newsome, *Giant at Bush House*, p.204.
8   'White House to become Brown House', 1 April 2014, norbertmiller. wordpress.com.
9   Kirkpatrick, *The Inner Circle*, p.148.
10   Memorandum, *Propaganda, Policy and Purpose*, 13 December 1939 (NA FO 898/4).
11   War Cabinet minutes, 20 November 1940 (NA CAB 61/10).
12   Kirkpatrick, *The Inner Circle*, pp.98–9.
13   Tangye-Lean, *Voices in the Darkness*, p.58.
14   K. Morrshead, *Beating Hitler with Humour*, BBC Radio 4, 31 August 2019.
15   Ibid.
16   V.M. Plock, *Erika Mann, the BBC German Service, and Foreign Language Broadcasting during WWII*.
17   H. Roberts, *Capture at Arnhem: A Story of Disaster and Survival*, pp.81, 97.
18   G. Mansell, *Let Truth Be Told: 50 Years of External Broadcasting*, p.155.
19   Plock, *Erika Mann, the BBC German Service, and Foreign Language Broadcasting during WWII*.
20   Morrshead, *Beating Hitler with Humour*.
21   Pickthorn, Hansard, HC deb, 17 February 1942, Vol. 377 c.1712.
22   Pickthorn, Hansard, HC deb, 7 July 1942, Vol. 381 c.663.
23   Tangye-Lean, *Voices in the Darkness*, p.194.
24   Newsome Directive, 7 July 1940 (CAC NERI 1/7/1).
25   War Cabinet minutes, 21 May 1943 (NA CAB 65/38).
26   Telegram from F.D. Roosevelt W. Churchill to Joint Chiefs of Staff, 24 May 1940 (NA CAB 65/38).
27   BBC Yearbook, 1944.
28   Ibid.

12. HEARTS AND MINDS – THE EASTERN SERVICE

1   Thurtle, Hansard, HC deb, 17 February 1942, Vol. 377 c.1690.
2   Briggs, *The History of Broadcasting in the United Kingdom, Vol. 3*, p.456.
3   War Cabinet minutes, 27 September 1939 (NA CAB 65/1).
4   Viscount Astor, Lords, 4 October 1939, Hansard.
5   *New Statesman*, 5 July 1941.
6   D. Stephenson, 'India a Picture?', BBC Yearbook, 1945, pp.88–9.
7   Grant-Duff, *The Man in the Street (of the BBC) Talks to Europe*, p.66.
8   P. Davison, *The Complete Works of George Orwell*, Vol. XVII, pp.451–2, 464.
9   Stourton, *Auntie's War*, p.313.
10   P. Davison, *The Complete Works of George Orwell*, Vol. XIII, p.93.
11   G. Orwell, Review of *Voices in the Darkness*, *Complete Works*, Vol. XV, pp.84–6.
12   G. Orwell (ed.), *Talking to India*, pp.8–9.

13   Ibid., p.9.
14   Ibid., p.7.
15   Ibid.
16   Kirkpatrick, *The Inner Circle*, p.97.

EPILOGUE - THE INVASION OF EUROPE

1   Verzetsmuseum, Amsterdam, Exhibit 6271.
2   Calder, Edinburgh University Spring Lecture, 1965.
3   A. Beevor, *D-Day: The Battle for Normandy*, p.43.
4   Briggs, *The History of Broadcasting in the United Kingdom, Vol. 3*, p.605.
5   Newsome Directive, 6 June 1944 (CAC NERI 1/3/8).
6   S. Nicholls, 'The British Press and D-Day: Reporting the Launch of the Second Front, 6 June 1944', *Media History*.
7   D. Hawkins, *War Report: D-Day to VE-Day*, p.11.
8   Ibid., p.13.
9   Nicholls, 'The British Press and D-Day: Reporting the Launch of the Second Front, 6 June 1944'.
10   War Cabinet Meeting, 2 January 1945 (NA CAB 65-49-1).
11   BBC Yearbook, 1945, p.16.
12   Briggs, *The History of Broadcasting in the United Kingdom, Vol. 3*, pp.625-6.
13   Ibid., p.611.
14   War Cabinet Meeting, 2 January 1945 (NA CAB 65-49-1).
15   J.P. O'Donnell, *The Berlin Bunker*, p.154.
16   Ibid., p.43.
17   BBC Yearbook, 1946, p.130.
18   Bracken, Hansard, HC deb, 8 April 1943, Vol. 388.

BIBLIOGRAPHY

PRIMARY SOURCES

BBC Written Archive Centre
Churchill Archive Cambridge (CAC)
Hansard
Imperial War Museum (IWM)
The National Archives/Public Records Office (NA)
Priestley Archive University of Bradford (PAB)
Verzetzmuseum, Amsterdam (VMA)

SECONDARY SOURCES

Aldgate, T. and A. Marwick, *Between Two Wars* (Milton Keynes: Open University Press, 2001).

Baade, C., *Victory Through Harmony: The BBC and Popular Music in World War II* (London: Oxford University Press, 2013).

BBC Yearbooks 1939/1940/1941/1942/1943/1944 (London: BBC Broadcasting House).

Beevor, A., *D-Day: The Battle for Normandy* (London: Penguin, 2014 edition).

Bloch, M., *Closet Queens: Some 20th Century Politicians* (London: Abacus, 2016).

Bouverie, T., *Appeasing Hitler: Chamberlain, Churchill and the Road to War* (London: Vintage, 2019).

Briggs, A., *The History of Broadcasting in the United Kingdom, Vol. 1: The Birth of Broadcasting* (London: Oxford University Press, 1961).

Briggs, A., *The History of Broadcasting in the United Kingdom, Vol. 3: War of Words* (London: Oxford University Press, 1995 edition).

Buittenhuis, P., 'J.B. Priestley: Britain's Star Propagandist in World War II', *English Studies in Canada*, 26.4 (2000).

Calder, A., *The People's War: Britain 1939–45* (London: Pimlico, 1992 edition).

Caplan, N.A., *Revisiting the Diary of Anne Frank* (New York: Blooms Modern Critical Interpretations, 2010).

Chadwick, K., 'Our Enemy's Enemy: Selling Britain to Occupied France on the BBC', *Media History*, 21.4 (2015).

Churchill, W., *Their Finest Hour* (London: Penguin Classics, 1985 edition).

Churchill, W., *The Grand Alliance* (London: Penguin Classics, 2005 edition).

Davison, P., *George Orwell: A Literary Life* (London: Macmillan, 1996).

Davison, P., *The Complete Works of George Orwell*, Vol. XVII (London: Secker & Warburg, 1998).

Davison, P., *George Orwell: Diaries* (London: Penguin Modern Classics, 2010 edition).

Ellis, P., *The Political Warfare Executive – A Re-Evaluation Based Upon Intelligence Work of the German Section*, PhD thesis, University of Sheffield (1996).

Emsley, C. et al., *The Impact of World War II* (Milton Keynes: Open University Press, 2001).

Fenby, J., *The Sinking of the Lancastria* (New York: Pocket Books, 2006 edition).

Fraenkel, H., *Vansittart's Gift to Goebbels* (London: Fabian Society, 1941).

Frank, A., *The Diary of Anne Frank* (London: Pan, 1954).

Frank, A., *The Diary of Anne Frank Critical Edition*, prepared by the Netherlands State Institute for War Documentation (New York: Doubleday, 1989).

Gardiner, J., *Wartime Britain 1939–45* (London: Review, 2004).

Gardiner, J., *The Children's War: The Second World War Through the Eyes of the Children of Britain* (London: Portrait, 2005).

Garfield, S., *We Are at War: The Diaries of Five Ordinary People in Extraordinary Times* (London: Ebury Press, 2005).

Garfield, S., *Private Battles: How the War Almost Defeated Us* (London: Ebury Press, 2006).

Gielgud, V., *Years of the Locust* (London: Nicholson and Watson, 1947).

Gies, M. and A.L. Gold, *Anne Frank Remembered* (London: Simon & Schuster Ltd, 1987).

Gildea, R., *Marianne in Chains* (New York: Picador, 2002).

Glees, A. (in Hirschfeld ed.), *Exile in Great Britain: Refugees from Hitler's Germany* (London/NJ: Berg/Humanities Press, 1984).

Goody, A., 'BBC Features, Radio Voices and the Propaganda of War 1939–1941' *Media History* 24.2, (2018).

Grant-Duff, S., *The Man in the Street (of the BBC) Talks to Europe* (London: P.S. King & Staples, 1945).

Hanson, N., *Priestley's Wars: Soldier, Broadcaster, Campaigner* (Ilkley: Great Northern Books, 2008).

Harman, N., *Dunkirk: The Necessary Myth* (London: Hodder & Stoughton, 1980).

Hawkes, N., *The Story of J.B. Priestley's Postscripts* (J.B. Priestley Society, 2008).

Hawkins, D., *War Report: D-Day to VE-Day* (London: BBC, Ariel edition, 1985).

Hickman, T., *What Did You Do in the War, Auntie?* (London: BBC Books, 1995).

Jackson, J., *France: The Dark Years 1940–44* (London: Oxford University Press, 2001).

Jenkins, A., *The Forties* (London: Book Club Associates, 1977).

Johnston, G. and E. Robertson, *BBC World Service: Overseas Broadcasting, 1932–2018* (London: Palgrave Macmillan, 2019).

Kavanagh, T., *Tommy Handley* (London: Hodder & Stoughton, 1949).

Kirkpatrick, I., *The Inner Circle* (London: Macmillan, 1959).

Knightley, P., *The First Casualty: The War Correspondent as Hero and Myth-Maker from the Crimea to Iraq* (London: John Hopkins University Press, 2004).

Lockhart, B., *Comes the Reckoning* (London: Putnam, 1947).

Lynn, V., *Vocal Refrain: An Autobiography by Vera Lynn* (London: W.H. Allen, 1975).

McLaine, I., *Ministry of Morale: Home Front Morale and the MOI in World War II* (London: Allen & Unwin, 1979).

McNeill, W.H., *America, Britain and Russia* (New York: Johnson Reprint Corporation, 1970).

Mansell, G., *Let Truth Be Told: 50 years of External Broadcasting* (London: Weidenfeld & Nicolson, 1982).

Martland, P., *Lord Haw-Haw: The English Voice of Nazi Germany* (Richmond: The National Archives, 2003).

Marwick, A., C. Emsley and W. Simpson, *Total War and Historical Change 1914–1955* (Philadelphia: Open University Press, 2002).

Mills, T., *The BBC: Myth of Public Service* (London: Verso, 2016).

Newsome, N., *Giant at Bush House: At the Heart of the Radio War* (Steyning: Real Press, 2019).

Nicholas, S. (in Hayes and Hill eds), *Millions Like Us: British Culture in the Second World War* (Liverpool: Liverpool University Press, 1999).

Nicholls, S., 'The British Press and D-Day: Reporting the Launch of the Second Front, 6 June 1944', *Media History*, 23.3 (2017).

O'Donnell, J.P., *The Berlin Bunker* (London: J.M. Dent & Sons, 1979).

Orwell, G. (ed.), *Talking to India* (London: Allen & Unwin, 1943).

Plock, V.M., *Erika Mann, the BBC German Service, and Foreign Language Broadcasting During WWII*, Vol. 5 (Baltimore, MD: Johns Hopkins University Press, 2019).

Porter, J., *Lost Sound: The Forgotten Art of Radio Storytelling* (Chapel Hill, NC: University of North Carolina Press, 2016).

Priestley, J.B., *All England Listened: The Wartime Postscripts of J.B. Priestley* (New York: Chilmark, 1967).

Roberts, Captain H., *Capture at Arnhem: A Story of Disaster and Survival* (Gloucestershire: Windrush, 1999).

Seaton, J., *The Media in British Politics* (Aldershot: Gower Publishing Co., 1987).

Seaton, J. and J. Curren, *Power Without Responsibility* (Abingdon: Routledge, 2018 edition).

Seul. S., *British Radio Propaganda against Nazi German during the Second World War* (Master's thesis) (University of Cambridge Faculty of History, 1995).

Shellard, D. and S. Nicholson, *The Lord Chamberlain Regrets: A History of British Theatre Censorship* (London: The British Library Publishing Division, 2004).

Sinclair, W.A., *The Voice of the Nazi* (London: Collins, 1940).

Sinke, O., *Verzet Vanuit De Verte: De Behoedzame Koers Van Radio Oranje* (Amsterdam: Augustus, 2009).

Steinbeck, J., *Once There Was a War* (London: Penguin, 1994 edition).

Stourton, E., *Auntie's War: The BBC during the Second World War* (London: Black Swan, 2018 edition).

Stuart, C., *The Reith Diaries* (London: Collins, 1975).

Tangye-Lean, E., *Voices in the Darkness: The Story of the European Radio War* (London: Secker & Warburg, 1943).

Thomas, J.A., *A History of the BBC Features Department 1924–1964* (Oxford: University of Oxford, 1993).

Toye, R., *The Roar of the Lion: The Untold Story of Churchill's World War II Speeches* (Oxford: Oxford University Press, 2013).

Van der Heide, D., *My Sister and I* (London: Faber & Faber, 1943).

Vansittart, Sir R., *Black Record: Germans Past and Present* (Toronto: Musson Book Co., 1941).

Wake-Walker, E., *A House for Spies: SIS Operations into Occupied France* (Leeds: Sapere Books, 2011).

Welch, D., *Propaganda, Power and Persuasion: From World War I to Wikileaks* (London: British Library Publishing, 2013).

Welch, D., *Persuading the People: British Propaganda in World War II* (London: The British Library, 2016).

Welch, D. and J. Fox, *Justifying War: Propaganda, Politics and the Modern Age* (London: Macmillan, 2012).

White, A., *BBC at War* (Wembley, Middlesex: BBC, 1942).

Wilkinson, E. and E. Conze, *Why War? A Handbook for those who will take part in the Second World War* (London: NCLC Publishing, 1939).

Winterton, Earl, *Orders of the Day* (London: Cassell, 1953).

Worsley, F., *ITMA 1939–1948* (London: Vox Mundi, 1949).

Yass, M., *This is Your War: Home Front Propaganda in the Second World War* (London: HMSO, 1983).

INDEX

INDEX

INDEX

The History Press
The destination for history
www.thehistorypress.co.uk